T0301415

On Economic Institutions

On Economic Institutions
Theory and Applications

Edited by

John Groenewegen
Associate Professor of Economic Organisation
and Modern Japanese Studies
Erasmus University
Rotterdam, Holland

Christos Pitelis
Barclays Bank Lecturer in Industrial and Business Strategy
Judge Institute of Management Studies, University of Cambridge
Cambridge, U. K.

Sven-Erik Sjöstrand
Matts Carlgren Professor of Management
Stockholm School of Economics
Stockholm, Sweden

Edward Elgar

Published by
Edward Elgar Publishing Limited
Gower House
Croft Road
Aldershot
Hants GU11 3HR
England

Edward Elgar Publishing Company
Old Post Road
Brookfield
Vermont 05036
USA

British Library Cataloguing in Publication Data

On Economic Institutions: Theory and
Applications
  1. Groenewegen, John
  338.6

Library of Congress Cataloguing in Publication Data

On economic institutions: theory and applications / edited by John
  Groenewegen, Christos Pitelis, Sven-Erik Sjöstrand.
    256 p. 23 cm.
    Includes index.
    1. Institutional economics. I. Groenewegen, John, 1949–
  II. Pitelis, Christos. III. Sjöstrand, Sven-Erik, 1945–
  HB99.5.063   1995
  330—dc20

94–43573
CIP

ISBN 1 85898 142 5

Contents

Contents

Figures

Tables

Contributors

JOHN GROENEWEGEN (Editor)

John Groenewegen (b. 1949) received his PhD in Economics from the University of Maastricht in the Netherlands. He is Associate Professor of Economic Organisation and Modern Japanese Studies at the Erasmus University Rotterdam. He is managing and consulting partner of the Group for Research and Advice in Strategic Management and Industrial Policy (GRASP), member of the steering committee of the European Association for Evolutionary Political Economy (EAEPE). President-elect of the Association of Post-Keynesian Economics. He has published in books and journals on the theory of the firm, Japanese economic system and several types of governance policies.

CHRISTOS PITELIS (Editor)

Christos Pitelis is the Barclays Bank Lecturer in Industrial and Business Strategy at the Judge Institute of Management Studies, and a Fellow in Economics at Queens College, both at the University of Cambridge (UK). He recieved his PhD in Economics from the University of Warwick 1984. He has held faculty positions at the Universities of Nottingham, St. Andrews, Cambridge, Athens, and the China-Europe Management Institute in Beijing. Further, he is a research co-ordinator at the EAEPE in the area 'The Theory of the Firm and Production Processes'. His most well-known publications include *Corporate Capital* (Cambridge University Press) and Market and non-Market Institutions (Blackwell).

SVEN-ERIK SJÖSTRAND (Editor)

Sven-Erik Sjöstrand (b. 1945) received his PhD 1973 and became Professor of Management at the Stockholm School of Economics (Sweden) in 1978. He is now Matts Carlgren Professor of Management at this school and chairman of its Department of Management and Business Administration. He is a member of several boards both in research associations and in large Swedish multinational companies. Furthermore he is the Vice President of the Society for the Advancement of Socio-Economics (SASE), research coordinator in the European Association for Evolutionary and Political Economics (EAEPE), and a member of several editorial boards of international scientific journals. His internationally most well known recent writings include *Organizational Myths* (Harper & Row, 1978), *Institutional Change: Theory and Empirical Findings* (M. E. Sharpe, 1993), and *The Janus of Management* (Routledge; 1995).

PAUL AUERBACH

Paul Auerbach (b. 1946) received his PhD in Economics from the University of Wisconsin (Madison). Since 1972, he has lectured at Kingston University (United Kingdom) and the Universtity of London, and since 1990 has been Reader in Economics at Kingston University. Research into the problems of Soviet type economies has resulted in lectures to the British Foreign Office, the Academy of Sciences, Moscow, and the University of the Far East in Vladivostok. The main focus of research has been into the economics of competitive processes (Competition: the Economics of Industrial Change, Basil Blackwell, 1989). Recent work has involved investigations of the dynamics of economic growth (*Cumulative Causation and the 'New' Theories of Economic Growth,* with P. Skott, Journal of Post Keynesian Economics).

HANS BERGER

Hans Berger (b. 1959) obtained his degree in Business Administration from the University of Groningen (the Netherlands). Since 1987 he is assistant professor in Marketing at the Faculty of Management and Organization at the University of Groningen. His research interests are in the area of transaction cost economics and hybrid vertical industrial relationships.

PATRIZIO BIANCHI

Patrizio V. Bianchi, b. 1952, is Professor of Economics and Finance of European Community at the University of Bologna. He became Research fellow at the University of Trento in 1980, Associate Professor at Bologna in 1986, Professor of Economics in 1990 at Udine. He is Senior Vice President of Nomisma, the largest economic research institute in Italy, Director of L'Industria, the Italian journal of industrial economics, member of the executive committee of the European Association of Research in Industrial Economics (EARIE), editor with R. Sudgen and K. Cowling of the Routledge Series on European Industrial Strategy. He is author of various books and articles on industrial economics and public policies in industrialized countries.

SHAUN HARGREAVES HEAP

Shaun Hargreaves Heap (b. 1951) received his PhD in economics from the University of California at Berkely. He has taught Economics in the School of Economic and Social Studies at the University of East Anglia since 1977 and he is currently Dean of the School. He has been Visiting Professor at Concordia University, Montreal (1981-2) and a Visiting Senior Lecturer at the University of Sydney (1990 and 1993). His major research interests are in Macroeconomics and at the interface between Philosophy and Economics. His recent work includes *Rationality in Economics* (Basil Blackwell 1989). *The Theory of Choice* (with others) (Basil Blackwell 1992). *The New Keynesian Macroeconomics* (Edward Elgar 1992) and *Game Theory: a Critical Introduction* (with Y. Varoufakis) (Routledge, 1995).

CLAES-FREDRIK HELGESSON

Claes-Fredrik Helgesson (b. 1964) studied telecommunications enginee-ring at Telia (Swedish Telecom), before entering Stockholm School of Economics for studies in economics and business administration. In 1994 he received a licentiate's degree on a thesis about industrial and technological change in telecommunications and he is currently continuing his doctoral studies at the department of marketing, distribution and industry dynamics at Stockholm School of Economics. He is spending the academic year of 1994/95 at Scancor at Stanford University and at CSI at Ecoles des Mines in Paris on a Hans Werthén grant provided by the Royal Swedish Academy of Engineering Sciences (IVA). His current interests are on the links between technological, industrial and regulatory change.

STAFFAN HULTÉN

Staffan Hultén (b. 1954) got his PhD at the Stockholm School of Economics 1988, and was appointed Associate Professor at the same school 1994. He has been a visiting researcher at École Centrale Paris 1991–94. Internationally, he has published chapters in editorials both on network theory (e.g., *Theories of Industrial Change and Markets as Networks*), and regarding communication systems (e.g., *High Speed Trains*).

JONATHAN MICHIE

Jonathan Michie got both his Bachelor of Arts and his PhD at Oxford University. He has been affiliated with several organizations, e.g., Economics Department, Trades Union Congress (London) and Cambridge University, and he is presently the co-ordinator, at Economic and Social Research Council. He is a current member of the editorial boards of *Cambridge Journal of Economics, The New Economy* and the *International Review of Applied Economics*. His most well known publications include *Wages in the Business Cycle — An Empirical and Methodological Analysis* (Frances Pinter, 1987), *Beyond the Casino Economy* (with N. Costello and S. Milne; Verso, 1989), *The Economic Legacy:* 1979–1992 (editor; Academic Press, 1992), and *Unemployment in Europe* (co-editor Grieve Smith; Academic Press, 1994)

LEE MILLER

Lee M. Miller is a Ph. D candidate at Yale University, Department of Sociology. Her dissertation explores the institutional foundations of innovation in Bologna's packaging machine sector. She is a co-editor of a forthcoming volume on systems of innovation, and co-author of a forthcoming article on collective action and institutional change. She is currently working on various projects focusing on the connection between economic activity and its institutional context.

NIELS G. NOORDERHAVEN

Niels Noorderhaven studied Dutch language and literature at the University of Amsterdam (BA) and business administration at Delft University of

Technology (MBA). In 1990 he obtained a PhD in business administration at the University of Groningen. He has worked for six years at the University of Groningen, as research assistant and as assistant professor. At present he is associate professor of business administration at Tilburg University. He is also a guest lecturer at the Institute Catholique des Hautes Études Commerciales in Brussels. His research interests include inter-firm relations, strategic decision making, and cultural influences on management and organization. His publication list comprises more than twenty articles in refereed journals and chapters in edited books, in English as well as in Dutch

BART NOOTEBOOM

Bart Nooteboom (b. 1942) studied mathematics in Leiden and econometrics in Rotterdam. He worked for four years with Shell in the Hauge and London. He has also worked for 14 years at the Dutch Economic Institute for Research of Small Business (EIM) — for the last four years as its scientific director. In 1980 he obtained his PhD on a thesis on retailing, Since 1987 he is professor at the faculty of Management & Organization, Groningen University, first as professor of Marketing and now as professor of Industrial Organization. He acted in several advisory committees, eg., committee on technology policy for the ministry of economic affairs. Since 1980 he published about one hundred articles in International and Dutch journals and books on: retailing, small business and entrepreneurship, pricing, technology and industry policy, innovation and diffusion of innovation, transaction costs, supply and contracting, methodology and the philosophy of economics and management.

DOUGLAS J. PUFFERT

Douglas J. Puffert obtained his PhD from the Department of Economics, at Stanford University 1991. His thesis *The Economics of Spatial Network Externalities and the Dynamics of Railway Gauge Standardization* won the 1991 Alexander Gerschenkron Prize, awarded annually by the Economic History Association for the best thesis in European or international comparative economic history. He is currently employed at the U.S. International Trade Commission, and has previously been visiting assistant professor at Swarthmore College and visiting instructor at the University of Connecticut.

ERNESTO SCREPANTI

Ernesto Screpanti (b. 1948) is professor of Economics at the University of Parma (Italy) and member of the steering Committee of the European Association of Evolutionary Political Economy (EAEPE). He has done extensive research in the fields of income distribution and capital dynamics and the history of economic thought. The following are three of his most recent books: *Rethinking Economics* (co-editor G. M. Hodgson; Edward Elgar, 1992), *An Outline of the History of Economic Thought* (co-editor S. Zamagni; Oxford University Press, 1993), and *Capital Accumulation and the Monetary Circuit, Dynamics,* (CNR Milan, 1993).

PETER SKOTT

Peter Skott (b. 1953) received his degree in Mathematical Economics from the University of Aarhus (Denmark). He has held appointments at the University of Copenhagen, and visiting positions at University College (London), University of Massachusetts, University of Nôtre Dame and EuroFaculty/University of Vilnius. He is on the editorial board of Review of Political Economy, and Britsh Review of Economic Issues, and International Papers in Political Economy. His published works include *Conflict and Effective Demand in Economic Growth* (Cambridge University Press, 1989), and *Kaldor's Growth and Distributions Theory* (Peter Lang Verlag, 1989).

DAVID YOUNG

David Young obtained his PhD from the University of Nottingham, U.K. His thesis title was 'OPEC stability and oil price behaviour'. He has been Tutor in Industrial Economics at the University of Nottingham, Lecturer in Economics at the School of Economic and Social Studies, U.E.A. Norwich, and is presently Lecturer in Economics at the School of Economic Studies, University of Manchester. His recent publications include several articles in well known journals and in international editorials as well as *Conflict in Economics,* (co-editor Y. Varoufakis; Harvester Wheatsheaf, 1990) and the forthcoming *Firms and Market Power: an Analysis of Method, Theory and Policy in Industrial Organisation* (Edward Elgar).

1. Introduction

John Groenewegen, Christos Pitelis and Sven-Erik Sjöstrand[1]

INSTITUTION — A CORE PHENOMENON IN THE ECONOMIC AND SOCIAL SCIENCES

In the 1980s and early 1990s interest was renewed in the idea of incorporating institutional analysis in the economic sciences, an interest which can be explained in part by some of the shortcomings of mainstream neoclassical theory (e.g., McCloskey, 1986; Swedberg, 1990; Mayer, 1993), and in part by the dramatic transformation of the socio-economic systems in Eastern Europe, including the former Soviet Union (cf. Sjöstrand, 1993).

In *economics,* important contributions appeared in both the more classical institutional tradition (e.g., Veblen, Commons, Ayres, Dewey, Myrdal, and Galbraith), and in writings more closely associated with the dominant neoclassical tradition. The former include, for instance, the work of Sjöstrand (1985) on the organization of societies, Hodgson (1987) on economics and institutions, Tool (1988) on evolutionary economics, Knudsen et al. (1989) on institutionalism in the social sciences, Bromley (1989) on economic interests and institutions, Hodgson and Screpanti (1991) on 'rethinking economies', Pedersen et al. (1992) on the negotiated economy, and Sjöstrand on 'rational' and 'irrational' institutions (1992).

Prominent writers trying to combine an institutional and neoclassical tradition include Williamson (1975, 1985, 1993a) on 'basic' institutions of modern capitalism, Sen (1981) on 'entitlements', Akerlöf (1980, 1984) on social customs and 'counteracting institutions', Schotter (1981) on the dynamics of institutions in a game theoretical setting, Axelrod (1984) on the evolution of co-operation, Leibenstein (1984) on the economics of conventions and institutions, Cyert (1988) on the economic theory of firms, Demsetz (1988) on the organization of economic activity, Rowe

1

(1989) on the economics of rules and conventions, Eggertsson (1990) on economic behaviour and institutions and Lane (1991) on the market experience. Much of this research is sometimes referred to as 'the New Institutional Economics'.

Institutionally oriented research is also an important and fairly recent tradition among *economic historians* such as Chandler (1977) in his writings on the visible hand, Braudel (1982) in his discussion of the wheels of commerce, Newman (1983) in his descriptions of pre-industrial societies, North (1973, 1981, 1990) in his works on structures and changes in modern economic history and on the institutional evolution in Europe, Koot (1987) in his reflections on English historical economics, Fogel (1989) in his analyses of American slavery, and Gustafsson (1991) with his reflections on (transitions to) capitalism. For an overview, see Sjöstrand (1993a).

In the other social sciences — especially *sociology, political science and law* — institutionalism has co-existed with other perspectives in a fairly non-dramatic and often productive way. In sociology, institutions have always been at the top of the research agenda. Writers as far back as Spencer and Weber focused on them, while important recent sociological contributions include DiMaggio and Powell (1983) on institutional isomorphism, Meyer and Scott (1983) on organizational environments, Perrow (1986) on complex organizations, Thomas et al. (1987) on institutional structures, Zucker (1988) on institutional patterns and organizations, Etzioni (1988) on the moral dimension and institutions and Meyer et al. (1992) on educational curricula.

A FOCUS ON ECONOMIC INSTITUTIONS

Partly as a consequence of the rapid growth in scientific literature in a variety of disciplines, somewhat diverging views on the institutional field have emerged. This need not mean, however, that the phenomenon is in itself particularly ambiguous or difficult to grasp. The variety is not in fact surprising when we remember that several disciplines have been and still are involved in extensive research in the field. It is quite clear, however, that in these studies the concept institution has been used in several different, albeit not necessarily contradictory, ways.

One basic difference between the various institutionalist research approaches in the economic sciences concerns the extent to which they distinguish their field of study from that of the other social sciences. Some scientists define their field more as an open learning system, while others are firm in excluding ideas and findings from other disciplines. In modern versions of the classical institutionalist tradition, the political and social frameworks for economic activities are not excluded from the analysis, nor is the past or the future. To regard economic action as part of a more general social action is in fact customary in modern institutional analysis (cf. Swedberg and Granovetter, 1992). Economic activities, as Parsons put it a long time ago, do not only take place in an institutional framework but are actually part of the institutional phenomenon itself (Parsons, 1937).

In most neoclassical theories the role of institutions has been marginalized because they define institutions as exogenous phenomena; that is, given a system of norms the optimal combination of, for instance, labour and capital will be based on utility maximizing agents operating in narrowly defined environments contributing to equilibria. This kind of logic still dominates writings in neoclassical micro-economics. To modern institutionalists continuous change processes, not states of equilibria, are the fundamental economic phenomena to be studied and explained.

In 1975, Oliver Williamson considerably advanced the analysis of economic institutions with his neoclassically flavoured volume 'Markets and Hierarchies'. Like Ronald Coase some forty years earlier, he focused on the costs associated with 'transactions' but he took the analysis one step further, at least theoretically. For instance, he raised the question of why transactions of capital as well as labour are sometimes co-ordinated through external markets, and sometimes through a kind of internal, 'miniature' market like the multi-divisional firm (i.e., hierarchy).

Although Williamson admits that explanatory variables other than efficiency have a role (especially in the organization of work), it is his strong conviction that economic efficiency is the most important explanatory variable for understanding the presence of markets and/or hierarchies (Williamson, 1995). His economic approach is, however, a *static* one. The question of how governance structures develop over time is not at stake. Apart from the so called 'fundamental transition' of a market (characterized by a large number of actors) to a situation of small numbers, dynamics is no part of his approach.

In the 1970s and 1980s, the new institutionalists and heirs of the old institutionalists[2] largely ignored each other, but from the late 1980s a scientific debate began to emerge (cf. Sjöstrand, 1985; Hodgson 1987; Williamson, 1985 and 1993b; and Groenewegen, 1995). Some of the scientists involved emphasized the need to extend the theoretical framework of transaction cost economics (=TCE) by integrating it with some findings from modern sociology and organization theory, for example, the significance of power relations (cf. Pfeffer and Salancik, 1978), the social embeddedness of human action (cf. Granovetter, 1985), the importance of history and evolution, and the presence of the complex, interactional individual (Sjöstrand, 1992).

Regarding the social embeddedness of economic actions, Granovetter (ibid.) and others claim that human activities cannot be explained by reference to individuals alone. Actions are not performed by atomized individuals, but are embedded in other kinds of relations, which attenuate the 'economic rationale' in action (cf. Sjöstrand, 1993b). Some researchers (e.g., Meyer, 1987 and 1990) even claim that there is actually a problem associated with the determination to find some sort of actor in social and economic life. Meyer refers to this disposition among researchers as 'the social construction of individual actorhood', and claims that it is one of the more important institutionalized modes of human thinking and perception of our times. However, his position is obviously not the only possible one to adopt.

Regarding the individual, Williamson considers bounded rationality and opportunism crucial. Some critics, however, discuss in several contributions the need for the endogenization of opportunism, and the importance of *trust* relationships. Several dimensions are then suggested for understanding trust, like attitudinal orientation, bases of power (coercive or legitimate), type of organization (cf. John, 1984), consistency, closeness, values, loyalty, and the like (see Sjöstrand 1993b, and Noorderhaven, 1994). Here some researchers emphasize the *homo oeconomicus* construct but add complexity by introducing various human 'attitudes' or motivations, while others abandon this simple assumption, and try instead to develop more complex notions like the one of *homo complexicus interactus* (Sjöstrand, 1992).

Another difference regarding humans refers to the degree of dynamics allowed for. Some researchers treat individuals as rather 'fixed' phenomena, while others perceive them as social phenomena which change and are malleable. Yet another discussion among institutionalists regarding humans concerns the ways they relate to institutions. Ideas differ as to the degree of autonomy (freedom) which should be ascribed to individuals — that is, to what extent action is determined by institutions — or, to reverse the issue, to what extent institutions are determined by human actions.

Furthermore, many neoclassically minded economists use economic action as a synonym for *rational* action defined in a traditional, although specific, 20th Century Western way (cf. Hirschman, 1977 and, for a criticism of such a platform, Sjöstrand, 1993b). Most institutionalists, however, regard such a conception of 'rationality' as an important — but incomplete — social construction institutionalized (!) in neoclassical analysis (cf. Sjöstrand, 1992).

With respect to the institutional environment Williamson, like Davis and North (1971), discriminates between the institutional *environment* (political, social and legal rules or norms) and institutional *arrangements* (governance structure that coordinate the way units cooperate and/or compete). According to Williamson the institutional environment defines the costs of (changes in) institutional arrangements (e.g. markets and hierarchies). Several critics claim that such a recognition is *not* sufficient, and that a detailed understanding of the institutional environment often has to be the starting point when studying institutional arrangements.

> For instance, an analysis of the subcontracting relations of a firm should start with a rather detailed study of the institutional *environment*, that is, the legal rules (e.g., contract law and competition law), the political pressures (ministries enforcing certain norms), the social attitudes towards co-operative business relations, the cultural-historical development of the country/region, and the like. When the conditions have been established to a reasonable degree, it may be possible to understand why firms in, for example, Japan choose subcontracting as the dominating governance structure, and why firms in the US more often use vertical integration. (Groenewegen, 1995).

To summarize, the critics who argue for extensions of TCE (Transaction cost economics) can be grouped into those who argue for other types of actors (individual level), those who argue for a more explicit attention to the institutional environment (macro level), and those who argue for an in-depth analysis of the 'organization as such'. It is becoming more and more recognized that the issue is not whether or not the 'old' or 'new' institutionalists have developed universal theories, but whether we are able to identify the conditions under which one theoretical approach could be preferable to another. The 'New Institutionalists' seem to be confident that in the majority of the cases, it is *economic efficiency* (objectively defined?) which explains the existence and dynamics of institutions, and that forces like cultural, legal, political, industrial, and other kinds of (systems of enforced) norms are of secondary importance. The contrary seems to hold for the 'Old Institutionalists'.

However, a more favourable attitude towards a more pluralistic approach in economics seems to be emerging. A plurality of theories is becoming increasingly accepted for the simple reason that none of the theories (neoclassical, 'old' institutional, 'new' institutional or 'neo'institutional) (see note 1) can be expected to be generally superior regardless of problem or situation. An aim is to allow for the co-existence of different theories which together — or as alternatives — could provide a rich understanding of economic phenomena in and across societies.

THE CONTENT OF THIS VOLUME — AN OVERVIEW

The central topic of this volume is '*economic* institutions' defined as systems of enforced norms, routines, conventions, legal rules and traditions in which individual economic activity is embedded. In this volume it is shown that the absence of institutions in most neoclassical economic analysis, both as explanatory variable and as variable to be explained, is often a shortcoming when trying to describe and understand crucial economic phenomena (and make policy recommendations).

Almost all of the twelve chapters included in this volume were selected from papers presented at a large international scientific conference (EAEPE; Barcelona, 1993) addressing economic institutions. All chosen papers were then reviewed and revised to qualify as chapters for this edited, *thematic* volume.

This volume *On Economic Institutions — Theory and Applications* focuses on four themes associated with institutions and institutional change. First of all, the rationalities involved in the emergence, change and dissolution of institutions are described and analysed. Then the inexhaustible explanatory variable in neoclassically flavoured kinds of institutional analysis — i.e., 'efficiency' — is problematized. Other explanatory variables are claimed to be needed too, and are therefore added to the traditional efficiency discussions. A third theme emphasized in this volume refers to institutional change processes in general. Here, discussions about path dependence, selection mechanisms, and institutional dynamics are introduced at some length. Finally, methodological issues are also put up front. A characteristic for several chapters of this volume is an emphasis on theoretical conclusions anchored in recent or even ongoing empirical studies.

In chapter 2, *Towards a Theory of Institutional Change,* Sven-Erik Sjöstrand develops the theory of institutional change, focusing on the more recent writings of Douglass North. He combines economic theory with some findings from macro sociology, thereby eliminating some of the circular qualities of the predominant institutional theories in the economic sciences.

Sjöstrand is very explicit about the meaning of the concept 'institution' and assigns its roots to human interaction. Thus to him an institution is constituted by human interaction and exchange, and represents a kind of infrastructure that facilitates — or hinders — certain co-ordination and allocation processes. Institutions then correspond to what could be named 'rationality contexts' and consequently they often are public goods characterized by non-excludability.

The focus of Sjöstrands's chapter is the dynamics of institutions and institutional change. He focuses on the recent theory developed by North (1990, 1993), and describes its basic ingredients, relationships and conclusions. Furthermore, Sjöstrand refers to parts of the criticism that has been raised both from economists and sociologists. He stresses the crucial weaknesses of the theory, and tries to add a few new ingredients to take care of the problems inherent in North's theory. He focuses especially on the potential sources for new, path independent institutions. Here North claims that endogenous forces are important but does not explain what forces and how they work ('preferences' change but we do not know how). The exogenous factors he pronounces also have limited explanatory power (changes in relative prices for land and labor).

Sjöstrand emphasizes that organizing institutions are being continuously shaped and reshaped (reproduced) as a result of historical, and emerging (inter)action patterns in society. They represent, and simultaneously provide, arenas for experiments, trial-and-error processes and learning among individuals at the 'micro' level, and perhaps also for organizations. The gaps or mismatches between the micro (individual) and macro (institutional) levels are then the driving-forces, the innovation-generators behind institutional changes. Thus, institutions, are social constructions that coordinate, regulate, and stabilize human activities at a kind of 'macro' (social construction) level, while simultaneously functioning as part of the raw material of change on the 'micro' level.

These patterns or infrastructures of human interaction absorb crucial uncertainties, while at the same time reducing the demands on the cognitive capacity of the human mind. Parallel with this, institutions also stabilize expectations and coordinate actions by assimilating certain cognitive maps. These become prescribed patterns for correlating behaviour in the performance of various tasks. Institutions facilitate the application of reliable knowledge to the performance of the continuing activities which a community has come to regard as significant, such as the production of food and goods, the determination of income shares, the transportation of people, and so forth. This diffusion of knowledge often explains the emergence and growth of an institution as well as its changes.

In chapter 3, *Rational Action and Institutional Change*, Shaun Hargreaves Heap begins with some brief background reflections on the relationship between institutions *per se* and rational action. These lead him to argue that an understanding of both institutional allegiance and institutional change requires an expanded notion of rational action. In particular, a sense of rational action is required which allows an important part to be played by shared sources of 'extraneous information'. By 'extraneous' is meant information which is not regarded relevant under the standard account of instrumental, rational decision-making. For example, the web of shared beliefs which often is referred to as a 'culture' could play a central role in the constitution of rational action.

He illustrates his argument with a particular theory of 'extraneous information' i.e., Mary Douglas's cultural theory. She essentially provides a taxonomy of possible beliefs which are in turn associated with four ideal-types of institutions. They are gained by fracturing the familiar opposition between the institutions of markets and hierarchies across two lines: what she refers to as the 'group' and 'grid' dimensions. The former captures the extent to which the institutions of a society involve an overlapping membership so that clear group boundaries can be drawn, and the latter refers to whether the institutions themselves make distinctions of rank between individuals who populate them. That theory helps him to explain the divergent income distributions in OECD countries observed over the last 10–15 years.

Later in his chapter he addresses more directly the core issues of this volume, namely economic institutions and institutional change. He is then concerned with whether to expect further entrenchment of market institutions and market values in OECD countries. In particular, Hargreaves Heap focuses on two arguments which point to continuing entrenchment. The first relates to the much noticed changes in shared 'extraneous' beliefs which are associated with the transition from 'modernity' to 'post-modernity'. The second is concerned with the impact on shared beliefs of the conspicuous shifts by governments over more than a decade towards pro-market policies.

In chapter 4, *Relative Rationality, Institutions and Precautionary Behaviour,* Ernesto Screpanti makes an attempt to put together suggestions and ideas coming from three different and seemingly contrasting streams of thought; the institutionalist, the Keynesian and the behaviourist. His aim is to develop a theory of economic agency capable of accounting, on the ground of an individualistic presupposition, for many economic phenomena, such as institutions and collective agents, that are often dealt with in holistic terms.

In many approaches to macroeconomics which treat social aggregates as the true actors of economic dynamics, collective agents are not — according to Screpanti — taken to be a *primum movens.* He claims that it is implicitly or explicitly assumed, even in most non-neoclassical models, that, since collective agents consist of groups of individuals, it is from the behaviour of the individuals that analysis must start. Furthermore, if one has to explain the social fabric tracing it back to the individual, then the individual is assumed to be a rational, autonomous and self-interested agent.

The hypothesis of individualistic rationality is reasonable although no one will deny that humans also are influenced by cultural and ethical factors which cannot easily be brought into the individualist viewpoint; it is equally well-known, Screpanti goes on, that irrational, instinctual and heterodirected behaviour exists in many forms of human activity. It is not, however, legitimate to assume that all behaviour is of this type. The fact is that, if rationality is intended as the capability to perceive means/consequence connections, it certainly cannot be denied that a good proportion of human choices are rational.

To Screpanti, the individualistic presupposition makes it necessary to attempt always first the explanation of behaviour in terms of rational, autonomous and egoistic behaviour. It should, furthermore, be clear that, when he speaks of the rationality, autonomy and egoism of individuals, he does not advocate the need to take the concepts to extremes. The hypothesis made is that the individual is a *relatively* rational and a *relatively* autonomous being. Screpanti assumes that, although the influence exerted on the individual by society is strong, the final decisions remain empowered in the individual themselves, and these are mostly of an intentional, voluntary and responsible kind.

The first behavioural hypothesis made by Screpanti is that the individual, in situations of uncertainty, orients him- or herself by using strategies of simplification. It is in this phase that Screpanti puts institutions on the

scene. The problem he states is which criterion to adopt in the simplification strategy? It is here that institutions play their main role: they make
life simpler for the individuals. People follow what he labels a criterion of
'institutional compliance'. This criterion of institutional compliance would,
according to him, lead to irrational behaviour if it were not accompanied
by one of 'institutional revision'. It is the criterion of institutional revision
that makes 'institutions function as a 'rationality context' of human
action, (Sjöstrand, 1992, p. 1011).

Screpanti is also able to clarify 'relative rationality'. One may, he states,
speak of *rationality relative to the given institutions*. In a perspective of
historical evolution, the criterion of institutional revision will lead to the
abandonment of obsolete institutions and the formation of new ones. The
new ones should be better than the old ones, at least from the point of
view of *some* individuals, but there is nothing to guarantee that they will
be *the best* as the evolution of institutions is a strongly path-dependent
process and therefore itself also historically determined. Screpanti
therefore also speaks of *rationality relative to past history*. Finally, he
makes the point that human choices, however much deliberate and self-
interested, are still conditioned by needs and interests whose formation is
strongly influenced by cultural factors. These influences are deeper than
those exerted by institutions in limiting the decisions about the means to
pursue human ends. Here is the very choices of ends that are at stake. In
this case Screpanti, finally, speaks of *rationality relative to a given
cultural setting*.

In chapter 5, *The Meaning and Role of Power in Economic Theories*,
David Young claims that the meaning and significance of power in
economic analysis seldom has been a subject which has engaged the
efforts of mainstream neoclassical theorists. That is not to say that the term
power is never used or that it does not play a significant role in certain
models. But Young proposes that it tends to be used in a very specific and
narrow way and that its alternative meanings and wider significance are
seldom acknowledged. The main objectives of his chapter are to consider
the alternative meanings of 'power' and to assess the different interpretations and roles of power in different types of economic theories. It is
argued that all the main schools of thought in economics adopt a particular
view of power and that this reflects fundamental differences in the nature
of the theories. It is also suggested that it is difficult to ignore the
significance of power in general for economic theory, and that attempts to
examine the nature and role of power more explicitly may lead to a more

satisfactory analysis of interactions between individual agents, and institutions.

Initially, Young discusses various meanings of 'power' and ends up with the concept proposed by Lukes (1974). Then Young goes on to relate these views of 'power' to different schools of economic thought. He concentrates on mainstream neoclassical analysis (especially game theory), Austrian economics (Hayek, Mises, and Rothbard), and Marxist or 'radical' theorists (e.g., Tucker, Poulantzas, Bowles and Gintis).

The general conclusion of this chapter is that all the types of economic theory which we have dealt with take a particular view of power either explicitly or implicitly, and that the recognition and discussion of this will furnish a better understanding of the principles/foundations of different economic theories and the ways in which they generate their conclusions.

In chapter 6, *Towards an Evolutionary Perspective of Institutional Crisis*, Christos Pitelis attempts to move away from conventional (neoclassical and Marxist) perspectives on economic crisis by providing a historical, institutional, and evolutionary approach to the issue of crisis. Following a critical account of neoclassical and Marxist perspectives on institutions and crisis, and having pointed to their largely static nature, the author proceeds to provide his own perspective. This is suggested to synthesize, in a non-eclectic way, major insights from previous approaches, but also breaks new ground.

For the author, institutional crises can be derived evolutionarily within a general framework of the principals' attempts to further their interests through achieving a more efficient (from their point of view) exploitation of specialization and the division of labour through trying to remove emerging constraints in doing so. The process is said to involve both transaction costs economizing, but also (often non-Pareto-efficient) reductions in production costs. The overall tendency which emerges from this is seen to be for an increasing profit share, which gives rise to a tendency towards a realization failure, and (in part) to internationalized production.

Along with, and in part because of, internationalization, realization crises are also said to lead to fiscal crises, and thus overall to a failure of three major capitalist institutions: the private sector of firms (1) and markets (2) and the public sector (the state) (3). The need for a new regulation regime arises in the modern epoch the tendency being for an 'austerity consensus'; a direct result of the dominance of international capital over labour, and the erosion of the relative autonomy of the nation state vis-à-

vis capital. The author concludes by pointing to some limitations of his
approach and the (related) need for further research on these issues.

In chapter 7, *Institutional Aspects of Regulating the Private Sector,*
Jonathan Michie deals with the issue of state regulation, in particular
significant 'increases in the state's regulatory activities over private
business following the privatizations of the 1980s in the United Kingdom,
Michie observes that there are reasons to believe that regulatory bodies
and regulation are not simply a transitory post-privatization phenomenon,
but they are here to stay. In the economy of the future, business will
therefore have to be conducted increasingly through regulated sectors.

Among other factors, is the need to foster confidence among those
establishing 'relational contracts' with newly privatized enterprises. This
renders important an analysis of the nature of the regulatory contract.
Having examined the recent history of privatization and regulation in
Britain, Michie views the 'regulatory contract' as delivering to the consumer some guaranteed level of service at a regulated price, while delivering
to the shareholders some guarantee against taxing away future profits. He
goes on to observe that such contracts will increasingly have to take into
account international business on both sides of such a contract, namely
customers and shareholders. All these point to the need for a 'new
research agenda', addressing issues such as pricing policy of regulated
enterprise and regulating the regulators, issues which are illustrated by the
author through a case-study analysis of the international communications
market.

In chapter 8, *Michael Porter's Inquiry into the Nature and Causes of
the Wealth of Nations — a Challenge to Neoclassical Economics,* Paul
Auerbach and Peter Scott explain why orthodoxy has failed in explaining
economic growth. The question about the nature and causes of the wealth
of nations is not answered by the macroeconomists of the 1950s (such as
Lucas). According to the traditional neoclassical approach the economy's
per capita rate of growth is not contingent on its rate of investment in the
long run. The second problematic notion is the non-existence of priority
sectors: the one sector is as good as the other due to the premise of
fungibility (factors can shift costlessly) and the premise of the absence of
non-convexities (unique equilibrium). The traditional neoclassical approach results in the prediction that the factor endowments determine what
a nation will produce and prescribes a policy of free trade and free
investment.

According to the new neoclassical growth theory, the rate is determined endogenously by the decisions to accumulate produced factors of production. As a result of the US losing important industrial sectors, the policy implications of the new neoclassical theory became rather radical: managed trade and the questionability of free investments. Auerbach and Skott point to a fundamental weakness in the new theory: like all neoclassical theories a competitive process is implicitly assumed, in which firms not producing at the production possibility frontier are eliminated. The authors question strongly whether the efficiency assumption in the present context of economic growth is a useful starting point. Moreover, the dominant view among contemporary economic historians that (the absence of) organizational innovation is crucial for explaining the economic growth of nations, is assumed away by the efficiency assumption. Auerbach and Skott use the Japanese steel case to show that superior organization and strategic competitive behaviour were crucial for their competitive advantage. An explanation of economic growth is not sufficient when the investments in R&D correlate with growth. On the contrary, fast growing countries are good at commercializing the innovations of others or at creating lock-ins by controlling complementary assets. The new neoclassical growth theory lacks such a genuine micro-foundation, a foundation which shows the history and specificity of the institutional setting in which firms operate.

Auerbach and Skott discuss the contribution of Michael Porter in that perspective, and conclude that Porter rightly points to the minor importance of factor endowments, and that he stresses the importance of historical and institutional factors. In his view competition is a process in which advantages are created. However, in his analysis Porter stresses the importance of the home market and the pressure of competition, but he fails to explain how such an aggressive, competitive environment is engendered. Drawing attention to the existence of it does not answer the question about the nature and causes of the wealth of nations. An institutional historical analysis is needed in order to find the real answers.

In chapter 9, *Standards as Institutions: Problems with Creating All-European Standards for Terminal Equipment,* by Claes-Fredrik Helgesson, Staffan Hultén and Douglas Puffert, the process of changing standards in the terminal equipment sector is discussed. Following Veblen, the authors consider standards as institutions that facilitate co-ordination and increase the possible scale of production. Also, standardization can enhance competition among suppliers, reduce transaction costs and decrease consumer dissatisfaction.

Although the creation of standards or the switch from one standard to another can be beneficial for society, several sources of inertia can be distinguished: technical restrictions, the users' reluctance to change equipment and the vested interests of the owners of production equipment. In order to understand the process of standardisation Helgesson et al. point to the importance of the institutional setting of the standard: they are delimited in both time and space. In industry, for example, standards are confined to the production plants and their historical evolution; in a nation state standards are (were?) delimited by the borders of a particular state. In other words, a standard is an institution, a widely accepted code facilitating co-ordination that is embedded in a regulatory regime. Vested interests and the momentum of the installed base enforce its further acceptance and conservation. In their contribution Helgesson et al. explain how markets and competition can facilitate but also hinder the process of standardization, whereas politics can also speed up the process (for instance at EU level) or slow down the process (by national governments). Three different kinds of regulatory regimes are discussed: the old nation oriented regimes, the emerging regime driven by market actors and the regime at EU level. These regimes are discussed with respect to the terminal equipment.

In chapter 10, *Collective Action, Strategic Behaviour and Endogenous Growth*, Bianchi and Miller critically review recent discussions on the issue of endogenous growth, with an ambition to developing new insights on the issue of public and, in particular, industrial policy. By observing that endogenous growth is not simply a technical problem of innovation but a socio-political problem of how groups react to change, they suggest the need to examine the link between individual behaviour and institutional change. They suggest that the 'trick' to successful competition through innovation is to ensure that agents' reactions to change do not induce instability. This is more difficult in the case of 'bottom-up' as opposed to 'top-down' innovation, but the former is likely to be more productive as it addresses specific local needs for change — it is the key to endogenous growth.

Bianchi and Miller provide a detailed analysis of factors facilitating bottom-up competition through innovation, with an ambition to propose 'A New Approach to Industrial Policy'. This entails social action aimed at regulating the openness of the social body to ensure that the selection process so activated does not transform itself into negative institutional changes, which favour monopolistic solutions or conservative reactions.

This can be facilitated by stimulating the creations of innovators, an idea currently favoured also by the European Union. Bianchi and Miller attempt to expand the scope of such policies by focusing on the institutional aspects of the issues involved, and go on to propose specific actions aimed at facilitating the implementation of their proposed policy.

In chapter 11, *Determinants of Supplier Dependence: An Empirical Study,* Hans Berger, Niels Noorderhaven and Bart Nooteboom address the question of how to understand the dynamics of economic organization; in particular attention is focused on subcontracting relations. The study of organization used to be the domain of sociology, anthropology and political science. Economists had reduced the question of organization to a technical issue of economies of scale. The firm was a production function until Oliver Williamson formulated an economic approach (Transaction Cost Economics: TCE) to organization in his well-known 'Markets and Hierarchies'. In time, the dichotomy changed into a classification of governance structures. The question of why organizations exist and change over time became a central problem definition for economists. TCE has been criticized mainly by sociologists. In their contribution, Berger et al. deal with the criticisms both theoretically and empirically.

Berger et al. develop hypotheses with respect to the determinants of supplier dependence and test the hypothesis in an empirical study of a large producer of photocopying machines. Their point of departure is the core of the New Institutional Economics: TCE. Institutions such as firms, hybrids of co-operation, classical market contracts are explained in TCE in terms of efficiency and in that sense the approach is of a neoclassical nature, in which a selection mechanism is assumed to select the fitter. Berger et al. extend the framework of TCE and add to the analysis variables like the embeddedness of the relation between buyer and supplier, the time dimension of the relation, and the degree of trust between the parties.

Another important aspect of TCE is the concept of perceived dependence of managers. The uncertainty which managers face is given a central role in their analysis: managers can only decide on the basis of their own imperfect perceptions. These perceptions are explicitly taken into account by Berger et al.

In the final chapter, *The Changing Japanese Market for Corporate Control,* John Groenewegen discusses the developments of a specific institution namely the Japanese market for corporate control: the stock market where outsiders can buy shares (ownership) of firms which can be made more profitable by reorganization and replacement of management. The threat of hostile take-overs puts pressure on management to be as efficient as possible. Such a market for corporate control hardly exists in Japan because 'stable stockholders' control about 70% of the shares.

Like in all other countries the Japanese economic institutions change. Of interest, especially for foreign firms, is the development of the market for corporate control. This market has to be studied in relation to other institutions like the industrial group (*keiretsu*) in which the main bank, the General Trading Company and the subcontractors are important elements. The Japanese business systems have other disciplining mechanisms which largely determine the 'institutional space' for the development of a market for corporate control. After having described the main elements of the Japanese system, attention is paid to the short term and long term pressures to change the system and the reactions of the main actors to these pressures (bureaucrats, government, banks and firms). Because of the existence of other disciplining mechanisms, the emerging market for corporate control is a very specific one fitting into the Japanese institutional space and serving the vested interests of especially the large business groups in particular.

NOTES

1. We are grateful for the economic support provided by *Humanistiskt Samhällsvetenskapliga Forskningsrådet* (Stockholm, Sweden) for making a final language check of all chapters in this editorial volume possible.
2. The successors of the old institutionalists (often called 'neo-institutionalists') can be found in the Association for Evolutionary Economics (AFEE) which sponsors the *Journal of Economic Issues* as well as in organizations like the European Association for Evolutionary Political Economics (EAEPE), and SASE (the Society for the Advancement of Socio-Economics) which sponsors the *Journal of Socio-Economics*.

REFERENCES

Akerlof, G. (1980), 'A Theory of Social Custom, of Which Unemployment May Be One Consequence', *Quarterly Journal of Economics*, 95, June, pp. 749–75.
Akerlöf, G. (1984), *An Economic Theorist's Book of Tales*, Cambridge University Press, Cambridge.
Axelrod, Robert (1984), *The Evolution of Cooperation*, Basic Books, New York.
Braudel, F. (1982), *The Wheels of Commerce, vol. 2*, London.
Bromley, D. (1989), *Economic Interests and Institutions*, Basil Blackwell, New York.

Chandler, A. (1977), *The Visible Hand*, The Belknap Press, Cambridge.
Cyert, R. (1988), *The Economic Theory of Organization and the Firm*, Harvester Wheatsheaf, New York.
Davis, L.E. and D.C. North (1971), *Institutional Change and American Economic Growth*, Cambridge University Press, Cambridge.
Demsetz, H. (1988), 'Ownership, Control and the Firm', *The Organization of Economic Activity*, vol. 1, Basil Blackwell, Oxford.
DiMaggio, P. and Powell, W. (1983), 'The Iron Cage Revisited', *American Sociological Review*, vol. 48., pp. 147–60.
Eggertsson, T. (1990), *Economic Behavior and Institutions*, Cambridge University Press, Cambridge.
Etzioni, A. (1988), *The Moral Dimension: Towards a New Economics*, The Free Press, New York.
Fogel, R.W. (1989), *Without Consent or Contract, the Rise and Fall of American Slavery*, W.W. Norton and Co., New York.
Granovetter, M. (1985), 'Economic Action and Social Structure. The Problem of Embeddedness', *American Journal of Sociology*, 91, pp. 481–510.
Groenewegen, J. ed. (1995), *Transaction Cost Economics and Beyond*, Kluwer Academic Publishers, forthcoming, Boston/Dordrecht.
Gustafsson, B. (ed.) (1991), *Power and Economic Institutions*, Edward Elgar, Aldershot.
Hirschman, Albert O. (1977), *The Passions and Interests: Political Arguments for Capitalism Before Its Triumph*, Princeton U.P., Princeton N.J.
Hodgson, G. (1987), *Economics and Institutions*, Polity Press, Oxford.
Hodgson, G. and Screpanti, E. (eds.), (1991), *Rethinking Economics*, Edward Elgar, Aldershot.
John, G. (1984), 'An Empirical Investigation of Some Antecedents of Opportunism in a Marketing Channel', *Journal of Marketing Research*, vol. XXI, August, pp. 278–289.
Knudsen, C. et al. (1989), *Institutionalismen i Samfundsvidenskaberne*, Samfundslitteratur, Gylling (in Danish only).
Koot, Gerhard M. (1987), *English Historical Economics, 1870–1926. The Rise of Economic History and Neomercantilism*, Cambridge University Press, Cambridge.
Lane, R. (1991), *The Market Experience*, Cambridge University Press, Cambridge.
Leibenstein, H. (1984), 'Property Rights and X-Efficiency Comment', *Economic Review*, vol. 73, no. 4, pp. 831–42.
Lukes, S. (1974). Power — A Radical View, Macmillan, London.
Mayer, T. (1993), *Truth versus Precision in Economics*, Edward Elgar, Aldershot.
McCloskey, D. (1986), *The Rhetoric of Economics*, Wheatsheaf Books, Brigthon.
Meyer, J. (1990), 'On Institutions', SCANCORE Meeting Conference Paper presented at Utö (Sweden), August 29–31.
Meyer, J. and R. Scott (1983), 'Centralization and the Legitimacy Problems of Local Government', in Meyer J.W. and W.R. Scott (eds.), *Organizational Environments: Ritual and Rationality*, Sage, Beverly Hills, pp. 199–215,
Meyer, J. et al. (1987), *Ontology and Rationalization in the Western Cultural Account. Institutional Structure: Constituting State, Society, and the Individual*, Sage Publications, London.
Meyer, J. et al. (1992), *School Knowledge for the Mass*, Falmer, Washington D.C.
Newman, K. (1983), *Law and Economic Organization: a Comparative Study of Preindustrial Societies*, Cambridge University Press, Cambridge.
Noorderhaven, N.G. (1994), 'Opportunism and Trust in Transaction Cost Economics' in J. Groenewegen (ed.), *Transaction Cost Economics and Beyond* (1995).

North, D. (1973), *The Rise of the Western World*, Cambridge University Press, Cambridge.

North, D. (1981), *Structure and Change in Economic History*, W. Norton, New York.

North, D. (1990), *Institutions, Institutional Change and Economic Performance*, Cambridge University Press, Cambridge.

North, D. (1993), 'Institutional Change' in Sjöstrand, S.E.. (ed.), *Institutional Change: Theory and Empirical Findings*, M. E. Sharpe, New York.

Parsons T. (1937), *The Structure of Social Action*, 2 vols, McGraw-Hill, New York.

Pedersen, O. et al. (1992), 'Privat Politik', Samfundslitteratur, Fredriksberg (in Danish only).

Perrow, C. (1986), *Complex Organization Theory*, Pitman, Marshfield.

Pfeffer, J. and Salancik, G. (1978), *The External Control of Organizations*, Förlag, New York.

Rowe, N. (1989), *Rules and Institutions*, Philip Allen, New York.

Schotter, A. (1981), *The Economic Theory of Social Institutions* Cambridge University Press, Cambridge.

Sen, A. (1981), *Poverty and Famines: An Essay on Entitlement and Deprivation*, Oxford University Press, Oxford.

Sjöstrand, S-E. (1985), *Samhällsorganisation*, Doxa, Lund (in Swedish only).

Sjöstrand, S-E. (1992), 'On the Rationale Behind Irrational Institutions', *Journal of Economic Issues*, vol. XXVI, no. 4, pp. 1007–40.

Sjöstrand, S-E. (ed.) (1993a), *Institutional Change: Theory and Empirical Findings*, M. E. Sharpe, New York.

Sjöstrand, S-E. (1993b), The Socio-Economic Institutions of Organizing: Origin, Emergence and Reproduction, *Journal of Socio-Economics,* vol. 22, no. 4, pp. 323–52.

Swedberg, R. (1990), *Economics and Sociology*, Princeton University Press, Oxford.

Swedberg, R. and M. Granovetter (1992), 'Introduction' in Granovetter, M. and R. Swedberg, (eds.), *The Sociology of Economic Life*, Westview Press, Oxford, pp. 1–28.

Thomas, G. et al. (1987), *Institutional Structure: Constituting State,. Society, and the Individual*, Sage, London.

Tool, M. (ed.), (1988), *Evolutionary Economics*, vol. 1, M. E. Sharpe, New York.

Williamson, O.E. (1975), *Markets and Hierarchies: Analysis and Antitrust Implications. A Study in the Economics of Internal Organization*, Free Press, New York.

Williamson, O.E. (1985), *The Economic Institutions of Capitalism*, Free Press, New York.

Williamson, O.E. (1993a), 'Comparative Economic Organization: The Analysis of Discrete Structural Alternatives in Sjöstrand, S.E.. (ed.), *Institutional Change: Theory and Empirical Findings*, M. E. Sharpe, New York.

Williamson, O.E. (1993b), 'Transaction Cost Economics and Organization Theory', *Industrial and Corporate Change*, vol. 2, no. 2, pp. 107–156, Oxford University Press, Oxford.

Williamson, O.E. (1995), 'Efficiency, Power, Authority and Economic Organization', in J. Groenewegen (ed.), *Transaction Cost Economics and Beyond*, Kluwer Academic Publishers, forthcoming, Boston/Dordrecht.

Zucker, L. (ed.) (1988), *Institutional Patterns and Organizations*, Ballinger, Cambridge.

2. Towards a Theory of Institutional Change

Sven-Erik Sjöstrand

Modern institutional economics should study man as he is, acting within the constraints imposed by real institutions. [... Then] modern institutional economics is economics as it ought to be. (Coase, 1984, p. 231)

[E]conomists have been slow to integrate institutions into their theoretical models [...] (North, 1990, p. 12)

INTRODUCTION

The concept 'institution' is crucial in this chapter, and therefore carefully defined in the first section, although the focus here is on improving the theory of institutional *change*. An institution is below described as a kind of *infrastructure* that facilitates — or hinders — human co-ordination and the allocation of resources. Institutions thus function as a kind of *rationality context*, which simultaneously emerges from and governs human interactions. Consequently institutions are public goods, relevant to and shared by many, and they are in principle characterized by non-excludability. Institutions simplify action choices; they are not separate from, but part of, the individual (inter)actions. Thus, institutions not only define and delimit the set of actions available to individuals; they are simultaneously shaped by individuals and make individual interaction possible.

In the following section institutional *change* is addressed. Previous contributions are discussed, as are excellent surveys addressing this vast research field. Quite a few of the neoclassical economists start from what they describe as 'market failures'. Institutions are then regarded as substitutes for or complements to (perfect or efficient) markets. One problem with all these neoclassical approaches is that the market is not regarded as an institution in itself, but is treated more as a kind of *preferable* (!) state.

In the third, main section of this chapter, there is an emphasis on the recent writings of Douglass North (1990 and 1993). His theory is described at some length, but also criticized in crucial areas. For example, North, too, uses the ideal type of market as *the* reference point when discussing (other kinds of) institutions. Furthermore, he does not give an explanation for what provides a break with path dependences in the ongoing (re)production of institutions. The way he describes the relationships between individuals and organizations is also problematic. Non-maximizing individuals in some way seem to be assumed to act as maximizers when organized.

Below, one way to deal with the problem of institutional change is suggested. The approach advocated here starts from two separate but related analytical levels in addressing human (inter)actions and exchanges, namely the 'micro' or individual level and the 'macro' or socially constructed level. Micro level situations refer to people's first-hand evidence in action of particular others and particular environments, while the macro level referes to indirect indicators, descriptions of or from generalized or unknown others, and/or formal (legal, physical) structures. Institutions, which generally represent macrophenomena, are continuously (re)produced by individuals in their daily activities and (inter)actions on the micro level.

It is suggested here that the ever present gap or '*mismatch*' between the micro and macro levels is the major force in institutional change processes. This mismatch is explained by the distance between the experiences, thoughts and actions of the many single individuals on the micro level on the one hand, and by the content and regulations embedded in the socially constructed institutions on the macro level, reflecting more general perspectives in society, on the other.

There are significant gaps between the social facts institutionalized at the macro level and those present at the micro level (see, for example, Zucker, 1988). The gaps — or mismatches — between the micro and macro levels are the driving forces, the innovation generators behind institutional changes. Thus, institutions are phenomena that coordinate, regulate, and stabilize human activities at a macro level, while simultaneously functioning as part of the raw material of change among individuals on the micro level.

INSTITUTIONS AS INFRASTRUCTURES OF HUMAN INTERACTION

As 'institution' is a root concept in this chapter it is worth trying to give it as clear a meaning as possible. A distinguishing feature of the institutional approach adopted here, relative to the basic controversies mentioned above, is that institutions in society are regarded as being founded or constituted in and by human interactions and exchanges. In the present chapter, therefore, an institution is described as an infrastructure that facilitates or hinders human co-ordination and the allocation of resources. Institutions thus function as a kind of 'rationality context', which simultaneously emerges from and governs human interactions (cf. Sjöstrand, 1993b). Consequently institutions are public goods, relevant to and shared by many, and they are in principle characterized by non-excludability. Further, an individual cannot avoid being part of the creation, reproduction, and destruction of institutions, since any interaction either enforces or creates a normative solution (or potential solution); institutional norms thus evolve from infinite interactions among individuals.

The position advocated here thus differs somewhat from that of Meyer and Rowan (1977), for example, who saw institutionalization as a social process in which individuals come to accept a shared definition of social reality — a conception whose validity is then regarded as independent of the actor's own view and actions, but is taken for granted as defining the way things are done and/or should be done (see also Scott, 1990). Our present position also differs from that of other prominent researchers, who prefer the notion that institutions constrain human interaction (e.g., North, 1990). This approach perceives the institution as an obstacle or hindrance to human beings, instead of a necessary and constituent element in all human activities. Instead, it is here proposed that institutions can be regarded as both restrictions and opportunities, in both cases facilitating action by reducing uncertainty. Institutions simplify action choices; they are not separate from, but are part of, the individual (inter)actions. Thus, institutions not only define and delimit the set of actions available to individuals; they are simultaneously shaped by individuals and make individual interaction possible.

Interactions are viewed as having both a physical and a mental/ psychological dimension (Stein, 1993). The former refers to the content of the interaction itself and includes both tangibles — the flow of goods or services — and intangibles — the transfer of information and knowledge.

The latter primarily refers to the normative content of interactions — the set of beliefs and values involved (e.g. feelings, affections, and emotions). Further, interactions encompass at the same time both substance and symbols, which means that they often provide both matter and meaning to individuals.

Human interaction and exchange arise for a variety of reasons. In this context it is relevant to consider both prerequisites and assumed aspirations among human beings. Among possible prerequisites, there is an obvious starting-point in the fact that individuals differ in their endowments and their experiences. Another prerequisite is that all human beings share some limitations or weaknesses (for an overview, see Sjöstrand, 1993b).

Human beings, it is further assumed, have aspirations in the form of desires, needs, and preferences, and when individual solutions are insufficient they favor the division of work and specialization. Specialization — a classic consequence both of cooperation and the division of labour — presupposes reliable exchanges between people to implement potential increases in wealth. The need for human cooperation is usually explained by the existence of indivisibles and the universality of situations. Specialization is also needed to exploit the possibilities of scale economies.

Yet another basic reason for human interaction is simply that people are social beings. Human action usually takes place in the presence of others. What is described here as interaction between individuals should be understood in this broader perspective. To emphasize and constantly recall this crucial point, 'interaction' will henceforth often be spelled '(inter)-action'. This perspective immediately introduces the expectations, pressures, norms and wishes of others — those present as well as those absent or even imagined (see Sjöstrand, 1993b). Finally, coercive force should be mentioned as one more dimension associated with interaction and exchange, implying that all such activities are not necessarily of a free and voluntary nature.

There are thus fundamental 'gaps' between individuals, and there are various reasons for making arrangements to bridge these. Gaps can be described in several dimensions, referring principally to space, time and preferences or ideals, illustrating the uncertainties generally inherent in interactive and exchange situations and constituting the ultimate explanation for the presence of institutions.

TOWARDS A MORE ELABORATED PERSPECTIVE ON INSTITUTIONS[1]

An intersubjective mental construct

In this approach, institutions are regarded not as objective phenomena but as mental constructions produced by human beings. This construction process can be described as a collective or intersubjective (social) phenomenon rather than an individual one. Further, it is continuous and on-going; social and economic theories, as well as experience, wisdom, popular beliefs and other sources of human knowledge are important inputs into the process. As institutions are regarded not as natural or objective physical phenomena but as mental, theoretical constructions, they cannot easily be observed by individuals as 'distinct wholes'.

Institutions have been described by researchers as embedded and 'stored' in many different phenomena. Thus, when interacting and exchanging, individuals experience institutions in both their mental and physical senses. Thus, institutions are embedded in concrete, empirical organizations as well as in the ideas and concepts which human beings use to sort out — construct — their views of reality. The latter include such things as rules of conduct and arrangements for facilitating communication.

Further, institutions sometimes express some of their qualities (values or norms) in buildings or in other physical arrangements or structured artifacts. Thus, all these mental and physical as well as cognitive and emotional aspects are intermixed, and will be closely linked in any discussion of institutions. Lastly, it is also important to focus on or identify regularities in human activities. This crucial point will be dealt with below.

As was noted above, empirical organizations are not the same as institutions. Organizations sometimes represent arenas for amalgamations of the rationales of a whole repertoire of institutions, and sometimes arenas for competing rationales. Thus, the members of a particular empirical organization usually express in their actions norms and values associated with several institutional forms. It is therefore important to distinguish between institutions and empirical organizations.

Expectations, norms and institutions

Institutions are related to human expectations. Sometimes these expectations assume a normative form, sometimes they express predictions. The first of these refers to situations in which values or ideals of individuals are involved as a basis for the (inter)actions, and the second refers to cases when expectations are founded on estimations or guesses and lack the same solid value basis (Sjöstrand, 1973). For example, we could expect somebody to win a tennis tournament (predictive expectation), or we could expect somebody to answer when addressed (normative expectation). In this last case some kind of potential enforcement method is always available. Expectations then — implicitly — become sanctions.

When there is no value basis for (inter)action, or it is weak as in the case of the predictive expectations above, people can fall back on what are usually described as 'conventions', which implies a situation of dependence between actors. The conventions may be quite simple, like 'driving on the left (or right)', or more complex, perhaps involving dependence on the coordination of stable but diverging expectations among several others (cf. Simon, 1991). In most scientific writing conventions refer to situations in which actors share the goals (not to crash when driving) but are indifferent to the means (left or right side of the road) (Bromley, 1989). Thus a convention does not reach — that is, does not provide guidance (ideals or values) for (inter)action — beyond a particular setting. Conventions do not provide meaning; institutions often do, as will be shown below.

Normative expectations, or norms, stabilize human (inter)action and make individual behaviour more predictable. Norms represent convergence processes in relation to human (inter)action, but with varying extension in time and space. Norms can be found in formal and articulated forms, as well as in forms that are more informal and tacit. Many concepts have been used by scientists to cover the whole range of possible 'groupings' of norms. Designations such as laws, regulations, rules, routines, conventions, traditions, customs, myths, and habits have been used. These (groupings of) norms often simultaneously express instrumental qualities (i.e., define efficiency) and values (i.e., provide meaning).

The 'locations' that Lane (1991) suggested for norms include laws, courts, interest groups and governmental agencies, preferences, myths (Meyer and Rowan, 1977), professions (DiMaggio and Powell, 1983), ideals and ideologies (Sjöstrand, 1992), material structures (Sjöstrand, 1993a), rules and routines (Nelson and Winter, 1982), culture (Zucker, 1988), technologies (Meyer and Scott, 1983), and educational curricula (Meyer et al., 1992).

An institution is defined here as a coherent system of norms. The word 'system' is used to convey the idea that the guiding norms are defined and interrelated in similar ways in the minds of different (inter)acting individuals. The norms may be secular and deriving from an ideology, for instance, or perhaps religious and linked to a belief system. A coherent system of norms, i.e., an institution, is usually linked to lengthy historical trends or to perduring cultures. Thus every norm has its own history which has produced its substance and its presence. Its very existence is a result of past conditions of power and the reference frames of various actors in history, individuals as well as collectives.

To qualify as an institution, this coherent system of norms also has to be shared and enforced. A shared norm may be taken for granted, implicit or unconsciously applied; or it may be explicitly and deliberately put into practice by the (inter)acting individuals. Several researchers perceive institutionalized activities especially associated with 'taken-for-granted' norms, defining the ways things are to be done. The norms then refer to the 'obvious' way to (inter)act, and concepts such as 'habit' and 'history' are commonly used (see e.g., Scott, 1987; Tushman and Romanelli, 1985; and Zucker, 1987). Sometimes these norms even refer to what can be described as shared, preconscious understandings (DiMaggio, 1988).

In the conscious and perhaps even intentional case, this sharing of a coherent system of norms indicates that the institution in focus represents values important to the individuals or collectives involved. Moreover, if the norms are shared, this could be a sign of the efficiency and/or legitimacy of the institution. However, there are also norms which dominate recurrent situations, despite lacking the qualities just described. Thus they are sometimes known and adjusted to, even though they are neither conscious, agreed on nor shared. The same applies to habitual (inter)action; institutions are (also) sometimes permeated with such actions.

Homo complexicus

An important part of the platform of most studies in the economic and social sciences consists of the particular chosen assumption regarding the human being. In institutional analyses *homo oeconomicus* is usually abandoned in favor of other conceptions, or the concept is at least modified in several important respects. The exclusive focus on interest-driven (inter)action, reflecting the behaviour of 'rational' *(homo oeconomicus)* actors, is abandoned. Some researchers, however, then tend to adopt the other extreme position, and to exclude interest-driven action from the institutional agenda (e.g., DiMaggio, 1988; Elster, 1989). In this type of approach, institutions are associated with a 'proceduralist' rather than a 'consequentialist' view of (inter)actions, i.e., it is assumed that interactions emerge independently of the goal orientations of the individuals involved.

The concept of 'interest' is central to almost all theories of human (inter)action. In mainstream economics, and in some sociological thinking, a rather simplistic utilitarian assumption dominates, while in institutional economics, many fields of sociology and in most organization theory, that assumption is abandoned in favor of others of a slightly more complex and empirically more substantial and relevant kind. There could be argument about which path to stress — interest-driven or uncertainty reducing behaviour (see below). Important in most modern institutional approaches, however, is the recognition of the presence and relevance of both. Maybe it is fair to say that institutionalists, at least over the last decade, have to a certain degree underestimated the merits of interest-oriented perspectives. In the theory developed here, however, humans are, conceived as both interactive and complex, in other words as *multirational*.

The notion of the multirational individual encompasses the idea that individuals are actors and that their actions are important in forming and organizing events, situations and environments. In their (inter)actions, individuals take into account experienced (inter)actions as well as the (inter)actions expected of others, both present and absent. The (inter)acting individual always includes others by way of socially constructed meanings; (inter)action is oriented toward and inspired by intersubjective representations (see Durkheim, 1984 [1893], p. 173; Weber, 1978 [1922], p. 4).

It was emphasized above that human (inter)action often takes place in some way in the presence of others. Obviously, the division of labour and far-reaching specialization make impersonal, occasional, and anonymous relations and exchanges necessary, thereby creating a need for an economizing and calculative rationale among humans (i.e., *homines oeconomics*). In economic analyses this calculative quality is traditionally associated with egoism and maximizing behaviour. It is not often very useful in scientific analysis, however, to claim that individuals are 'egoists' or that they act selfishly. Perhaps individuals do what they perceive is best for themselves; that is to say, they try to act in a *subjectively* 'rational' way. In such a perspective, all actions must then by definition be 'selfish', and the concept of 'egoism' becomes omnipresent and scientifically useless. It provides neither distinctions nor variances, and consequently has no distinct meaning. It would not then be possible to study or imagine non-selfish or 'altruistic' behaviour. Instead it is suggested here that altruism should be understood as referring to situations in which the primary consequences of human action are utility or wealth also for (some) others (even though, rightly or wrongly, such actions often could be described as simultaneously beneficial to the actor).

Uncertainty in human (inter)actions is thus reduced at least partly or temporarily as a result of calculations, but we have to bear in mind that frequent, continuous calculations incur a significant cost. Moreover, this calculative capacity is usually considered to be limited, in the sense that people cannot be assumed to be perfect calculators with infinite information processing capacities (cf. bounded rationality). In most economic analysis, however, this calculative logic is regarded as by far the most important way in which uncertainty is handled (Sjöstrand, 1992).

Historically, uncertainty has also been reduced or absorbed by various kinds of status or positional systems, by 'genuine' relationships such as those in a family or clan, or among neighbours and friends. Such (dependence) relations with *known* others are still highly relevant, but during the present century at least, they have been diluted by other forms associated with calculative action. These non-calculative ways are also sometimes available when uncertainty exists in relation to unknown others, particularly when calculations are difficult to make. Uncertainty can then also be reduced by way of relations and exchanges founded on the sharing of ideals and norms which create a common understanding and thus contribute to more trusting relationships, as well as hampering opportunistic behaviour and 'moral hazard'. These relationships then partially transform unknown others into (better) known others. Both the status or positional relationships, and those founded on shared ideals, are of great importance in emergent (inter)actions between individuals. As they are not founded on the calculative rationale, however, they represent what most neoclassical economists would describe as 'irrational' qualities (Sjöstrand, 1992). Finally, a fourth basic way of trying to absorb or regulate uncertainty is suggested here, involving the use of physical force or violence (coercive relationships).

Individuals thus try to reduce or absorb uncertainty not only by way of (a) calculative relations (= interest-driven — 'rational' — *homo oeconomicus* kind of behaviour), but also by (b) selected, value-impregnated interactions (relations anchored in shared values or ideals), by (c) genuine relations, and, finally, by (d) coercive relations (cf. Sjöstrand, 1985, 1992, and 1993b).

Although all the four kinds of relationships between individuals described here cope with uncertainty, they fulfill somewhat different purposes. The calculative rationale is associated to a greater extent with *exchange*. Relationships founded on shared ideals and values indicate *redistributive* purposes, while 'status' or genuine relationships signify *reciprocity*. Coercive relations, finally, indicate *repression*. There are thus several rationales involved when people relate to each other and engage in more or less continuous exchange (for an in-depth description of these rationalities see Sjöstrand, 1993b).

Actors and institutions defined

It has been suggested above that institutions influence human (inter)-actions, but this is not synonymous with a declaration of environmental determinism. Rather, reciprocity between individual actions and institutions is proposed, in the sense that each influences and constitutes the other. Institutions are not imposed on individuals, but provide the matrices in which individuals live and act. Consequently, the institutional setting does not define the actions undertaken by an individual in a mechanical and deterministic way; there is some freedom of action. Institutions open the way for human action, as well as restrict it, by representing structures which individuals can enforce, trespass upon or violate.

A definition of 'institution' emerges from the above discussion, and this will be used in the following attempt to formulate a theory. An institution is defined as *a social construct for a coherent system of shared and enforced norms*. Obviously the scope of institutions varies. Some institutions refer to less common but very important situations, while others represent more frequent but less crucial events (cf. p. 41 below).

EMERGENCE, REPRODUCTION AND DISSOCIATION OF INSTITUTIONS

Dynamics — previous attempts

In discussions on the dynamics of institutions and institutional change, a concept that appears quite often, especially among the New Institutional

Economists, is that of the 'game'. This concept has regained popularity in economic analysis in recent years, probably due to the slowly growing interest among neoclassically oriented researchers in trying to explain institutions without being forced to give up conventional basic assumptions. Research in the New Institutional Economics thus often describes institutions as ways of solving social coordination games, that is to say of preventing individual rational actions from leading to 'irrational' collective outcomes.

The main drawback to this game-theoretical tradition, in the context of institutional analysis, is that games allow neither for very complicated dynamics nor for *homo complexicus*. Change is, paradoxically, an important ingredient in the use of the institution concept in economic analysis, in that constitutional norms emerge in a continuous — albeit usually very slow and gradual — process, which is in turn affected by the outcomes of the simultaneous microlevel (inter)action processes in which individuals are involved. A game cannot cope with this more sophisticated type of interactive dynamics.

Other important contributions apart from game theory have of course been made to the theory of institutional change (i.e., the emergence, reproduction and dissociation of institutions) by neoclassically inspired institutional economists. Excellent surveys addressing these vast research fields have been presented by Bush (1987), Bromley (1989, ch. 2) and Gustafsson (1991, ch. 1). Quite a few of these neoclassical economists start from what they describe as 'market failures'. Institutions are then regarded as substitutes for, or complements to, (perfect or efficient) markets. Several reasons are suggested for these market failures (for an overview, see Sjöstrand, 1993b).

One problem about these approaches is that the market is not regarded as an institution in itself, but is treated more as a kind of preferable state and general reference point. It is defined in accordance with the neoclassical theoretical 'ideal type'[2], and is then used primarily for analytical purposes. Another problem about this perspective can be illustrated by stating the basic question the other way round, starting instead from 'hierarchical or organizational failures' and trying to explain the presence of (different kinds of) markets. Why not investigate instead why closed circles (e.g., couples, families, friends and neighbours), kinship (e.g., clans and dynasties), and other positional or status relationships, fail? Why not try to find out why and how these impersonal, calculative relationships, that characterize (ideal type) markets, emerge?

There has also been some significant institutional research in the economic sciences that stresses changes in relative prices (e.g., land and labour) and technology as important exogenous sources triggering institutional change and development (see Bush, 1987, for an overview). Most of these studies simultaneously add other crucial factors to their theory-building. Discussion of 'property rights' and 'transaction costs' is often introduced, as well as factors like 'resource endowment' and product demand (see North and Thomas 1970, 1973; North 1981, 1990; and Rowe, 1989). In the following theoretical exposition there will be an emphasis on the recent writings of Douglass North (1990 and 1993).

On North's theories of institutional change

North's ideas have become more sophisticated over the years. From a rather simplistic theory (1973), in which efficient institutions were told to be established mainly as a result of relative prices between land and labour, he went on to introduce technology, asymmetries, inefficient institutions, the economic entrepreneur, organizations, individuals with more complex motives (including ideals) and varying in their resource endowments (1990 and 1993).

North's current theory of institutional change is founded on individual choices. That is what makes it an economic theory and not part of the social sciences (North, 1990, p. 5). Integrating individual choices with the constraints that institutions represent is at the very heart of his theory of institutional change. Institutions, together with the technology employed, influence the performance of an economy by affecting the costs of exchange (= transaction costs), and production (= transformation costs), which add up to the 'total costs'.

Institutional change is according to North, a consequence of changes in rules, informal constraints, and in the kind and the effectiveness of the enforcement procedures (ibid., p. 6). In his view, institutions usually change gradually, due to the embeddedness of informal constraints in societies. This incremental change springs from a perception of entrepreneurs in organizations that they could do better by altering the existing institutional framework. This perception is dependent on the information which these individuals receive and the way it is processed (ibid., p. 8). Actors then have to rely on incomplete information and use mental constructs which could result in inefficient institutional paths.

North continues to develop his theory by abandoning the classical notion of the wealth-maximizing actor. In doing so he refers to experimental economics, surprisingly not to the vast experience provided by social scientists. He revises the assumptions regarding *homo oeconomicus* in several ways. North sees actors' motivations as a complicated phenomenon, and similarly the fact that individuals make choices based on incomplete information, and that they use diverging and subjectively derived models. He abandons the belief in rational choice, and rejects the conventional assumption of the economic sciences that individuals behaving in that famous 'rational' way will ultimately survive in competitive situations.

In describing his assumptions about human beings, North makes a distinction between human 'motivation' and the 'deciphering' of the environment by actors. As regards motivation, he adds further dimensions to the notion of *homo oeconomicus,* in particular ideologies, altruism and self-imposed constraints, and in connection with the deciphering of the enviroment he adds pre-existing mental maps. On the question of motivation, however, he concludes that these added dimensions or qualities do have a 'price', and that the trade-off between 'wealth' and these other qualities is a negatively sloped function; they will loom large when the price is low, i.e., when 'wealth' is only slightly affected. North then also tries to show that institutions alter the prices that individuals have to pay for 'non-rational' actions.

On the question of deciphering the environment, he emphasizes the subjective side of the activity, and the imperfection of human processing capacities. Complexities and uncertainty are then coped with by using simplified models or rules of thumb. Institutions, thus, exist to solve two problems at the same time: the complexity of the problems that face individuals, and the limitations in human information processing (bounded rationality). This complexity can be seen, for instance, in the number and variety of attributes attaching to services, commodities and actors, which then represent asymmetries in human (inter)actions or exchanges. In most situations, it is too costly for individuals to identify these attributes.

When it comes to exchanges between individuals North assumes that these are not without cost (cf. Coase's classical article, 1937). Nor is information. The 'total cost' according to North (1990), includes all the resource inputs (land, labour and capital) involved in the transformation of the physical attributes of goods, and the transactions connected with the corresponding exchanges (including the definition, protection and enforcement of the property rights associated with the good). The most observable form of institution according to North, is transaction costs, but he points out that most of these are hard to measure. In this chapter, therefore, norms are introduced as the tangible building blocks of institutions.

North sees institutions as providing the structure for exchange. How well they solve the organizing or coordinating of human effort is then determined by the motivation of the actors (their utility function), the complexity of the environment, and the ability of the actors to decipher and order this environment. Institutions structure economic exchanges in a variety of forms. North focuses on three general types: personalized exchange, (small-scale production; local trade), impersonal exchange (when parties are constrained by kinship ties, or exchanging hostages or following commercial codes of conduct), and impersonal exchange with third-party enforcement. These three types all focus on different modes of enforcement but North takes for granted that ideals (codes) and kinship are constraints, rather than something valuable which could be preferred *as such*.

An alternative way of distinguishing exchange and (inter)actions was proposed above, namely according to the different rationales involved. Four of these were defined as the calculative (cf. impersonal exchange with third-party enforcement), idealistic (cf. constrained impersonal exchanges), genuine (cf. constrained impersonal exchanges), and coercive rationales (cf. impersonal exchange with third-party enforcement). In his classification and theory-building, North thus leaves out some important kinds of interaction and exchange situations, probably partly because he perceives institutions as constraints only, and therefore describes genuine and idealistic relationships as 'constrained' preferred others (= calculative relations). Maybe another explanation for this exclusion of some rationales is North's assumption that 'economic' exchanges can be separated from their social settings, and that relationships anchored in ideals and genuine relations do not exist in 'economic' exchanges.

'Informal' constraints (those outside the state sector and legislation) come, according to North, from the socially transmitted information called 'culture'. There are many names for these norms: routine, custom, rule, tradition, ritual, etc. Their roots are habitual behaviour (ibid., p. 83). 'Formal' constraints, on the other hand, include political and judicial rules, economic rules (!), and contracts. The basic difference between formal and informal constraints seems to be connected with differing means for enforcement.

Enforcement is generally motivated on grounds of making the effects of specialization and the division of labour available to people. Each individual has to be confident (has to be able to enforce) that most of the others carry out their part of the whole. Enforcement, according to North, has principally three main sources: the self (internally enforced codes of conduct), the other person (second-party retaliation), and a third party ('societal sanctions'; e.g., the state). The state, then, represents a monopolistic coercive force (i.e., institution) socially constructed to monitor property rights and to enforce contracts effectively.

North generally uses the 'market' as the (sometimes implicit) reference point in his analysis. Thus the market is not regarded as one institution among others. It is pre-eminent, as it is defined as a 'mixed bag of institutions' (ibid. p. 69). Some effective institutions will appear which will reduce the 'total cost', while others which are inefficient will raise costs. North explains the existence of inefficient institutions on the grounds that the market (!) is imperfect; in other words it is not an ideal type but is like 'a mixed bag of institutions'. But these 'mixed institutions' could not select or reproduce constructions other than those which are identical or similar to themselves. Thus his reasoning here goes in a circle. Or is there a meta-market somewhere (the ideal type?), which decides which actual markets (institutions, perhaps mixed?) will survive?

According to North, institutional change occurs by way of various norms and the way these are enforced. Path-dependence, however, is prominent. North sees this institutional change as being primarily triggered by changes in relative prices or in human preferences. The former include changes in the cost of information, in technology (competences) and in (relative) factor prices. Thus, one explanation is again the exogenous one suggested in his early works (e.g., North, 1973). But according to North himself the most important explanation is endogenous, and it reflects the continuous efforts of entrepreneurs. The agent of change, the innovation-generator, is the individual (entrepreneur) who makes use of certain knowledge which he or she can command (e.g., regarding patent law, etc). The institutional framework shapes the direction of the individual competence acquiring activities.

When it comes to changes in preferences North resigns, and admits that 'we know very little about the sources of changing preferences' (ibid. p. 84). He suggests, again, that these arise from changes in relative prices (cf. above). In this context the notion of the organization is introduced as a maximizing tool for the entrepreneur. Organizations shape institutional change by investing in certain (individuals') competences, choosing within existing constraints, or altering them. Organizations will also engage 'society' to invest in what is beneficial to them. This would lead to convergence processes. Over time the strong or 'large' institutions will swallow the weak ones because of the presence of asymmetries (= power relations), which at least temporarily and probably for fairly long periods, may preserve 'inefficient' institutions. There is always this element of inefficiency — what some neoclassical economists would label 'slack' — in societies. Sometimes it increases and sometimes it decreases, there is a continous path dependent fluctuation.

The interaction between organizations and institutions is crucial in North's theory of institutional change. He discusses the mechanisms for institutional change, i.e., how adaptive efficiency arises and how it works. Unfortunately this is again a circular argument. The institutional setting at a certain moment represents the individuals' (organizations') incentives to act. At the same time the institutions represent the standards for eliminating 'failing' attempts, either individual or organizational (or organizing). What then explains the possible motive for an individual to do something new, something which is not part of the incentives built into the existing institutions? Success based on such efforts is impossible, since the existing institutions define the criteria. In other words, it seems difficult to find any reason why entrepreneurs should go beyond the existing institutional frames.

How, then, is it possible to change institutions, to develop new paths, when the institutions themselves (as constraints) define both incentives and outcomes? Ultimately North fails to explain how an existing structure of incentives (as prevailing in institutions) changes, i.e., he never explains the transformation from one path to another. Gustafsson (1991) adds to this criticism, which was originally raised by Bromley (1989).

Gustafsson (ibid.) stresses the fragmented character of most of these neoclassically inspired 'neoinstitutional' theories. Descriptions of the relationships between the crucial concepts are often ambiguous, if they exist at all. North is once again the main target for criticism, although in many respects his approach is probably the best developed yet. In particular, according to Gustafsson, North neglects or fails to state in any straightforward way the relationships between institutions, endowments and technology, which according to North all define the opportunity sets for actors wanting to alter institutions in a society. Nor does North provide an unambiguous discussion of the important relationships between changes in relative prices, preferences and organizational actions, even though he suggests all three factors as those which initiate changes in institutions. Perhaps the most fundamental weakness, according to Gustafsson (ibid.) concerns the lack of information about the source of an organizational commitment to change institutions. Nor is there much comment on the tensions and conflicts often involved in these processes of change, or on the reasons for the continual development and existence of inefficient institutions.

TOWARDS A THEORY OF INSTITUTIONAL CHANGE

In seeking to understand institutional change we start from the assumption that institutions, as described above, refer to norms for organizing rather than to any a priori defined organizational norms. Institutions do not 'provide' structures for exchange or interaction; they constitute generalized regularities in the organizing activities themselves. Thus, for example, if the physical manifestations of institutions suddenly break down, it could be a sign of institutional change but is not necessary so, since institutions represent norms for organizing rather than concrete structures.

A critique of North

In this concluding section, I will attempt to tackle some of the weaknessess inherent in the theory of institutional change proposed by several institutionalists, foremost by Douglass North (1990 and 1993). In particular, I will address the problem of what makes institutional change possible, i.e., how is it possible to break the above-mentioned path-dependence? To do this it will be necessary to reformulate some of North's assumptions. Although he has, for example, abandoned some of the basic conventional neoclassical assumptions regarding human beings these changes are not sufficient to explain the triggering forces behind institutional change. Moreover, in this chapter the (inter)action concept is preferred to exchange, in line with the argument that economic changes cannot be separated from their social context(s). This is usually referred to as the problem of embeddedness (cf. Granovetter, 1985).

There are basically two ways of conceiving the emergence of institutions: (a) by considering the outcome of competition between existing institutions, or (b) by considering the processes constituting a particular institution. The first one refers to some kind of 'natural' selection, and there are several reasons why this will not be efficient (see below). Other explanations include 'adverse selection', whereby short-term conditions, random or otherwise, which differ significantly from long-term conditions, may wipe out certain institutions, thus sooner or later producing inefficient institutions. Frequency could generate similar problems. It is possible to single out at least two problems intrinsic to institutional reproduction, which may provide the primary stuff of its dynamics: one is the socialization of new members, the other is the difficulty in maintaining intense commitment for very long.

Some of North's positions need to be developed further. In his recent writings he adopts three stances which could be questioned. First, he is not interactional in his theory-building; i.e., he does not regard the complex relationship(s) between the exchanging actors as crucial. In fact he tries to separate 'economic' exchanges from their social embeddedness, as is made clear in his discussion of exchange types based on enforcement variations rather than individual motives or rationales. The same attitude emerges from his discussion of three sources of enforcement, where he adopts a simple, atomistic perspective. Finally, he also often describes institutions as 'providing' structures for interactions, rather than representing or constituting the on-going human interactions themselves.

Another problem, not unrelated to the first is that according to North 'wealth' does not include activities associated with altruism, ideologies or self-imposed constraints. He tries to identify one kind of wealth, not surprisingly the one connected with the notion of *homo oeconomicus,* and then to treat other ingredients as trade-offs, as having a 'price'. But why not the other way around? Why (always?) adopt the *homo oeconomicus* assumption (the calculative rationale) as the reference point or preferred state? Why not try to treat all 'wealth ingredients' in a similar way, without pre-set rankings?

In the same spirit, at least implicitly, North adopts the ideal type of market as the reference point in discussing institutions. This (ideal type of) 'initial state' then becomes more complicated when, in practice, it is filled with 'institutions' (constraints). Thus, the ideal type of market is treated as the preferred state rather than as one theoretical or empirical institution among several (cf. Sjöstrand, 1992). According to North, institutions appear on the stage when human beings do not act in accordance with the assumption of *homo oeconomicus.* This 'deviant' behaviour is then said to be due to 'constraints' (institutions) in the situation.

Another problem in using North's theory of institutional change is that it does not provide a theoretical explanation of what makes 'entrepreneurs' change existing path-dependent institutions. The only exogenous force suggested in his current (1990, 1993) theory is the one presented as far back as the early 1970s (diseases of various kinds). Endogenous sources are important, he claims, but he makes no attempt to explain in what way. 'Preferences change, but we do not know how' (p. 84).

North introduces the concept and the entity of 'the organization', which is supposed to be able to maximize as a result of the behaviour of its non-maximizing actors. The relationship between actors and organizations, however, is not clear. The main impression is that the organization is a tool for the entrepreneur, but that makes the maximizing logic of the organization come as a surprise. However, organizations invest in (human) competence, and they try to choose among, and to break, institutional norms. But, again, how is this possible? The institutions themselves, as we have seen, define what is efficient action.

If instead we accept the idea that institutions represent interaction patterns between humans rather than 'provide structures' for the various human exchanges, and if we also accept the notion that economic and social exchanges — i.e., interactions — are amalgamated (cf. the notion of *homo complexicus*), then could the problem of what makes institutional change possible be solved. In other words, a truly dynamic perspective has to be introduced.

The core of this theory — micro macro tension[3]

In any discussion of institutional change it is important to try to identify the potential sources of such change. Thus, an innovation generator is needed. The approach advocated here starts from two separate but related analytical levels in addressing human (inter)actions and exchanges, namely the 'micro' (inividual) and 'macro' (socially constructed) levels. Micro level situations refer to people's first-hand evidence of particular others and particular environments, while the macro level refers to (indirect) indicators, descriptions of or from generalized or unknown others, and/or formal (legal, physical) structures. Further, microlevel situations tend to be limited in scope, and their coherent system of shared and enforced norms often relates in a direct way to some or even most of the interacting individuals in the experienced contexts, while macro level information tends to be grand in scope, referring to a rather abstract and attenuated coherent system of shared norms (cf. Zucker, 1988).

Institutions, which generally represent macrophenomena, are continuously (re)produced by individuals in their daily activities and interactions on the microlevel. The use of the prefix '(re)' indicates that this reproduction on the micro level is usually an extended process (i.e., it is imperfect), and thus over time it sometimes modifies or even alters the significant norms and their interrelationships, thereby also changing the existing institutions on the macro level.

It is suggested here that the ever-present mismatch between the micro and macro levels is the major initiating force in institutional change processes. This mismatch is further explained by the distance between the experiences and thoughts of the many single individuals on the micro level (some of the more active human beings are often called 'entrepreneurs') on the one hand, and the content and regulations embedded in the more formalized institutions on the macro level, reflecting a more general perspective in society, on the other. There are significant gaps between the social facts institutionalized at the macro level and those present at the micro level. These gaps or differences between the two levels arise primarily from their different origins (cf. Zucker, 1988).

The micro (individual) level

The role of the individual entrepreneur now has to be elaborated. Change, from an individual and interactional point of view, must include at least three steps. First of all we have to assume that an individual describes his experiences and thoughts with the help of concepts ('social construction of reality'). Second, as a result of interaction or communication, these concepts become to some extent shared intersubjectively, and are in that sense 'objectivized'. They then acquire 'a life of their own' and have to be interpreted by the actors (creating variation). Third, individuals internalize the use of a concept, perhaps making it part of their 'cognitive schemes' and thereby contributing to what provides meaning for them. Institutional change thus very much concerns micro level interactions and (communicative) exchanges.[4]

Here, five ways are suggested as to how individuals make institutional change possible, breaking the path-dependence and circularity inherent in the theory presented by North (1990). The basic mechanisms suggested are human *perception*, human *imagination*, human *limitations*, human *mobility* and human *commitment*.

Regarding the first of these, human perception, a source of variation is that institutions are not always 'activated' (i.e., 'perceived'), from the perspective of the single individual. They are not continuous phenomena in the perceptions of actors. Only now and then do individuals relate in their interactions to a specific institution, thereby contributing to its (re)production, creation or destruction. There are several reasons for this. Which norms, associated with certain institutions, are appropriate to a particular activity is often a dubious question. An activity could also have multiple meanings to different individuals, thus becoming the focus of conflicting institutional definitions and demands. The definition or demarcation of particular situations contributes to this uncertainty or conflict. Different individuals often perceive a particular situation in dissimilar ways, and each one therefore acts on his or her own presumptions. Thus they act in a specific situation as if they were being influenced by different institutions. This variety creates confusion and even tension.

There is usually a common and instinctive understanding among individuals of how to group or cluster situations, and consequently what institutions to refer to. This understanding could then be described as human 'instituting ideas' (cf. Neale, 1987), which in turn are usually based on notions of necessary and sufficient requisites for identifying and classifying a situation, and are very often based on considerations of time and space. But such a common understanding does not solve the problem of the normative ambiguity inherent in most microlevel situations. Situations are not always similarly known and defined; different individuals may perceive a single situation as belonging to a different cluster, and consequently to another institutional setting.

Thus, in almost every particular situation, the individual can 'choose' among several simultaneously existing but often unrelated or sometimes even conflicting norms. One important source of this (partial) individual freedom of action, the capacity to 'choose', rests on the ability of people to discriminate between *what is* and *what should or could be*. It rests on the human capacity of imagination. Some claim that this freedom of action is very limited, that most action is performed by routine, while others stress instead the opportunities for human discretion. In this chapter it is assumed that *some* freedom does exist for the individual, not least because the norms specified and enforced by way of an institutional setting are always incomplete. Thus individuals at least have a choice between different coherent systems of norms. They sometimes even face the problem of how to select and fit a norm to a situation.

Another way to explain institutional change processes is by introducing the idea of the existence of flows of norms between contexts. These flows are produced by meetings between previously unrelated individuals, which give rise to creative, imitative or destructive institutional processes. Individuals move physically and perhaps also mentally from one context or setting to another. As a result of these continuous streams of human experiences and ideas across previously unlinked or relatively autonomous settings, conflicts between differing or even antagonistic systems of shared and enforced norms tend to appear.

If the situation is such that the various institutions cannot co-exist, if the 'gaps' are too big in the minds of those involved, then sometimes the old structures will live on more or less unchanged, and sometimes they will break down and new ones will emerge. The outcomes of these processes are then dependent on the nature of the possibilities for identification (cf. commitment) provided by the competing emergent institutions, and on expectations about other people's inclination to comply to this or that alternative. Screpanti (Chapter 4 of this volume) suggests 'institutional involvement' or 'institutional compliance' as useful concepts to adopt in analysing these questions. Moreover, as human beings have their shortcomings (cf. p. 22, above), at least some variation is certain to occur in the actions taken. This variation could be intentional or it could be unconscious. It could also sometimes arise by accident (cf. bounded rationality), and sometimes by chance.

The frequency with which an individual practices a certain rationale, for example conforming to a social norm, depends on many things. Important factors are the frequency with which it has been practiced in the past, and (or) the frequency with which it is practiced by other social units. If a multiplicity of competing institutional forms exists at one point in time, frequency-dependency effects may lead to the dominance of a particular institution by virtue of the prevalence of certain initial conditions rather than because of the efficiency of the institutions (cf., for example, Hodgson, 1991).

Some researchers point out, as an example of the importance of frequency, that under capitalism, norms associated with the collective interest are regularly 'selected away' by the self-reinforcing norm of self-interest. This process occurs despite the fact that a collective-interest approach may help solve problems of cooperation and coordination, and hence may ultimately promote/flavour the workings of a capitalist political economy. If an economy becomes 'locked in' to self-selecting, inefficient institutions, there is a risk that these will subsequently persist for a long time.

The macro (socially constructed) level

Some institutions encompass larger sectors of a society than others. In that sense there are dependencies or at least weak ties (partial overlaps at various levels in society). Consequently, there is a certain institutional interrelatedness, which to some extent explains institutional stability and path dependence. The cost of changing a specific institution at one level could depend on the degree of its connection with the next level, and so forth. Institutional stability is then secured by this interconnectedness, by the web of institutions overlapping with each other sometimes even in hierarchical relationships. In this last case each higher level, with its greater scope, becomes more difficult and therefore more costly to change than the previous lower level.

But the situation does not always resemble the one described above, which could be described as a situation of harmony between various hierarchically connected institutions. At the same time, it is important to remember that different institutions tend to intermix in the micro level arenas, for example, in organizations of various kinds. This mixture could very well reflect conflicts between rationalities in the individual institutions involved. Harmony does not necessarily exist between various existing institutions, and outcomes at the macro level are thus also determined by actual or potential competition between institutions in the micro arenas.

Finally: the reproduction of institutions

In seeking further understanding of institutional change, a possible starting point is to analyse the way institutions are reproduced over time. In the basic concept and definition of the 'institution' stability and pattern maintenance are both important factors. But this stability varies between different kinds of institutions, and is seldom indefectible. For example, the understanding of societywide culture constituting concepts such as 'democracy', 'rationality', and 'efficiency' is often solidly institutionalized (cf. Gustafsson, 1994), while institutions of a more finite or limited scope may be relatively unstable and fluid. Thus, in order to last, institutions have to be continuously (re)produced.

A short summary

What has been emphasized in this chapter, but what may not have been immediately obvious from the formal definition given, is that organizing institutions are being continuously shaped and reshaped or (re)produced as a result of historical, and emerging (inter)action patterns in society. They represent and simultaneously provide arenas for experiments, trial-and-error processes and learning among individuals at the micro level, and perhaps also for organizations. The gap or mismatch between the micro and macro levels is the driving force, the innovation generator behind institutional change. Institutions are thus phenomena that coordinate, regulate, and stabilize human activities at a macro level, while simultaneously functioning as part of the raw material of change on the micro level.

These patterns or infrastructures of human interaction absorb crucial uncertainties, while at the same time reducing the demands on the cognitive capacity of the human mind. Parallel with this, institutions also stabilize expectations and coordinate actions by assimilating certain cognitive maps or charts. These become prescribed patterns for correlating behaviour in the performance of various tasks. Institutions facilitate the application of reliable knowledge to the performance of the continuing activities which a community has come to regard as significant, such as the production of food and goods, the determination of income shares, the transportation of persons, and so forth. This application of knowledge is often the primary reason for the existence of an institution and for any changes that occur in it.

NOTES

1. Cf. Sjöstrand, 1993b.
2. Ideal type then refers to a theoretical construction (cf. the related German term *Gedankenbild*) which is formed by an accentuation of selected points of view. Here, an ideal type expresses conceptual purity, and each single ideal type is an elaborate construct which (usually) cannot be found as a unit anywhere in the empirical world. It is neither separate from empirical sources nor simple reflections of empirical phenomena. An ideal type, however, is often based on scientific knowledge that explicitly or implicitly involves empirical ingredients. Then it is

not irrelevant whether to base its ingredients on the best scholarly knowledge existing or making use of pure fantasy constructions. Its fruitfulness in the continuously ongoing theoretical discussion is therefore crucial for each ideal type construct. The value of a construct of this kind is not decided through the testing of single ideal types against single empirical organizations. Its value is shown when the whole theoretical repertoire (= the related ideal types) as such is confronted with an empirical material for analyses. To sum up: the relationship between theory and empirical sources is an analytical one — ideal types represent a kind of 'as if'-tools when theoretizing.
3. This part was inspired by Zucker (1988).
4. There is an interesting article by Elsner (1989) which discusses how Adam Smith explained the emergence of institutions. This discussion is connected with the imaginative capacity of humans in interactive situations, and Elsner explains successively how 'initial normative rules', 'positive rules', 'sophisticated normative rules', and '(normative) institutions' evolve.

REFERENCES

Bromley, D. (1989), *Economic Interests and Institutions*, Basil Blackwell, New York.
Bush, P. (1987), 'Theory of Institutional Change', *Journal of Economic Issues*, vol. XXI, no. 3. pp. 1075–1116.
Coase, R. (1937), 'The Nature of the Firm', *Economica*, vol. 4, pp. 386–405.
Coase, R. (1984), 'The New Institutional Economics', *Journal of Institutional and Theoretical Economy*, March, pp. 229–32.
DiMaggio, P. (1988), 'Interest and Agency', in Lynne G. Zucker (ed.), *Institutional Patterns and Organizations*.
DiMaggio, P. and Powell, W. (1983), 'The Iron Cage Revisited', *American Sociological Review*, vol. 48, pp. 147–70.
Durkheim, E. (1984) [1893], *The Division of Labor in Society*, Free Press, New York.
Elster, J. (1989), *The Cement of Society*, Cambridge University Press, Cambridge.
Elsner, W. (1989), 'Adam Smith's Model of the Origins and Emergence of Institutions', *Journal of Economic Issues*, vol. XXIII. no. 1, pp. 189–213.
Granovetter, M. (1985), 'Economic Action and Social Structure, The Problem of Embeddedness', *American Journal of Sociology* 91, pp. 481–510.
Gustafsson, B. (ed.) (1991), *Power and Economic Institutions*, Edward Elgar, Aldershot.
Gustafsson, C. (1994), *Om Produktion av Allvar*, N&S, Stockholm (in Swedish only).
Hodgson, G.M. (1991), 'Economic Evolution: Intervention Contra Pangloss', *Journal of Economic Issues*, vol. 25, pp. 519–33.
Lane, R. (1991), *The Market Experience*, Cambridge University Press, Cambridge.
Meyer, J. and B. Rowan (1977), 'Institutional Organizations: Formal Structure as Myth and Ceremony', *American Journal of Sociology*, vol. 83, pp. 340–363.
Meyer, J. and R. Scott (1983), 'Centralization and the Legitimacy Problems of Local Government' in Meyer J.W. and W.R. Scott (eds.), *Organizational Environments: Ritual and Rationality*, CA, Sage, Beverly Hills, pp. 199–215.
Meyer, J. et al. (1992), *School Knowledge for the Mass*, Falmer, Washington D.C.
Neale, Walter (1987), 'Institutions', *Journal of Economic Issues*, vol. XXI, no. 3, pp. 1177–1206.
Nelson, R. and Winter, S. (1982), *An Evolutionary Theory of Economic Change*, Belknap Press, Cambridge, Mass.

North, D. (1981), *Structure and Change in Economic History*, Norton, New York.
North, D. (1990), *Institutions, Institutional Change and Economic Performance*, Cambridge University Press, Cambridge, Mass.
North, D. (1993), 'Institutional Change — A Framework for Analysis' in Sjöstrand, S-E. (ed.) (1993a), *Institutional Change: Theory and Empirical Findings*, M. E. Sharpe, New York, pp. 35-46.
North, D. and R. Thomas, (1970), 'An Economic Theory of the Growth of the Western World', *Economic History Review*, vol. 23, pp. 1-17.
North, D. and R. Thomas, (1973), *The Rise of the Western World*, Cambridge University Press, Cambridge, Mass.
Rowe, N. (1989), *Rules and Institutions*, Philip Allen, New York.
Scott, R. (1987), 'The Adolescence of Institutional Theory', *Administrative Science Quarterly*, vol. 32, pp. 493-511.
Scott, R. (1990), 'Institutional Analysis: Variance and Powers Theory Approaches', Paper presented at SCANCORS' Conference in Stockholm, Sweden, August 1990, pp. 29-31.
Simon, H. (1991), *Models of My Life*, Basic Books, Alfred P. Sloan foundation series, (biography), New York.
Sjöstrand, S-E. (1973), *Företagsorganisation*, EFI, HHS Stockholm (in Swedish only).
Sjöstrand, S-E. (1985), *Samhällsorganisation*, Doxa (available in Swedish only), Lund.
Sjöstrand, S-E. (1992), 'On the Rationale Behind Irrational Institutions', *Journal of Economic Issues*, vol. XXVI, no. 4, pp. 1007-40.
Sjöstrand, S-E.. (ed.) (1993a), *Institutional Change: Theory and Empirical Findings*, M. E. Sharpe, New York.
Sjöstrand, S-E.. (1993b), 'On Institutional Thought in the Social and Economic Sciences', in *Institutional Change: Theory and Empirical Findings*, M. E. Sharpe, New York.
Stein, J. (1993), *Strategy Formation and Managerial Agency*, EFI (the Stockholm School of Economics), Stockholm.
Tushman, M.L. and Romanelli, E. (1985), 'Organizational Evolution: a Metamorphosis Model of Convergence and Reorientation' in Cummings L.L. and Staw, B. (eds.), *Research in Organizational Behavior*, pp. 171-222, JAI Press, Greenwich CT.
Weber, M. (1978) [1922], *Economy and Society*, University of California Press, Berkely.
Zucker, L.G. (1987), 'Institutional Theories of Organizations', *Annual Review of Sociology*, vol. 13, pp. 443-464.
Zucker, L. (ed.) (1988), *Institutional Patterns and Organizations*, Ballinger, Cambridge.

3. Rational Action and Institutional Change

Shaun Hargreaves Heap

INTRODUCTION

This chapter is concerned with institutional change and its relationship to rational action. I begin with some brief background reflections on the relationship between institutions per se and rational action. These lead me to argue that an understanding of both institutional allegiance and institutional change requires an expanded notion of rational action. In particular, a sense of rational action is required which allows an important part to be played by shared sources of 'extraneous information'. By 'extraneous', what is meant is information which is not regarded as relevant under the standard account of instrumentally rational decision making. Thus, for instance, the web of shared beliefs which cultural anthropologists refer to as a group's culture could play a central role in the constitution of rational action.

The third section provides an illustration of this argument. It is concerned with how one particular theory of 'extraneous information', Mary Douglas's Cultural Theory, helps explain the divergent income distributions in OECD countries observed over the last 10–15 years. The fourth section addresses more directly the question of institutional change. It is concerned with whether to expect the further entrenchment of market institutions and market values in OECD countries. In particular, it focuses on two arguments which point to continuing entrenchment. The first relates to the much noticed changes in shared 'extraneous' beliefs which are associated with the so-called transition from 'modernity' to 'post-modernity'. The second is concerned with the impact on shared beliefs of the conspicuous shifts by governments over more than a decade towards pro-market policies.

INSTITUTIONS AND RATIONALITY

Throughout this discussion, institutions are understood broadly. They are the rules or procedures which in one way or another supplement the standard instrumental account of rational action. Thus we typically respect or use a variety of shared rules, some formal and some informal, as constraints upon our actions or as guides to how we should process information. This is particularly so when forming expectations regarding what others will do. Indeed, without these guides, the actions which serve our interests would be opaque because the world in which we operate would lack the requisite shape or order for making such calculations.

The recognition of institutions in this respect begs a question about their relationship to rational action and there are two broad types of answer. One keeps faith with the instrumental model of rational action and suggests that these practices have evolved to serve our instrumental concerns (see for instance, Schotter, 1981, and Sugden, 1986). Thus a convention emerges at the metaphorical crossroads of life because it serves everyone's interest. It is the unintended consequence of us experimenting or learning from experience (in a procedurally rational sense) with respect to how best to act. Nobody thinks about why it should be 'giveway to the left' rather than 'giveway to the right', even though each would coordinate the traffic at the crossroads as well as the other. We simply accept whichever has emerged historically. In this sense the evolutionary account treats us as institutional dopes, which is unsatisfactory in two respects.

Firstly it seems that we do think, at least occasionally, about the merits of conventions; we don't just accept their emergence. For example, we do think about whether it is better to have 'capital hiring labour' or 'labour hiring capital'. Yet both are plausibly conventions which could serve us by establishing a property right (in this instance over residual incomes) because we typically benefit from clear rather than opaque property rights; and so there would be no reason on these grounds for distinguishing between them. Or to give an example which connects with the discussion in section III, most bargaining problems are indeterminate in the sense that there are any number of possible expectations 'x' regarding what share of the pie you should get which will prove consistent with those of other claimants provided their expectations sum to '1–x' (i.e.,one for each possible value of 'x'). It is in each person's interest that there is an agreement on 'x', since conflict is thereby avoided, but we do not typically accept without question a figure which emerges from an evolutionary historical process. We reflect on 'x' and like to think that it has some merit, usually in terms of how it coheres with our shared notions of justice.

Secondly, it is not obvious that even if we were motivated in the standard instrumental way, that we would be best served by such an unreflective attitude since there seems to be no reason for supposing that evolutionary processes will deliver the best convention. Indeed, this is now much better appreciated both theoretically, through the formal analysis of evolutionary game theory, and through practical examples like the QWERTY keyboard arrangement or the failure of Betamax to become the industry standard for videos (VCRs).

Both problems suggest that a recognition of institutions requires a fundamental re-working of our notions of rational agency as has long been argued by institutionalists (see Sjöstrand, 1993). In a sense we have to act not just because it serves our interests, as there is more than one convention which when followed by all would fulfil this function, but also because we believe that one way of acting is 'right'. Thus, on this account, institutions could not always simply be conventions writ large (that is, rules which it makes instrumental sense to follow because others follow them). Instead, they often embody some further shared normative commitments which makes the following of the rule seem 'right' to those who inhabit the institution and this, in turn, means that we shall need a model of rational action which renders such normative commitments intelligible. In other words, our actions in an institutional context draw on some other, non-instrumental vocabulary (for further discussion of what this might entail, see Hargreaves Heap, 1991).

These points can be made in a more formal game theoretic way. Many games have multiple Nash (or Nash refinement) equilibria (as in the earlier example of the bargaining game). These are the equilibria which are standardly taken by game theorists to be consistent with agents being instrumentally rational and having common knowledge of that rationality. Thus the instrumental conception of rationality is not sufficient to fix behaviour. To fix behaviour (and so understand which equilibrium emerges) the agents will have to draw on shared sources of 'extraneous information'. Why? The information will have to be extraneous to the way that the interaction is defined by game theory because this description has thrown up the problem of indeterminacy; and the extraneous information will have to be shared by the agents, otherwise it will not do the job of selecting the same equilibrium for both players.

The importance of the contrast between these two approaches is perhaps clearest when we turn to questions of institutional change. With the approach which maintains the exclusive reliance on instrumental rationality and turns to evolutionary accounts of conventions, there is little more to be said about institutional change. Evolutionary processes depend too heavily on matters of chance and contingency and we must effectively sit back and see what happens. In contrast, the second approach suggests that the key to understanding institutional change lies not only in how chance and contingency make one way of doing things seem a more effective servant of our preferences but also in understanding how those sources of 'extraneous information' may contribute to how we come to see certain ways of doing things as more effective and how those sources of extraneous information themselves change.

In short, if the latter argument is accepted, then we need to know about the sources of 'extraneous information' which influence our current actions and our receptivity to certain sorts of change and we need to know more about how these sources of 'extraneous information' are changing.

(MARY DOUGLAS'S) CULTURAL THEORY AS A THEORY OF EXTRANEOUS BELIEF

In some of my previous work, I have argued that Mary Douglas's Cultural Theory provides a ready source for economists to draw on if they wish to understand the 'sources of extraneous information' which contribute to equilibrium selection. Thus, I have argued that her cultural theory is particularly helpful if we wish to understand why different economic agents or groups respond variously to different kinds of risks, as they often seem to do, for instance, in the evaluation of environmental risks (see Hargreaves Heap, 1986). Likewise, I suggest that her theory can contribute to the explanation of the recent changes in competitiveness among the major OECD ocuntries by providing an understanding of why some countries have been more receptive to the technological change associated with so-called flexible manufacturing systems (Hargreaves Heap 1991, 1993). In this section, I provide a further illustration and it is probably sensible if I begin with a very brief sketch of her cultural theory.

Mary Douglas essentially provides a taxonomy of possible beliefs which are in turn associated with four ideal-types of institutions. Figure

3.1 sets out the types. They are gained by fracturing the familiar opposition between the institutions of markets and hierarchies across two dimensions: what she refers to as the 'group' and 'grid' dimensions. The former captures the extent to which the institutions of a society involve an overlapping membership so that clear group boundaries can be drawn, and the latter refers to whether the institutions themselves make distinctions of rank between individuals who populate them. So, for instance, 'individualist' institutions are typically populated by people who have no ties to a shared (and possibly larger) group and they expect interactions within the institution to be free-wheeling and unscripted by considerations of class, caste or other sources of rank.

Figure 3.1   Cultural ideal type institutions (from Mary Douglas)

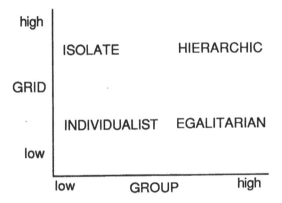

Thus there are four broad types of institutions and Mary Douglas associates them respectively with a variety of 'extraneous beliefs', ranging from particular views about nature through attitudes about education to their respective views on justice (see Douglas, 1978 and 1986 for more details). In part these mappings are held to be empirical regularities and in part they seem to stem from a requirement that each web of belief should be internally coherent in the support which it lends to its institutional type.

Now consider the changes in income distribution which have been observed in OECD countries over the last 10–15 years (table 3.1). The income distribution changes differ markedly across these countries and it would be nice to know what accounts for these differences as they seem somewhat puzzling from a conventional viewpoint. Broadly speaking, on a conventional neoclassical account, one would expect a change in income distribution to result from some change in the exogenous variables: the 'givens' of technology, tastes and the population. Yet most of these countries have been exposed to broadly similar technological and demographic changes over this period. For example, every economy has faced the challenge which some refer to as the technological shift from 'Fordist' to 'Post-Fordist' techniques and most economies have a similar demographic profile with a concentration around the so-called baby-boomers of the immediate postwar years.

Table 3.1. Wage inequalities in OECD countries (ratio of top 10 % of earners to bottom 10%)

COUNTRY	1980/81	1987/90	CHANGE OVER 1980s	
Italy	2.11	2.08	−0.03	(males, 80–87)
Canada	3.48	3.98	+0.50	(males, 81–90)
Ireland	na	na	na	
USA	4.75	5.63	+0.88	(males, 80–89)
Australia	2.02	2.27	+0.03	(males, 80–90)
UK	2.67	3.37	+0.70	(males, 81–90)
Belgium	2.47	2.53	+0.06	(both, 86–88)
France	3.25	3.21	−0.04	(males, 80–90)
Denmark	2.14	2.15	+0.01	(males, 80–90)
Sweden	2.15	2.15	±0.00	(males, 81–91)
Japan	2.59	2.83	+0.24	(males, 79–90)
Norway	2.05	1.97	−0.08	(both, 80–91)
Germany	2.40	2.32	−0.08	(males, 81–90)
Netherlands	2.21	2.29	+0.08	(males, 79–90)

So why have there been such divergences? One possible explanation draws on the differences in the cultures of the various economies. Extraneous information could play a role in two ways on this account. Firstly, it would not be surprising to find that culture influenced the institutional arrangements (with respect to provision of human capital programmes and the like) which affect how these basic economic changes in technology and the working population translate into actual demand and supply developments in individual labour markets. Secondly, even when economies have the same configuration of supply and demand in individual labour markets, the structure of wages can vary as a result of differences in culture. The point here is that typically wages are set either implicitly or explicitly through bargaining and few people now believe that bargaining problems have unique solutions (see section II). Instead, there are multiple equilibria and the selection of one rather than another is likely to turn on the sources of extraneous information which the bargainers share. When these vary across countries, so will the solution selected in their respective bargaining problems.

To test whether Mary Douglas's specific cultural theory potentially contributes to understanding these divergent developments in this way, we need to reflect on what differences in income distribution it would predict and we need some independent assessment of where each country's culture lies in grid-group space. The first part of this is relatively easy. Mary Douglas's theory appears to yield two predictions:

1. 'egalitarian' countries will, *ceteris paribus,* have more equal distributions than both 'hierarchic' and 'individualist' ones.

2. 'individualist' societies will, *ceteris paribus,* have income distributions which are more sensitive to changes in the underlying economic parameters of the bargaining problem.

This is not the place for a complete explanation of these predictions (see Douglas, 1978). Nevertheless, a quick intuition can be gained by noting firstly that 'individualist' societies typically hold 'procedural' notions of justice rather than 'end state' notions. That is to say, they hold ones which appeal to the justice of the procedure which generated the outcome rather than the attributes of the outcome itself. The reason is that 'end state' theories of justice cannot avoid making interpersonal comparisons of welfare at some point and it is simply very difficult to make such comparisons when there is not the resource of either a high group identity or a status hierarchy to provide the basis for such comparisons. In contrast, the other two types can draw on these resources and are more likely to hold 'end state' theories.

Thus when the operation of markets throws up unequal outcomes or changed outcomes, 'individualist' societies are less likely to find a reason in their sense of justice for intervening. Their interventions are cued by transgressions of valued procedural principles, like voluntary exchange, and, unlike the other types, not by the attributes of the outcomes. Secondly, we can quickly note that the 'end state' notion of justice associated with 'egalitarian' societies is likely to be more egalitarian than 'hierarchic' ones simply because they do not respect the rank sources of differentiation which are the hallmark of 'hierarchies'.

Figure 3.2 gives Grendstad's (1990) attempt to fit the cultures of Europe into the cultural theory's grid/group space. To help evaluate the predictions, it is probably sensible (and not too controversial) to supplement figure 3.2 by locating the US and Canada in the 'individualist' quadrant, Sweden in the 'egalitarian' box (along with the other Scandinavian economies Grendstad identifies there) and Japan in the high-group column.

Figure 3.2   European cultures and ideal type institutions (cf. figure 3.1)

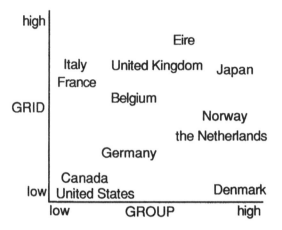

Source: Grendstad(1990) with the insertion of the US, Canada and Japan by the author.

The two predictions can now be evaluated, albeit in a rough and ready fashion, through the use of table 3.1 and figure 3.2. Prediction one does reasonably well. The broadly 'egalitarian' cultures like Netherlands, Norway, Denmark and Sweden (and possibly Germany) do seem to have more equal wage distributions than the more 'hierarchic' cultures of Ireland, UK, Belgium (and perhaps France); and they are more equal than the 'individualist' ones of the US and Canada. Likewise prediction two fares well. In many economies, for instance the US, the UK, Australia and Canada, the position of the low-paid deteriorated markedly and this is often explained with reference to changes in the economic fundamentals as unskilled workers in OECD countries increasingly competed (as a result of falling trade barriers and increased capital mobility) with similar workers in non-OECD countries who were paid considerably lower wages (see Davis, 1992, Katz, Loveman and Blanchflower, 1993, and OECD, 1993).

Interestingly the same changes in fundamentals occurred in other OECD economies, such as France, Germany, and Japan, and yet there was not the same stretching of the income distribution in these countries.

General differences of this sort are precisely what is entailed in the second prediction above. However, there is one anomaly: the UK. If Grendstad is right then one would not expect such sensitivity to the changes in economic fundamentals. Australia provides another example of a country which has *not* been traditionally regarded as individualist and yet its income distribution has also been stretched by the economic changes of the 1980s. One possible explanation is that the cultures of both countries have been moving significantly in the individualist direction over this decade and this has not been captured by Grendstad. Alternatively, it is possible that institutional change has occurred in these countries as a result of political change which does not reflect (or is in advance) of any general changes in belief. This is a possibility which I consider in more detail below.

Fortunately, we are not attempting to provide anything like a definitive empirical test of cultural theory. The point is to see whether there are *prima facie* grounds for taking the claims of cultural theory and its taxonomy of beliefs and institutions in this regard any further. On this basis, the evidence with respect to cross-country differences in income distribution is promising.

CHANGES IN CULTURAL BELIEFS AND THE DECLINE OF NON-MARKET VALUES

I have argued for the recognition that institutions encode shared sources of extraneous belief (and they are not mere convention writ-large). In particular it is important if we want to explain features of the social world, such as institutional allegiance and the equilibrium selection, and if we want to understand better the process of institutional change. It is important in two respects for the analysis of such change. Firstly, the shared sources of extraneous belief within a group sensitise that group to certain sorts of change. It encourages them, for instance, to respond (sometimes by modifying their institutions) to certain types of technological or demographic change and not others; and I have given an illustration of this influence at work in the previous section. Secondly it opens up interesting questions regarding the relation between institutional change and changes in the shared sources of extraneous belief. Do beliefs ever evolve independently of their institutions to cause tensions which contribute to institutional change? Alternatively, do institutions sometimes change and so cause an adjustment in the supporting beliefs? Or do we see examples of both types of influence?

It would be nice to report that there is a ready theory for economists with respect to *changes* in cultural beliefs and their relation to institutional change. Unfortunately, this is not the case. Instead in this section, I address a rather narrower issue relating to whether we should expect a decline in non-market values as the ideology of the market sweeps all before it. The question is, of course, of broad interest and it connects directly with certain arguments which I might loosely connect with Etzioni (1988): to the effect that the contemporary celebration of the market undermines the non-market values which enable markets to operate smoothly (for example through the destruction of traditional sources of trust).

I shall argue that there are reasons for being rather more sanguine about the survival of non-market values than either contemporary events or Etzioni might allow. I do not pretend to offer anything like a comprehensive counter here, but I do want to take issue with two particular arguments (or pointers) which sometimes fuel doubts about the endurance of non-market values.

The first argument draws on the change in cultural beliefs associated with the transition from modernity to post-modernity. The change has been much remarked upon and we do not need to theorise how it has arrived in order to treat it as a 'fact'. In particular, as one of the hallmarks of this transition is the collapse of the 'grand narrative' (that is, the attempt to construct any sort of universal knowledge), it is tempting to ally this change with a wholesale celebration of the market. After all, leaving things to markets would seem to be exactly what is demanded once a thoroughgoing pluralism denies a consensus over some set of non-market values that the State can intervene in the market to support. Or as everyone knows, the great thing about markets is that people can pursue their own ends and they do not need to agree on anything.

If the argument is allied in this way, then the prospects are rather gloomy. Or at least they are so long as the post-modern turn seems inescapable; and this explains why much post-modern writing has such a depressing nihilistic ring (see Baudrillard, 1989).

I want to claim, in contrast, that it is wrong to make the cultural change associated with post-modernity synonymous with the advance of the ideology of the market. There is a long and a short version to this part of the argument. The short argument goes like this. It relies on the thought that the post-modern turn does *not* suggest that we can do without moral or other values. Rather it emphasises that there is no overarching set of values by which we can judge the correctness of any individual point of view and this entails a commitment to valuing pluralism.

So while post-modernity means many different things, for the purposes of this chapter, it is associated with valuing pluralism because this is the only way, in the presence of more than one value system, to avoid constructing a ('modernist') 'grand narrative' which subordinates one view to another. The question is: does anything substantive flow from accepting value diversity? O'Neill (1989b) suggests the following answer.

> What does justice require of such a plurality? At least we can claim that their most basic principles must be ones that *could* be adopted by all. If they were not, at least some agents would have to be excluded from the plurality for whom the principle can hold, whose boundaries would have to be drawn more narrowly (p.18).

In other words to accept the existence of a plurality of agents necessarily commits one to be guided by principles which are universal, otherwise the application of the principle would undermine the plurality.

This seems reasonable enough but does a condition of universality have any bite? It rules out the practices of Nazis (since they denied moral status to the Jews and other groups and so their principles were never designed to be universalisable), but we would also like it to adjudicate in disputes between coherent moral positions — that is, ones which satisfy the condition of being potentially universalisable. Is it capable of doing this and if it is, does it provide support for market outcomes? And even if it is capable of 'bite' in this way, should we be worried by the thought that we must have smuggled some absolute 'modernist' source of value back into the argument to arrive at such a conclusion?

To offer the baldest of answers to the last question first: of course, we have. The condition of universalisability comes from accepting the value of plurality. But at least this has the virtue of being based on a presumption that we are ignorant of what could constitute moral (or other) knowledge. (The contrasting claims of either absolute knowledge or relativism are notoriously difficult to render coherent, whereas a foundation in ignorance avoids both pitfalls, see O'Neill, 1989a.)

To turn to the more substantive part of the question: does anything useful follow from the condition of universalisability? It does under certain conditions. Let us suppose that there is a conflict between two groups over, say, the development of a resource which arises because they have very different conceptions of the 'good' or justice. Further, we assume that each view of the world is coherent in the sense that it can evaluate the relative merits of the various ways that the resource might be developed by attaching a utility number to each outcome (where these numbers are arbitrary up to any positive linear transformation).

In other words, each group has a cardinal 'utility' ordering over the possible uses of the resource. Such numbers are, of course, strictly incommensurable between groups (as indeed they must be if we are to keep with the spirit of post-modernity). The utility numbers for the groups in the event of non-development are (d_1, d_2). Now suppose the best possible development for group 1 which leaves group 2 feeling no better-off than non-development yields that group I_1. Likewise the maximum return possible for group 2 is I_2. Various compromise paths of development between these two extremes are possible and they yield a continuous set of possible utility combinations for the two groups, given by the frontier in figure 3.3.

Figure 3.3 Conflict between two groups

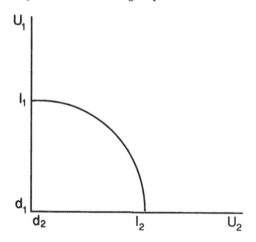

This is a standard representation of a bargaining problem and we would like to be able to choose one of the paths represented by a point on the utility frontier as this represents an improvement for both groups over non-development. The problem is that the group do not share the same views with respect to justice or the good and so they cannot use such a view to adjudicate in this dispute over how to develop this resource — indeed the dispute here arises precisely because they do not share such a view. However, I shall assume that both groups value pluralism and so seek a rule for dispute resolution which can be universalised. If I further require that the rule operates for a group only on the preferences which the group itself holds, then there is only one rule which universalises. It is the Kalai–Smorodinsky (1975) principle of equal relative concession. This principle selects that option for development which yields the utility pair (u_1, u_2) on the frontier such that

$$(u_1-d_1)/(I_1-d_1) = (u_2-d_2)/(I_2-d_2)$$

It will be obvious that this satisfies the condition of universalisability since it requires every group to be treated in the same relative way. Thus any group's relative concession is matched by all other group's concessions and so the application of the principle to one group does not preclude its application to another group. (See Hargreaves Heap, 1994, on what is perhaps less obvious: that this is the only principle which satisfies the universality condition.) It is also known from Kalai and Smorodinsky (1975) that this solution is the only one which satisfies the following axioms:

1. invariance under affine transformations of the utility scale,

2. pareto optimality,

3. symmetry, and

4. monotonicity.

This, in a sense, provides a useful cross-check on the principle. Condition one tells us that the solution will not change with affine transformations of the utility scale used by each group. Thus, the solution requires only that each group can represent its preferences with a Von Neumann–Morgenstern cardinal utility function — it does not depend on any intergroup comparison of utility numbers, each group can attach what numbers it likes to the outcomes provided they are affine transformations of each. Thus the solution respects each group's value system and makes no attempt to compare one with another, which is exactly what we would want from the perspective of post-modernity.

Condition two is also useful because it is unlikely that groups would be happy with an arbitration rule which is not pareto optimal. Condition three means that when two groups are identical in terms of utility information, then the result is that each group is treated equally. Again this is useful because it shows that the equal relative concession generalises the universalisability condition to cases where groups from a Von Neumann–Morgenstern utility point of view think identically about some issue even though they may use different languages (that is, utility scales). Finally, condition four states that when the decision problem changes so that the feasible set is improved for one player then the player should not end up losing out as a result. This might be thought to embody an elementary form of natural justice in the sense that if the options improve for one agent, he or she should enjoy some benefit from this improvement.

To summarise, the equal relative concession principle is universalisable and thus ought to commend itself to all groups which recognise the value of plurality (and it has what seem in the circumstances to be the desirable properties of avoiding any comparison of values between groups, of being pareto optimal, of being symmetric and of embodying an elementary form of natural justice). Thus if post-modernity is correctly identified with the valuation of pluralism, then it should favour the adoption of the principle of equal relative concession in such circumstances. Granting this inference, the question is: how does such a principle relate to the operation of markets? In particular, does it suggest an outcome which differs from that of the market or does it provide a further source of support for the market outcome?

It is usually argued in mainstream game theory that voluntary inter-action in such circumstances yields the so-called Nash solution to the bargaining problem. This is the outcome which maximises the product of the utility gains from agreement and so generally differs from the Kalai–Smoridinsky solution. The so-called generalised Nash solution allows for power differences between the players with the result that an outcome is selected which maximises the weighted product of the utility gains, where the weights are indexes of relative power. Again the generalised Nash solution will only coincide with the Kalai–Smorodinsky solution as a matter of pure serendipidity (i.e., there will always be a particular power distribution which generates the same result as Kalai–Smorodinsky, but there is no reason to suppose that it will be obtained). Hence, it could scarcely be argued on this account that a post-modern inclination towards equal relative concession works in favour of market outcomes.

This completes the first part of my argument against a wholesale pessimism. The second part is concerned with a particular view of how government policy is encouraging the demise of non-market values. The view goes something like this: the pro-market policies of governments, especially in the Anglo-American economies, are driving non-market sentiment out-of-business as there is simply no space for alternative values to flourish when profit is valued above all else.

The view will be familiar enough, but I am suspicious of it for a variety of related reasons. To return initially to the argument which was made in the section II, it is wrong to imagine that the spread of market relations could ever simply or smoothly force out non-market values. If market values are values which lend support to outcomes which come from agents interacting in pursuit of their own interests, then this is not an adequate general complement to the operation of markets. The point is that market interactions do not always generate unique outcomes when they involve instrumentally rational agents and so it is not going to help fix an outcome in these markets to give agents pro-market values. This would simply reproduce the problem of indeterminacy. To fix an outcome, the agents in these markets must draw on shared sources of extraneous information: they must be able to appeal jointly to something which goes beyond the characterisation of markets in terms of an interaction between agents who are simply pursuing their own interest.

Noting this only means that we should not expect a smooth decline of non-market values in the wake of pro-market policies. It still leaves the way open for the kind of pessimistic view which I sketched at the beginning of this section. After all, if pro-market policies do succeed in undermining non-market values, then it carries the implication that markets will begin to flounder as participants lose their sources of shared extraneous information. There remains, however, the important prior question over whether the advance of market relations in one way or another does actually lead to the decline of non-market values. I have two reasons for being suspicious on this score. On Polanyi's (1944) classic account of this matter, for instance, the contest between the extension of the market and non-market values has never been quite so simple or one-sided. Non-market values do not simply disappear. Rather, they tend to reassert themselves (not always in pleasant ways, which in turn may be the source for a rather different kind of pessimism) through political changes which constrain the advance of market relations.

Likewise, there is some support from cognitive psychology for the view that non-market values could remain in place now despite the current policy shift towards the market. For example, Festinger's (1957) cognitive dissonance theory suggests that beliefs (about what is worthy) are likely to change whenever a dissonance is created between one's actions and one's beliefs; this may seem to support the idea that our beliefs will follow our market-directed behaviours. However, this theory also predicts that beliefs will not change when the individual can find external reasons which explain the dissonance. In particular, if you do something which conflicts with your beliefs, then according to the theory it is less likely that your beliefs will change when you can explain that the action was 'forced' upon you by the external environment. For example when the material incentives are such that you seem to have no sensible option but to behave in a particular way, then you are less likely to change your beliefs to accommodate or validate this action.

This theory has interesting implications, in particular, for the Anglo-American countries (the US, the UK, Canada, New Zealand and Australia). The governments in these countries have been in the vanguard of a worldwide pro-market move and they have witnessed very significant growths of income inequality. The rhetoric of these changes is that behaviours and attitudes have changed irrevocably, but cognitive dissonance theory would counsel greater caution. Insofar as people have changed their behaviour because income distributions have been stretched, then this theory suggests that belief changes are unlikely to follow the changes in behaviour. The greater material incentives of the 1980s provides the external reason for changes in behaviour and thus beliefs are not called upon to change in validation of the new types of behaviour. If this is right, then the stage in these countries seems more likely to have been set for the kind of Polanyi-like confrontation between the consequences of extending the market and the still vibrant non-market values.

This prospect may not appear to be very encouraging, but suppose it yields an outcome where income distributions narrow again, then perhaps somewhat paradoxically these would be precisely the circumstances where the non-market values might begin to change. If we follow the logic of cognitive dissonance theory, then people will be left behaving in 'enterprising' ways for no apparent external reason once income distributions narrow and so they will have to find reasons of their own through changes in belief. What might such a change be? Well, to connect this thought speculatively with an earlier one, is it too much to suppose that we might begin to think of 'enterprise' as a form of post-modern 'playfulness'?

CONCLUSION

The starting point for this chapter is thought that the explanation of how institutions affect behaviour and how they change depends on an improved understanding of how individuals draw on their cultures and how these webs of extraneous beliefs evolve.

Towards this end, I have argued that Mary Douglas's Cultural Theory provides a taxonomy of beliefs which can be used to help explain the somewhat surprising (from the point of view of economic fundamentals) divergent income distribution developments of OECD countries in the 1980s. I have also argued that there are reasons for suspecting that the decline of non-market values has been much exaggerated in recent times. In particular, reflection on what is entailed by the much observed post-modern change in beliefs and on what we know from cognitive dissonance theory with respect to how beliefs move to accommodate behaviours suggests an alternative conclusion. Non-market values of some sort seem likely to survive both the post-modern turn and the aggressive pro-market policies of some governments.

REFERENCES

Baudrillard, J. (1989), *America*, Verso, London.
Davis, S. (1992), 'Cross Country Comparisons of Changes in Relative Wages', *Macroeconomic Annual*, NBER.
Douglas, M. (1978), *Cultural Bias*, Royal Anthropological Society, London.
Douglas, M. (1986), *How Institutions Think*, Syracuse University Press, Syracuse.
Etzioni, A. (1988), *The Moral Dimension*, Free Press, London.
Festinger, L. (1957), *A Theory of Cognitive Dissonance*, Stanford University Press, Stanford.
Grendstad, G. (1990), *Europe by Culture*, University of Bergen.
Hargreaves Heap, S. (1986), 'Risk and Culture: a Missing Link in the Post Keynesian Tradition', *Journal of Post Keynesian Economics*, vol. 9, pp. 267–78.
Hargreaves Heap, S. (1989), *Rationality in Economics*, Basil Blackwell, Oxford.
Hargreaves Heap, S. (1991), 'Entrepreneurship, Enterprise and Information in Economics' in S. Hargreaves Heap and A. Ross (eds.), *Understanding the Enterprise Culture: Themes in the Work of Mary Douglas*, Edinburgh University Press, Edinburgh.
Hargreaves Heap, S. (1993), 'Culture and Competitiveness', in K. Hughes (ed.), *European Competitiveness*, Cambridge University Press, Cambridge.
Hargreaves Heap, S. (1994), 'Conflict Resolution in Plural Societies', *UEA Discussion Paper*.
Kalai, E. and M. Smorodinsky (1975), 'Other Solutions to Nash's Bargaining Problem', *Econometrica*, vol. 43, pp. 513–18.

Katz, L., G. Loveman and D. Blanchflower (1993), 'A Comparison of Changes in the Structure of Wages in Four OECD Countries', *NBER Working Papers no.* 4297.

OECD (1993), *Employment Outlook*, OECD, Paris.

O'Neill, O. (1989a), *Constructions of Reason: Explorations of Kant's Practical Philosophy*, Cambridge University Press, Cambridge.

O'Neill, O. (1989b), 'Justice Gender and International Boundaries', WIDER, Working Paper, vol. 68.

Polanyi, K. (1944), *The Great Transformation*, Farrar and Rinehart, New York.

Schotter, A. (1981), *Economic Theory of Social Institutions*, Cambridge University Press, Cambridge.

Sjöstrand, S-E. (ed.) (1993), *Institutional Change. Theory and Empirical Findings*, M.E. Sharpe, New York.

Sugden, R. (1986), *The Economics of Rights Cooperation and Welfare*, Basil Blackwell, Oxford.

4. Relative Rationality, Institutions and Precautionary Behaviour

Ernesto Screpanti

INTRODUCTION

In this chapter an attempt is made to bring together suggestions and ideas from three different and seemingly contrasting streams of thought: the institutionalist, the Keynesian and the behaviourist. The aim is to develop a theory of economic agency capable of accounting, on the ground of an individualistic presupposition, for many economic phenomena, like institutions and collective agents, that are often dealt with in holistic terms.

In many approaches to macroeconomics that treat social aggregates as the true actors of economic dynamics, collective agents are not taken to be a *primum movens*. Implicitly or explicitly it is assumed, even in most non-neoclassical models, that, since collective agents consist of groups of individuals, it is from the behaviour of the individuals that analysis must start. But the individualistic presupposition is not limited to this area. If one has to explain social fabric, and the social fabric of a capitalist economy, tracing it back to the individual, the latter has to be considered as a decisional agent who is in some way rational, autonomous and self-interested.

It goes without saying that this is an abstraction. It is, however, a justified abstraction. Man, as has been observed in history, is an agglomeration of social and cultural influences whose behaviour is rarely explicable in terms of purely individualistic and rational choices. But it is also true that, with historical development, the set of actions explicable in rational and individualistic terms tends to widen, the more so if the field of investigation is restricted to the economic sphere. Gradually, emerging from the darkness of the centuries, humans improve their ability to orient themselves in society rationally and autonomously (Tool, 1993, p. 2).

There is another justification for the hypothesis of individualistic rationality. No one will deny that humans are easily influenced in their behaviour by cultural and ethical factors which cannot be brought into the individualist viewpoint; it is equally well-known that irrational, instinctual and heterodirected behaviour is observable in many forms of human activity. It is not legitimate, however, to assume that all behaviour is of this type. The fact is that, if rationality is intended as the 'capability to perceive means/consequence connections' (Tool, 1993, p. 2), it certainly cannot be denied that a good proportion of human decisions are rational. And this is more than sufficient to justify the efforts aimed at the construction of a theory of such decisions[1].

We must not exaggerate, however. The individualistic presupposition requires that we first attempt to explain behaviour in terms of rational, autonomous and egoistic behaviour. Furthermore it should be clear that when speaking of the rationality, autonomy and egoism of individuals, there is no need to take concepts to extremes. To be precise, the hypothesis made here is that the individual is a *relatively* rational and *relatively* autonomous being.

The notion of 'relative rationality' comes from Commons, but is used with some freedom in this essay. At any rate, it will be necessary to read the whole essay in order to understand what is meant here by 'relative rationality'. On the contrary, something can be said straight away on 'relative autonomy'.

RELATIVE AUTONOMY

Here the notion of 'autonomy' refers to the capability of individuals to choose preferences, needs, interests, values, in other words: the ends of their actions. The term 'choices', in this context, does not refer to decisions to be taken in order to pursue some given ends. The problem of the *choice* of ends must be clearly distinguished from that of *decisions* about the means. In the former context the question is posed of the individual's autonomy or independence from the social environment. In the latter, the rationality of his behaviour is the question at issue.

No one is a Robinson Crusoe: the perfectly autonomous individual is an abstraction[2]. The very capacities of perception and knowledge, inasmuch as they are conditioned by language and culture, are socially determined. On the other hand, it is well-known that the famous hypothesis of no externalities is in no case so absurd as in that of the formation of individual preferences. The very phenomena of advertising, hidden persuasion, fashions, demonstration effects etc., are only the most superficial and obvious manifestations of a fact of wider significance. The fundamental question is that the very notion of 'need' is difficult to define except in terms of processes that are socially, culturally and historically determined.

But besides this generic and general type of social influence, there is another that deserves special attention in a theory aspiring to explain the evolution of institutions[3]. There is a very widespread phenomenon, that might be called 'institutional involvement', which is the tendency of individuals to change their own needs and interests according to the specific institutions to which they belong. It is often the institutions themselves that work systematically to mould the needs of the individuals who 'use' them. Just think of the contribution made by the great religions to the formation of human character and aspirations. But often it is the individuals themselves who, by deciding to join an institution, voluntarily and more or less consciously modify their own purposes in relation to the exigencies of the institution. Conversion to a religion is the case that springs immediately to mind.

It is not, however, necessary to move far from the economic sphere to find some illuminating examples. One thinks of the official or the manager of a firm who, in the course of his career, changes his vision of the world to the point that he can consciously act against his own personal interests. He may identify with the firm to such an extent that, let us say, in the case of a high bankruptcy risk, instead of accepting the offer of a better job with another firm — better, for example, in terms of salary, power and prestige — he will decide to go on struggling to save 'his' firm.

In this approach to the formation of human needs and interests, however, it is assumed that, although the influence exerted on the individual by society is strong, the final choices remain empowered in the individual himself, and these are mostly intentional, voluntary and responsible choices. Individual autonomy implies the intentionality of actions, that is, the fact that actions aim at ends which are freely chosen by the individual agents.

Intentional behaviour presupposes freedom of choice. And it consists, to be precise, of the choice of the purpose of the action. The individual always has a wide range of possible alternative ends open to him. It is for this reason that he has freedom of choice. Basically, what is assumed is that culture and institutions are not in fact totally able to determine human behaviour (Sjöstrand, 1992, p. 1013). And that this is so, above all, for a rather simple reason: despite what is implied by an inveterate linguistic use, *culture* does not exist. What *do* exist are culture*s*: different cultures, different collective agents, different group interests etc. And each of these social factors gives rise to different, and often conflicting, influences. Thus, the possible purposes of individual action remain multifarious, even though culturally influenced (Sjöstrand, 1993, pp. 10, 14).

For this reason individual actions remain genuinely intentional. But it is also clear that the kind of autonomy deriving thereof can only be defined in relative terms: the individual is autonomous only within the limits posed by the, possibly very large, set of institutional and cultural factors that influence the formation of his needs, interests and values. This is the sense in which we speak of 'relative autonomy'.

THREE ELEMENTARY CRITERIA OF BEHAVIOUR

The problem of individual behaviour arises from the context of uncertainty in which a decisor takes decisions. Uncertainty exists if the individual does not possess all the information and/or all the computational ability necessary to take decisions.

The first behavioural hypothesis made is that the individual, in situations of uncertainty, orients himself by using strategies of simplification[4]. For a better understanding of this, recourse to a mathematical metaphor may be helpful. The decision-making problem could be posed in terms of the solution of a system of equations in which the unknowns represent decisional variables, while the parameters and the forms of equations incorporate the basic factors that affect those variables. Lack of information means that the agent does not know all the parameters and all the functional forms of the system of equations he must solve. Lack of computational ability means that the individual does not possess the time and the capability to master all the equations so as to find a determined solution; or, in other words, that, even if there were no lack of information, the dimension and the complexity of the system are too big for the individual to be able to manage it. Thus the difficulty of decision-making in conditions of uncertainty takes on the meaning of a problem of underdetermination[5]. The simplification strategy consists of disregarding some excess variables, or of treating some variables as parameters, by making simplifying hypotheses on their values. In this way the individual tries to make the solution determinate, or, at least, to reduce the degree of indeterminacy.

However, many determinate systems can be derived from an underdetermined one, according to which variables are chosen as parameters. In a certain sense, therefore, the problem increases in difficulty: the number of sub-problems derivable from the original one may be very large. A second aspect of the simplification strategy consists in reducing the number of options, or sub-problems, on which decisions have to be taken. It goes without saying that such a reduction of options can only be based on criteria which are to a certain extent *arbitrary*. This arbitrariness is made inevitable by the fact that the simplification strategy derives from the very impossibility of taking decisions on the basis of a determined solution, i.e., a solution containing no arbitrariness.

It is in this phase that institutions enter the scene. The problem is: which criterion to adopt in the simplification strategy? The hypothesis made is that the individual, as a first and unmindful move, will tend to follow a conservative policy. He will tend to stick to the options which have been tested socially. In following such a practice he will make wide use, more or less consciously, of the support of institutions. In this way, a significant quantity of potentially perturbing decisional options will be done away with, and a restricted set of options considered feasible will be selected[6]. It is on this very ground that institutions play their main role: they contribute to solving the decision problem by making life simpler for the individuals. This first behavioural criterion will be called the 'criterion of institutional compliance'. As will be seen further on, it is not necessary, for the validity of this criterion, to assume awareness.

Once the decision-making options have been so restricted, it is necessary to identify a criterion of action. The use of the criterion of institutional compliance contributes to reducing the complexity of a decision, but can hardly eliminate all complexity. Therefore the individual who has to take the decision still has to carry out some problem-solving activity after complying with an institution. In any case a criterion of action is needed. The hypothesis made here is that, given the options selected, the one considered to be the best will be singled out. This will be called the 'criterion of conditional improvement'. The status quo *may* be included among the possible 'best' options, so that it would be more precise to speak of 'non-worsening' rather than 'improvement'.

It will be necessary to assume that individuals possess 'subjective evaluators' (Egidi, 1989, p. 44; 1992, p. 151), that is rules to find the best option among the feasible ones. Many evaluators can exist[7]; they can be different in different individuals, and can change with time in each individual. Here it is not necessary, however, to choose a particular evaluator. It is sufficient to assume that such a choice has been made by any individual in any given situation.

Thus, given the restrictions on the decision-making options allowed by the institutions the individual complies with, the option which will be chosen will be the one considered the best in terms of the evaluator adopted. This is the criterion of conditional improvement. *Improvement*, because it aims at moving the individual to the action which is considered to be the best, and therefore at enabling him to improve his situation, or at least not to worsen it. *Conditional*, because the improvement is conditional on the constraints posed by the institutions complied with.

It will be noted that the improvement criterion does not lead to maximizing behaviour. In fact, it is not the best of all the available options that will be chosen, but the best of those selected as relevant by the institutions. It is, therefore, an improvement conditioned by a limited set of options. And since the criterion of reduction of options is not a maximization criterion, there is no guarantee that the final decision will be the best one possible. Furthermore, since various evaluators may exist, the final decision need not be the optimum, even within the limits posed by institutions. This is why the term 'improvement' rather than 'maximization' is used. Nor can it be expected that, with the passing of time, the accumulations of solutions considered best at each time will lead to the optimum solution, or even approximate to it. Firstly, in fact, each decision changes the data of the problem. Secondly, many solutions may turn out to be wrong *ex post*, as is inevitable in a context of uncertainty. There is, therefore, nothing to prevent the data from changing in such a way that a succession of solutions considered best at each time will lead to a final solution which could be considered even worse than the initial one. Thirdly and most importantly, since the criterion of institutional compliance restricts the decisional options in a non-optimum way, the possibility cannot be excluded that some options which are scrapped are better than those singled out. Therefore, with the passing of time, the ongoing decisional process could follow a path-dependent course from which optimum outcomes are repeatedly rejected.

Finally, a third behavioural hypothesis is made: that the individual will stick to the behaviour induced by the two previous criteria as long as the final result does not involve a systematic worsening of the situation. Otherwise, he will abandon the preceding simplifying strategy and start to search for others. The worsening has to be systematic, i.e., not attributable to chance or to an error in applying the improvement criterion. If a systematic worsening occurs, it must be attributed to the adoption of the criterion of institutional compliance, and it will be the institutions adhered to that will have to be revised. It has already been said that the criterion of institutional compliance does not necessarily imply awareness. The individual will remain attached to an institution, and maintain a conduct of passive and habitual adaptation, but only as long as the institution 'works'. However, when this type of behaviour systematically produces bad results, the individual will tend to take up more active and critical attitudes, will be able to abandon his habits and will start searching for new strategies of simplification. This behavioural criterion will be called the 'criterion of institutional revision'. As will shortly be seen, it is a fundamental mechanism of institutional change.

The third behaviour criterion is perhaps the most important of the three, and contributes to giving the other two a rational content they would not otherwise have. The criterion of institutional compliance would in fact lead to irrational behaviour if it were not accompanied by that of institutional revision. The presence of this third criterion means that behaviour governed by the first takes on the sense of an unconscious rationality. It is the criterion of institutional revision that makes 'institutions function as a rationality context' of human action (Sjöstrand, 1992, p. 1011). Individuals who let themselves be guided by institutions are not necessarily stupid if they know that the institutions function, at least in part, in their interests. This knowledge, even if maintained at an unconscious level, is implied by a mental reserve according to which, if the institution does not work well, it can always be abandoned and replaced by another one. In fact, the criterion of institutional revision, like that of conditional improvement, does presuppose awareness of decisions.

Behaviour governed by the three mentioned criteria, even if not maximizing, cannot be considered irrational in the context of uncertainty in which it takes place: it is, at any rate, behaviour governed by the urge to 'do better', moved by the objective of improving the existing situation.

PRECAUTIONARY BEHAVIOUR

An important problem arising in relation to the criterion of institutional revision is to define the guidelines on the basis of which the revision is put into practice. In order to tackle this problem in the correct manner, it is necessary to understand that behaviour governed by our three criteria is a form of *precautionary behaviour*.

In the face of uncertainty agents tend to build up safety reserves to protect themselves from possible surprises brought about by future events[8]. 'Reserve' is used here in the twofold sense of 'goods stored for future use' and of 'limiting condition'. The decision to hold inventories of goods to protect against future oscillations of their prices or of those of their substitutes is precautionary. Also, precautionary is the decision to join an institution or to comply with a convention which could limit the possibilities of decision. And between these two cases there are fewer differences than there may appear to be at first sight. In fact, the decision to hold inventories of goods is none other than the decision to stick to a rule that limits the possibilities of investing wealth in some other way.

Precautionary behaviour, so defined, is normally coupled with the definition of a tolerance threshold tracing out the benchmark for the revision of behaviour. This threshold often takes the form of a reservation price or premium[9] such as to induce the agent to remain faithful to usual behaviour if the current price or yield is compatible with the threshold itself. Only if the actual price or yield trespasses that threshold will the agent be induced to modify his behaviour.

A very well-known type of institutional behaviour has already been mentioned, and consists in accumulating inventories of goods. In this way, precautions are taken against the possibility of some variables taking on actual values which are different from the expected ones, thereby forcing the agent to revise his own decisions with, at times, disastrous effects. Inventories perform the role of shock absorbers for decisional errors and unforeseen effects, allowing agents to continue operating or to continue without relevant losses, even when expectations are partially disappointed. Reservation premiums or prices fixed in relation to the decision to accumulate inventories are expedients for avoiding the difficult task of determining accurately the values of the decisional variables and, above all, for avoiding continual modifications of decisions because of small variations in those values.

The institutional nature of precautionary behaviour can easily be understood by reflecting on the fact that the fixing of reservation prices, to which this kind of behaviour is always associated, is often done through compliance to social habits and conventions. In establishing the tolerance thresholds for the holding of inventories, individuals do not decide in a social vacuum, but willingly use conventions and habits formed collectively. On the other hand, reservation prices heavily depend on expectations, and these are widely influenced by social and psychological interactions and the decisions of collective agents. So, for example, the liquidity premium can be interpreted as a reservation rate of return such that the agent is not induced to modify his liquid balances until the differential between the long and short-term interest rates is lower than the reservation premium itself. This will differ from one agent to another, but the difference will be small. And it will depend on expectations about the prevailing mood, the degree of bearishness and instability of the market, the policy of the monetary authority, and still other social and political processes. These are all phenomena that, given the conventional and collective character of their formation, take on the meaning of institutional factors.

Among the devices of simplification strategies, the routine ones are important. Here individuals let themselves be governed by consolidated rules of behaviour. This, too, insofar as routines are socially accepted, is institutional behaviour. And, insofar as they are adopted to avoid continually revising decisions in the face of uncertainty, it is precautionary behaviour.'Another type of action induced by simplification strategies that can be interpreted in terms of precautionary behaviour is heterodirected action. Here collective agents are important. From this point of view, they can be considered as social aggregates which, preordaining the behaviour of the individuals who form part of them, allow them to simplify decision-making problems in the face of uncertainty.

EVOLUTIONARY CHANGE OF INSTITUTIONS

Now a problem has to be tackled which is crucial to any theory of institutions that wishes to avoid holistic slips. What guarantees that institutions serve individual interests? In other words, does a social mechanism exist that acts in such a way that institutions contribute to pushing individuals to adopt a kind of behaviour which is individualistically rational even when they act unconsciously?

There is a solution to this problem, and it is well-consolidated in the institutionalist tradition, even though the very economists who adopted it have often shown unawareness of its individualistic implications[10]. It is the evolutionary solution. No institution can survive for long if it systematically induces to error the individuals who comply with it. Such a result is ensured by our third behavioural hypothesis, the criterion of institutional revision. It is a simple and potent result, which performs a double theoretical function. Whilst providing a rational foundation for routine behaviour, it also nurtures an important mechanism of institutional evolution: institutions change when they no longer serve the individuals.

An important mechanism of institutional change is that which could be defined as 'change due to ineffectiveness'. It can be triggered off by a mutation in individual attitudes and aspirations or by environmental variation. In either cases the individuals may be induced to change their reservation prices. As a consequence the strategies of simplification may have to be modified because of the change in the relevant decisional factors. Thus, it may occur that an old institution is no longer capable of guaranteeing a restriction of the decisional options which permits an improvement or, at least, a non-worsening of the situation. When this happens, the institution becomes ineffective from the individual point of view. Therefore, the individual himself puts into practice the strategies of institutional revision that lead him to abandon the old institutions. Then a diffusion process begins (Witt, 1993). As this process gradually extends to an increasing number of individuals, the old institution loses its social grip, and, sooner or later, will disappear from the scene.

But there is another type of institutional change, one which is no less important than that due to ineffectiveness, and which can be defined 'change due to innovation'. Innovation is by definition a type of behaviour that cannot be reduced to parametric decisions. There are cases of improvements that are brought about by breaking the restraints imposed by institutional compliance, improvements which can not be planned or predicted. There comes into play, here, the 'idle curiosity' to which Veblen referred in *The Instinct of Workmanship* (1914), and which Hodgson (1992, p. 289) places at the basis of the production of diversity and variation in the processes of economic evolution.

In recent literature, in the wake of Nelson and Winter (1982), the technical dimension of production has been studied in terms of routine behaviour[11]. In this theoretical context innovation is by definition a nonroutinizable behaviour. Indeed an innovation consists in the abandonment of an old routine and the adoption of a new one. The conception of the new routine is an invention. An institution, then, is a routine which has passed through a process of social diffusion and has become a social habit.

To understand how innovations can be generated by a behaviour governed by the criterion of conditional improvement, it is necessary to reflect on the fact that this criterion does not normally lead to Pareto efficiency, nor to global maximization for the individual point of view. Furthermore, since different individual agents have different evaluators of what is considered a good solution, it is possible to obtain different solutions to a given problem even among individuals who comply with the same institution. This is so because institutions, as has already been argued, do not completely determine human behaviour: they merely restrict decisional options. Therefore, the final actions of the decisions of different agents who comply with the same institution may differ, even if not dramatically. This would mean that an institution is a routine adopted by many agents but applied by each of them in slightly different ways obtaining slightly different results. On the other hand, since routines are adopted as forms of problem-solving procedures, it is always possible that, in applying them, some individuals will succeed in arriving at new routines which enable them to obtain better results than the old ones.

An innovation is a decision that can only be put into practice by breaking the limitations of the decisional options imposed by existing institutions. This is a definition which, incidentally, immediately makes clear the institutional and evolutionary character of the processes of technological change. But it goes without saying that, 'innovation' here not only refers to technological processes.

In the process of institutional change, an important role is played by learning and imitation, two practices normally used by individuals and organizations to improve their own performances. Learning is based on observation of the results of an action. If success is observed, the action will be repeated; if there is a failure, the action will be changed. Learning, especially when applied to routines, is very important in the processes of institutional consolidation and the processes of change due to ineffectiveness. Individuals who observe the success of the criterion of institutional compliance will insist on it. When, however, this kind of behaviour results in failure, and probably when this failure has been observed long enough to appear to be systematic, the individuals who have learned the lesson will prompt institutional revision.

Imitation is similar to learning, except for the fact that it is based on observation of the success of others (Selten, 1991, p. 14). Obviously, neither learning nor imitation can be invoked to explain innovations, above all if these are of the radical type that modifies institutions. Yet imitation plays a fundamental role in the diffusion of innovations and, therefore, in the process of institutional change due to innovation. In fact, innovation as such is not sufficient to create a new institution. It can only trigger off the change. But in order to be fully implemented to the point of creating a new institution, the innovation must spread, and this result is ensured by imitation.

The use of biological and evolutionary metaphors is spreading more and more among contemporary economists, as the faults of Walrasian mechanics are gradually realised and, above all, as the role played by institutions in moulding economic behaviour is understood[12]. But care should be taken not to extend the metaphor too far. A good deal of economic behaviour is motivated by rational, as opposed to biologically determined actions. This means that the right metaphor, in economics, is not the Darwinian 'natural selection'. The type of institutional change dealt with in this section, inasmuch as it is ultimately determined by rational decisions, is arguably closer to 'artificial selection'. In the sphere of human activity, evolution comes about mainly through the creation and destruction of institutions by cognizant individuals, not through individuals' births and deaths (Simon, 1981).

The relevance of this clarification can be better appreciated in the light of another of the advantages offered by this theory of rational behaviour. The three elementary criteria of behaviour can be used to give a rational basis to the concepts of 'robustness' and 'evolutionary stability'; concepts that, since being proposed by Maynard Smith (1974), have received increasing attention from economists, especially from students of evolutionary models in game theory. In the approach proposed here, there is no need to assimilate human behaviour to that of microbes; nor is there any need to make inappropriate use of the concepts of 'natural adaptation' and 'fitness'. The criterion of institutional revision, together with the mechanism of imitation, is sufficient to account for the robustness of an institution in terms of individual decisions. A new institution spreads out and eventually becomes well established if and when, being able to satisfy the needs of many individuals, it is accepted by them as a guide for behaviour. On the other hand, both the criteria of institutional compliance and revision, together with both the mechanisms of learning and imitation, can be used to account for evolutionary stability and instability. An institution is collectively stable if it satisfies the needs of many individuals better than any other competing institution. It becomes collectively unstable when it induces individuals to systematic error so that it is abandoned by a growing number of them[13].

There is one last important problem of evolutionary political economy that can be worked out satisfactorily by using the theory of behaviour outlined here. It is widely held that a theory of evolutionary dynamics implies the adoption of a principle of efficiency. The alternative is to fall into tautology: evolution comes about by selection of the fittest; the fittest is the individual selected[14]. This is a serious problem. Its solution, however, does not necessarily have to be the neoclassical one. The principle of maximization is not the only valid principle of evolutionary efficiency; and, actually, it is not the real one (Selten, 1991, and Hodgson, 1991).

The three elementary criteria of behaviour elucidated here offer a principle of regulation of the evolutionary process that is equally sound and far more realistic than that of maximization. It could be defined as the 'principle of improvement'. It consists in the rule that the replacement of an old institution with a new one occurs only if it contributes towards improving the situation of some individuals. The new institution does not necessarily have to be the best possible, since individuals do not maximize, and since, as it will be seen in the next section, many other strange phenomena may occur, such as lock-in, path-dependence, institutional involvement and so forth. However, even if it is not the best, the new institution will be better than the old one. And this is enough to sustain an evolutionary process.

INVOLUTION, IRRATIONAL BEHAVIOUR AND ALL THAT

It has been argued in this essay that much of human behaviour, even that which appears to be irrational, like precautionary behaviour and allegiance to institutions, can be justified in terms of decisions that are basically rational, though boundedly so. As it was declared in the introductory section, however, no claim is laid of explaining all behaviour as rational, and now it can be explicitly stated that irrational behaviour is admitted. Nor is it claimed that all institutional change can be accounted for in terms of evolutionary processes governed by the principle of improvement. *Involution* is admitted too. This is a process of institutional change involving the decoupling of selection and adaptation. It comprises lock-in phenomena, institutional adverse selection, institutional stickiness, bad adaptation due to frequency dependence (Hodgson, 1991) and other similar oddities: all cases in which the principle of improvement does not work, namely, cases in which individuals comply with institutions that prevent them from improving their conditions, even when alternative and better courses of action are available. Clearly, they are manifestations of irrational behaviour.

The problem is: how do we account for irrational behaviour, if individuals are assumed to be basically rational? The solution to this problem is to be sought mainly in the field of the formation of human ends and values. As it has already been elucidated, individuals' autonomy is a very relative characteristic: it is relative to the cultural and social influences that agents have undergone in the formation of their preferences. Most actions are purposeful and intentional, in the sense that individuals freely and deliberately choose their ends. But choices are restricted to a limited set of possibilities, the limitations being posed by the contrasting drives coming from the social context.

Social influences, however, do not just work towards framing the set of possible human choices. They work also in other, more perverse ways. One such case is that which could be called 'teleological dissonance'. This occurs when an individual lets himself be governed by two, or even more, contrasting influences, to the point of clinging to contradictory ends or values. For example, in a capitalist economy in which religious sentiments survive, it is conceivable for an individual to act by aiming at both usurious profits and God's grace. In situations of this kind, whatever the means chosen to pursue one of the contradictory ends, if it is rational with respect to that end, it could be irrational with respect to the others.

Another case of contradictory behaviour could be called 'operational dissonance', and occurs when cultural and social influences push individuals to prefer or to avoid certain particular means independently of the ends they can be made to serve. The difference between teleological and operational dissonance is simple: in the former case a contradiction arises which involves different ends (or values attached to them), whilst in the latter it is the consistency between ends and means (or values attached to them) that is impaired.

The scene is complicated by the fact that we live in a conflictual society, namely, one in which the pursuit of some individuals' ends may require the frustration of those of some other individuals. Worse: one in which some individuals could form coalitions in order to exploit others. Most collective agents are formed with the aim of strengthening the power of some individuals in the struggle for survival. And since the pursuit of individual interests and ends is widely framed by institutions, the latter can be used by some coalitions of agents as a means to perpetrate the exploitation of others. This result can be achieved by inducing teleological or operational dissonance, and then irrational behaviour, in the exploited people. An obvious example is that of the use of religious sentiments as a means to persuade the exploited classes to accept peacefully their conditions of life.

It is now easy to explain various kinds of perverse evolutionary processes. And there are three that are particularly interesting. One of them is institutional adverse selection. This occurs when some old institutions are supplanted by new ones that are conducive to the improvement of the situation of some individuals, call them 'winners', but detrimental with respect to the interests of some other individuals, call them 'losers'. The latter could be prevented by operational dissonance from activating the logical attempt at institutional revision.

Another case is institutional lock-in. This occurs when allegiance to a certain basic institution prevents individuals from adopting better routines that might have been easily accessible had other basic institutions been complied with. The abandonment of the conservative institution could be made impossible by either teleological or operational dissonance.

A third case is stickiness of institutions due to institutional involvement. This occurs when some individuals let their ends be moulded by the institutions to which they belong to the point of avoiding changing their institutional allegiance even when a better institution is available. In this case, teleological or operational dissonance could be assumed to be at work.

It goes without saying that the deterioration of the situation of some individuals might be compatible with an improvement of that of others. Therefore the problem is posed of the stability of an involutional kind of institutional change. This problem cannot be worked out here, mainly because of the high level of abstraction of the analysis developed in this essay. However, a few words can be said.

First of all, since an institutional change, or non-change, could be involutional for some individuals and evolutional for others, the new situation can survive as long as the latter, i.e. the winners, succeed in keeping hold. On the other hand, struggle is incessant. Thus we have here a case of temporary stability. But the period of permanence of the involutional institution could be very long.

Secondly, the deterioration of the situation of some individuals brought about by an involutional change could well lead to the extinction of the losers, which is a case of strong stability. But clearly this is a case of stability of evolution, since survivors obtain an improvement from the change. Most probably therefore, if individuals are assumed to be basically rational, in the very long run only evolutionary changes will turn out to be collectively stable. But I admit that such a conclusion may well have been prompted by a helpless optimism as regards the fate of human free will.

CONCLUSIONS: WHAT IS RELATIVE RATIONALITY?

We are finally able to clarify what is meant by 'relative rationality'. By definition, we would consider the conduct governed by our three elementary criteria of behaviour to be relatively rational. 'Relatively', in a threefold sense. First of all, it is observed that if even the individual maximized in the neoclassical manner, _in applying the criterion of conditional improvement_, he would do so by accepting institutional constraints that are historically determined. Nothing would guarantee that overall and absolute maximization would be achieved. In any given historical situation one may, therefore, speak of _rationality relative to the given institutions_.

Secondly, in a perspective of historical evolution, the criterion of institutional revision will lead to the abandonment of obsolete institutions and the formation of new ones. The new ones should be better than the old ones, at least from the point of view of some individuals, but there is nothing to guarantee that they will be _the best_. Most of them emerge from Veblenian 'idle curiosity' applied to the search for new ways of 'doing better'. They are therefore influenced both by the historical and institutional context within which the search is carried out, and by pure and simple chance.

Furthermore, various phenomena of dissonant behaviour could push individuals into taking decisions which sometimes conflict with their own real interests and may lead to the survival of some institutions well beyond the point at which they fail to satisfy individual interests. It is difficult, hopefully, for such survival to be protracted. And yet this is a form of institutional stickiness which contributes to undermining the absoluteness of the rationality of evolution. In short, the _evolution_ of institutions, as already pointed out, is not governed by the maximization principle. It is, rather, a strongly path-dependent process and therefore itself also historically determined. Consequently, it is impossible to conceive of an absolute rationality, even in the perspective of extremely long-lasting evolutionary processes. We will speak, instead, of relative rationality[15]: in this case, of *rationality relative to past history.*

Thirdly, there is a more general sense in which one may speak of relative rationality. The point is that human choices, however deliberate and self-interested, are still conditioned by needs and interests whose formation is strongly influenced by cultural factors. These influences are deeper than those exerted by institutions in limiting the decisions about the means to pursue human ends. Here, it is the very choices of ends that are at stake. In this case, we will speak of *rationality relative to a given cultural setting.*

A final caveat is necessary. It is the case to be cautious about the unintentional nature of institutions. An institution is an unintentional result of individual action, when it is such, only in the sense that no particular individual may have intentionally created it *as an institution.* To become an institution, a routine needs diffusion, and such a process might not result from a plan. But it remains true that all the routines from which institutions emerge 'are products of human reflection, formulation and election' (Tool, 1993, p. 3). Furthermore, it is also true that an institution, although it may not have originated from the decisions of a social planner (Schotter, 1981, p. 118), exists and can continue to exist only inasmuch as, and for as long as, some individuals conform to it. Finally, an institution disappears and is replaced by a new one only if a certain number of individuals abandon it and conform their behaviour to the new one. The actions of such individuals need not be unintentional. On the other hand, a new pattern of behaviour, actually, 'becomes habitual through repetition, but its initial performance requires conscious direction' (Fagg Foster, 1981, p. 933). In conclusion, even if no single agent may normally produce an institution according to a plan, it remains true that the institution exists by virtue of the intentional and conscious actions of individuals.

NOTES

1. In this sense, see also Axelrod (1984, pp. 6–7) and Williamson (1986, pp. 176–7). It is necessary to declare explicitly that the concept of individualism used here admits not only *self-interested behaviour*, but also so called 'opportunism', and is traceable to the argument of Georgescu-Roegen (1971, pp. 319–20) according to which 'casual observation of what happens in the sphere of economic organizations, or between these organizations and individuals, suffices to reveal phenomena that do not consist of *tâtonnement* with given means toward given ends according to given rules. They show beyond any doubt that in all societies the individual also continually pursues an end ignored by the standard framework: the increase of what he can claim as his income according to his current position and distributive norms. It is the pursuit of this end that

makes the individual a true agent of the economic process'. The emphasis here should be placed on the 'given rules' and 'norms' which the individual would naturally be disposed to infringe upon in the pursuit of his personal ends.

2. For an examination in greater depth of the themes dealt with in this section the reader is referred to Hodgson (1988, chaps. 4, 5, 6).

3. Some terminological clarification is necessary here on the concept of 'institutions'. In the recent institutionalist revival this term is used with a threefold meaning: in the sense of 'social habits' or 'socially diffused routines'; in the sense of 'social norms'; in the sense of 'organisations' or 'collective agents'. The first meaning is the most common. The following is a definition by Mitchell (1937, p. 373): 'institution' is merely a convenient term for a more important among the widely prevalent, highly standardized social habits'. A somewhat more precise definition is offered by Hamilton (1963, p. 84), who says that an institution is 'a way of thought or action of some prevalence and permanence, which is embedded in the habits of a group or the customs of a people'. A similar definition is used in many models of institutional evolution based on game theory: see, for example, Schotter (1981, p. 11) and Witt (1993, pp. 1–2).

    Sometimes the term is used in the sense of Commons, namely as meaning 'social norms and rules' or, rather, 'collective action in control (...) of individual action' (Commons, 1931, p. 651; see also Commons, 1934, p. 69). This is the second meaning. Actually, institutions do consist in the two kinds of phenomena, and this is why 'it would be advisable to adopt the (...) option that (they) comprise both rules and regularities' (Mäki, 1993, p. 13)

    The use of the term 'institutions' also in the third meaning, namely, in the sense of organizations or collective agents, is more controversial (North, 1990 pp. 3–5, Sjöstrand, 1993, p. 11, Pitelis, 1995, note 1). At any rate, it could be motivated by the fact that an organisational structure is defined by the normative apparatus which regulates it and the routines followed by the individuals who belong to it. For this reason, it is quite legitimate to use the term in all three meanings referred to above. See also Lachmann (1971, p. 81) Hayek (1973, pp. 30 and 50) Nelson and Winter (1982, chs. 4 and 5) Langlois (1986b, p. 15) and Hodgson (1988, p. 10).

    So here, too, we shall comply with this usage. Often, however, it will be necessary to refer to certain institutions (in the third sense) such as firms, unions, etc., treating them as agents or sets of agents, rather than as sets of norms and routines. To avoid confusion, in these cases it is better to use another term. Here the expression 'collective agents' will be adopted.

4. The origin of this idea must be sought in Simon (1955; 1957). Similar versions of the hypothesis of bounded rationality in conditions of uncertainty are provided by Shackle (1955; 1972) and Boulding (1956). Other interesting treatments, among the most recent, are those of Loasby (1976), Earl (1983), Heiner (1983), Hodgson (1988) and Dosi and Egidi (1991). It is worth noting that Simon's theses on behaviour in conditions of uncertainty explicitly claim, although somewhat shyly, an institutionalist ascendancy (see Simon, 1979, p. 499; 1982, p. 718). In the present essay such a claim is taken seriously; more seriously than the behaviourist Simonians tend to do; and perhaps even more seriously than Simon himself.

5. It is admitted that the system includes equations for the possible reactions of other agents to the actions of the decision-maker. Thus, to say that the system of equations is underdetermined is compatible with excluding parametric behaviour. In other words, this mathematical metaphor is capable of accounting also for strategic behaviour in conditions of uncertainty.

6. A similar thesis is argued by Hayek (1964), Agassi (1975), Langlois (1986c), Schotter (1986), Hodgson (1988) and Vanberg (1993).
7. Game theory offers illuminating examples. The notion of the 'decision-making rule', which is used in this theory, can be interpreted in terms of a rule to evaluate the best strategy, or a rule of behaviour that implicitly contains a rule of evaluation. Even in the simplest static games different decision-making rules can be adopted by an individual, depending on whether, e.g., he follows a minimax criterion or points to a Nash equilibrium or adheres to a cooperative behaviour.

   In repeated games, decision-making rules can proliferate. Just think, for example, of the various 'tit for tat', 'grim', 'all D', etc. The interesting thing to note is that different rules, when applied to the same game, can bring the individual to different situations, each of which could be considered to be the best in terms of a rule.
8. This idea goes at least as far back as Menger (1959). See also Loasby (1993, p. 7).
9. Here we develop, although in a different direction from the one pointed out by Simon, the ideas he put forward with regard to acceptance prices and aspiration levels, for which the reader is referred to Simon (1955). Berg (1974) obtained interesting experimental results with the thesis according to which investment decisions are based on criteria using aspiration levels rather than on the maximization criterion.
10. Veblen himself, despite his insistence on the intentionality of human action, and notwithstanding the conviction that 'economic action is teleological' (1919, p. 75), rather leans towards an evolutionary conception in which instinctual behaviour prevails. On this question see Commons (1934, p. 654 et passim), Seckler (1975, p. 56 et passim) and Hodgson (1992).
11. For a justification of this approach on the ground of the theory of bounded rationality see Dosi and Egidi (1991) and Egidi (1992). An interesting experimental study on the formation of routines is Cohen (1991).
12. For a wide review of evolutionary theories produced by economists see Hodgson (1993).
13. Perhaps it was the very need to preserve a rational foundation for the evolutionary processes of human institutions that led Axelrod (1984, chap. 3) to replace the concept of 'evolutionary stability' with that of 'collective stability'. Axelrod is actually not very clear on this point. To the extent to which such an interpretation is valid, however, his terminological innovation deserves to be followed by social scientists.
14. For an extended analysis on this point see Langlois (1986b, p. 21; 1986c, pp. 236, 247, and 251).
15. In this aspect, the present notion of 'relative rationality' undoubtedly resembles the one worked out by Commons. See Biddle (1990, pp. 36–37) and Vanberg (1993, p. 174).

REFERENCES

Agassi, J. (1975), 'Institutional Individualism', *British Journal of Sociology*, vol. 26, pp. 144–55.
Axelrod, R. (1984), *The Evolution of Cooperation*, Basic Books, New York.
Berg, C.C. (1974), 'Individual Decisions Concerning the Allocation of Resources for Projects with Uncertain Consequences', *Management Science*, vol. 21, pp. 98–105.

Biddle, J.E. (1990), 'Purpose and Evolution in Commons Institutionalism', *History of Political Economy*, vol. 22, pp. 19–47.

Boulding, K.E. (1956), *The Image: Knowledge in Life and Society*, University of Michigan Press, Ann Arbour.

Cohen, M.D. (1991), 'Individual Learning and Organizational Routine: Emerging Connections', *Organization Science*, vol. 2, pp. 135–139.

Commons, J. (1931), 'Institutional Economics', *American Economic Review*, vol. 21.

Commons, J. (1934), *Institutional Economics: Its Place in Political Economy*, Macmillan, New York (reprint: Transaction Books, New Brunswick).

Dosi, G. and Egidi, M. (1991), 'Substantive and Procedural Uncertainty: An Exploration of Economic Behaviour in Changing Environments', *Journal of Evolutionary Economics*, vol. 1, pp. 148–168.

Earl, P.E. (1983), *The Economic Imagination: Toward a Behavioural Analysis of Choice*, Wheatsheaf, Brighton.

Egidi, M. (1989), 'Bounded Rationality and the Theory of the Firm: An Interview with Herbert Simon', *Annali Scientifici del Dipartimento di Economia*, University of Trento, vol. 2, pp. 41–6.

Egidi, M. (1992), 'Organizational Learning, Problem Solving and the Division of Labour' in M. Egidi and R. Marris (eds.) (1992), *Economics, Bounded Rationality and the Cognitive Revolution*, pp. 148–173.

Fagg Foster, J. (1981), 'Syllabus for Problems of Modern Society: The Theory of Institutional Adjustment', *Journal of Economic Issues*, vol. 15.

Georgescu-Roegen, N. (1971), *The Entropy Law and Economic Progress*, Harvard University Press, Cambridge Mass.

Hamilton, W.H. (1963), 'Institutions', in E.R.A. Seligman and A. Johnson (eds.), *Encyclopedia of the Social Sciences*, vol. 7, Macmillan, London.

Hayek, F. (1964), 'Kinds of Order in Society', *Individualist Review*, vol. 3, pp. 3–12.

Hayek, F. (1973), *Law, Legislation, and Liberty*, vol. 1: *Rules and Order*, Chicago University Press, Chicago.

Heiner, R.A. (1983), 'The Origin of Predictable Behaviour', *American Economic Review*, vol. 73, pp. 560–95.

Hodgson, G.M. (1988), *Economics and Institutions*, Polity Press, Cambridge.

Hodgson G.M.(1991), 'Economic Evolution: Intervention Contra Pangloss', *Journal of Economic Issues*, vol. 25, pp. 519–33.

Hodgson, G.M. (1992), 'Thorstein Veblen and Post-Darwinian Economics', *Cambridge Journal of Economics*, vol. 16, pp. 285–301.

Hodgson, G.M. (1993), *Economics and Evolution*, Polity Press, Cambridge.

Lachmann, L. (1971), *The Legacy of Max Weber*, Glendessary Press, Berkeley.

Langlois, R.N. (ed.) (1986b), 'The New Institutional Economics: An Introductory Essay', in Langlois (1986a), *Economics as a Process, Essays in the New Institutional Economics*, pp. 1–26.

Langlois, R.N. (1986c), 'Rationality, Institutions, and Explanation', in Langlois (ed.) (1986a) *Economics as a Process, Essays in the New Institutional Economics*, pp. 225–55.

Loasby, B.J. (1976), *Choice, Complexity and Ignorance: an Enquiry into Economic Theory and Practice of Decision Making*, Cambridge University Press, Cambridge.

Loasby, B.J. (1993), 'Organizational Capabilities and Interfirm Relations', Paper presented at the workshop on *The Notions of Competition and Cooperation in Economics*, Fondazione Levi, Venice.

Mäki, U. (1993), 'Economics with Institutions: Agenda for Methodological Enquire' in Mäki U., B.Gustafsson and G. Knudsen (eds.), *Rationality, Institutions and Economic Methodology*, Routledge, London, pp. 3–42.

Mäki, U., B. Gustafsson, and G. Knudsen (eds.) (1993), *Rationality, Institutions and Economic Methodology*, Routledge, London.

Maynard Smith, J. (1974), 'The Theory of Games and the Evolution of Animal Conflict', *Journal of Theoretical Biology*, vol. 47, pp. 209–21.

Menger, C. (1959), *Principles of Economics*, Free Press, Glencoe, Ill.

Mitchell, W.C. (1937), 'The Prospect of Economics', in *The Backward Art of Spending Money and Other Essays*, New York.

Nelson, R.R. and Winter, S.G. (1982), *An Evolutionary Theory of Economic Change*, Harvard University Press, Cambridge Mass.

North, D.C. (1990), *Institutions, Institutional Change and Economic Performance*, Cambridge University Press, Cambridge.

Pitelis, S. (1995), 'Towards an Evolutionary Perspective of Instituional Crises', in Groenewegen, J., C. Pitelis, and S-E Sjöstrand (eds.), *On Economic Institutions — Theory and Applications*, Edward Elgar, London.

Schotter, A. (1981), *The Economic Theory of Social Institutions*, Cambridge University Press, Cambridge.

Schotter, A. (ed.) (1986), 'The Evolution of Rules', in Langlois (1986a), *Economics as a Process, Essays in the New Institutional Economics*, pp. 117–34.

Seckler, D. (1975), *Thorstein Veblen and the Institutionalists: A Study in the Social Philosophy of Economics*, Macmillan, London.

Selten, R. (1991), 'Evolution, Learning, and Economic Behavior', *Games and Economic Behavior*, vol. 3, pp. 3–24.

Shackle, G.L.S. (1955), *Uncertainty in Economics*, Cambridge University Press, Cambridge.

Shackle, G.L.S. (1972), *Epistemics and Economics*, Cambridge University Press, Cambridge.

Simon, H.A. (1955), 'A Behavioral Model of Rational Choice', *Quarterly Journal of Economics*, vol. 69, pp. 99–118.

Simon, H.A. (1957), *Models of Man: Social and Rational*, Wiley, New York.

Simon, H.A. (1979), 'Rational Decision Making in Business Organization', *American Economic Review*, vol. 69, pp. 493–512.

Simon, H.A. (1981), 'Economic Rationality: Adaptive Artifice', in *The Science of the Artificial*, pp. 31–61, MIT Press, Cambridge Mass.

Simon, H.A. (1982), 'Economics and Psychology', in *Models of Bounded Rationality*, vol. 2, *Behavioral Economics and Business Organization*, MIT Press, Cambridge Mass.

Sjöstrand, S-E. (1992), 'On the Rationale Behind Irrational Institutions', *Journal of Economic Issues*, vol. 26, pp. 1007–40.

Sjöstrand, S-E. (1993), 'On Institutional Thought in the Social and Economic Sciences', in S-E. Sjöstrand (ed.) (1993), *Institutional Change: Theory and Empirical Findings*, pp. 3–31, M. E. Sharpe, New York.

Tool, M. (1993), 'Institutional Adjustment and Instrumental Value: with Observations on 'Reform' in Eastern Europe', paper presented at the Fifth Annual Conference of the EAEPE, Barcelona.

Vanberg, V. (1993), 'Rational Choice, Rule-following and Institutions', in U. Mäki, B. Gustafsson and C. Knudsen (eds.) (1993), *Rationality, Institutions and Economic Methodology*, Routledge, London, pp. 171–200.

Veblen, T.B. (1914), *The Instinct of Workmanship, and the State of Industrial Arts*, Kelley, New York (reprint: Transaction Books, 1990, New Brunswick).

Veblen, T.B. (1919), *The Place of Science in Modern Civilization and Other Essays*, Huebsch, New York, (reprint: Transaction Books, 1990, New Brunswick).

Williamson, O.E. (1986), 'The Economics of Governance: Framework and Implications', in Langlois (ed.) (1986a) *Economics as a Process, Essays in the New Institutional Economics*, Cambridge University Press, Cambridge, pp. 171–203.

Witt, U. (1993), 'Path-dependence in Institutional Change', paper presented at the Fifth Annual Conference of the EAEPE, Barcelona.

5. The Meaning and Role of Power in Economic Theories

David Young

INTRODUCTION

The meaning and significance of power in economic analysis has seldom been a subject which has engaged the efforts of mainstream neoclassical theorists. That is not to say that the term power is never used or that it does not play a significant role in certain models. But, it tends to be used in a very specific and narrow way and its alternative meanings and wider significance are seldom acknowledged.

In 1971 Rothschild commented that as 'in other important social fields we should expect that individuals and groups will struggle for position; that power will be used to improve one's chances in the economic 'game'. Power should, therefore, be a recurrent theme in economic studies of a theoretical or applied nature. Yet if we look at the main run of economic theory over the past hundred years we find that it is characterised by a strange lack of power considerations' (Rothschild, 1971 p. 7). This state of affairs has fundamentally changed very little. To a large extent, this neglect has continued almost uninterrupted as mainstream economists refine and extend the basic model postulated by neoclassical theory. Despite more common usage of the term power in mainstream game-theoretic analysis, the meaning of power is still constrained by the conception of neoclassical competition, and so the general neglect of 'power' in mainstream analysis remains.

The main objectives of this chapter are to consider the alternative meanings of 'power' and to assess the different interpretations and roles of power in different types of economic theory. It will be argued that all the main schools of thought in economics adopt a particular view of power and that this reflects fundamental differences in the nature of the theories. It will also be suggested that it is difficult to ignore the significance of power in general for economic theory, and that attempts to examine the nature and role of power more explicitly may lead to a more satisfactory analysis of market interactions between individual agents, firms and other institutions.

DIFFERENT SCHOOLS OF ECONOMIC THOUGHT AND DIFFERENT NOTIONS OF 'POWER'

The relative neglect (at least until recently) of the notion of power in mainstream economics is not shared by alternative schools of thought. In general, economic theorists of a Marxist or 'radical' persuasion have long emphasised the importance of 'power' for explaining economic phenomena. Similarly some other heterodox economists (who we might refer to as institutionalists) such as those works collected in Samuels (1979) have also discussed various aspects of power, although from a somewhat different standpoint and in very diverse ways. By contrast, Austrian economists have long denied the importance of power for explaining the workings of competitive market economies.

Neither the Marxist or the Austrian view of power accord with mainstream theory. To attempt to elucidate the different meanings of power and its general importance to economic theory it is helpful to consider the different conceptions of power adopted by these three schools of thought: Marxian, Austrian and neoclassical. Although there are a number of different alternative approaches, it may be contended that these three bodies of theory can be regarded as the most clearly defined and distinctive approaches to economic theory. They have different philosophical presumptions and give rise to distinct policy prescriptions. Other approaches (and there are many) may be regarded as less than distinct schools of thought. They do not have such clearly defined foundations, either philosophically or in terms of their historical roots and some have emerged specifically as a criticism of particular aspects of mainstream theory rather than being grounded in a different tradition or mode of thought. This may be so with respect to the institutionalist approach, which is clearly the most relevant in the present context.

Institutional economics encompasses a variety of different theoretical perspectives (based on correspondingly different philosophical foundations) united by an emphasis or an explicit discussion of institutions and institutional change. The three schools identified here may be regarded as having different views regarding the role and importance of institutions, and much of the content of what is often described as being an institutionalist approach may be regarded as being influenced by one or another of these schools. So the nature of power which varies so much within institutionalist theories may be clarified by considering the meaning of power as it relates to these three schools of thought. This is not to say that there are no important alternative ideas and that these do not provide some basis for future progress but, for the moment, the three schools we have identified may be taken to represent the basis of competing contemporary theories.

Before examining the views of power inherent in these different schools of thought it is necessary to consider the meanings which we might attach to the term power, and to consider some basis for comparing the different views of power which have emerged in economic theory.

THE MEANINGS OF POWER

As noted in the introduction the term 'power' has been used in numerous ways and can be taken to involve a number of diverse dimensions. Within economics specifically, the term has been applied to 'power' over resources (e.g., the means to produce), purchasing power, monopoly power, and the power of the state. More generally it is also used with reference to natural powers (e.g., wind, waves) and to coercion or violence. The two latter meanings are normally not the concern of social theory and will not be of concern here, except in as much as some reference will be made to coercion in the discussion of economic power.

The issue of power has been widely discussed in social theory over a number of years, and particularly since Dahl (1957) has received considerable attention in sociological studies. One study which is widely regarded as having provided an important approach to considering power is Lukes (1974), which argued for a more 'radical' approach. Though there are problems involved with this view, which have subsequently been discussed in sociological theory, Lukes (1974) does still provide a framework for thinking about different types or dimensions of power, which have generally not been recognised by economists in their modelling of problems which utilise some conception of power.

Lukes (1974) provides a detailed account of the dimensions of power which are often mentioned but largely neglected by liberal analysts. In particular we are offered a more 'radical' analysis which considers some of the more subtle and indirect ways in which power may be exercised. Lukes specifies three principal dimensions of power. The one dimensional view concerns the ability to win in overt conflict through sheer 'weight'. This is the most obvious and most widely recognised dimension of power, although there may still be difficulties in modelling such conflicts. The two dimensional view includes consideration of cases where, say, A has power over B if A can prevent B's wants from reaching the stage of overt conflict and decision, i.e., rigging the 'game' before it starts or setting the agenda. This is clearly a less direct but potentially very important aspect of power, and continuing in this vein a three dimensional view is defined which involves situations where A can manipulate B's preferences, in such a manner that they are then contrary to B's interests. This is perhaps the most controversial dimension and in practice (as Lukes, 1974, discusses) involves establishing the appropriate counterfactuals in order to establish that such power has been exercised.

In addition we may also wish to draw a clear distinction between wants or preferences and interests. If this is so, then one may wish to divide Lukes' three dimensional view into two categories, one involving the manipulation of wants and the other the manipulation of wants in the subversion of that agent's interests. Following Hollis (1987) we may then distinguish four clear categories which may be useful in thinking about what is meant by 'power' and the ways in which we might consider its significance. These categories may be summarised as follows. Consider two individuals (agents), A and B. A has power over B if:

1. A has the ability to win in overt conflict with B.

2. A is able to divert B's wants.

3. A is able to reconstitute B's wants.

4. A is able to reconstitute B's wants against B's interests.

Although not uncontroversial, such a classification does seem to capture most of the important aspects or dimensions of power which we might wish to discuss in economic theories. It should be acknowledged however that there are a number of desirable characteristics which any conception of power might involve, namely a positive as well as a negative dimension and a more dynamic or process quality. Although these aspects are not developed here it should be emphasised that power may be an enabling as well as a restraining relation and the ways in which it emerges is within the context of an evolving process of relations between agents and institutions. These aspects of power may also be important in distinguishing between different economic theories but in general some Lukes-type classification will suffice for the purpose of examining the views of power adopted within the different schools which have been specified.

THE DISTINCT VIEWS OF 'POWER' INHERENT IN DIFFERENT SCHOOLS OF THOUGHT

Having sketched the different attitudes to 'power' adopted by the three principle schools of thought which we have identified, and having considered what we might mean by 'power' we may begin to develop a categorisation of the different views of power embedded in each approach and to illuminate the key differences between them.

If we begin by considering mainstream neoclassical analysis, then it is clear that the term power has long been in common usage but has seldom been explicitly considered; its meaning has often been specific but very narrow, arising out of the particular models within which it appears. As noted by Rothschild (1971) much of early microeconomic analysis was built around the model of perfect competition. As is well-known, this model (contestability aside) still forms the basis of welfare judgments with respect to monopolistic and oligopolistic markets. Game theory has developed models of firms' strategic behaviour but the conception of 'power' is linked to the old idea of monopoly or market power which is itself conceived of in terms of a departure from a competitive state. Similarly the neoclassical conception of dominance relies heavily on the concept of market power and price leadership.

For example, the standard dominant firm-price leadership model is based on the idea that a particular firm or group of firms has a sufficiently large market share to set prices as a monopolist would, but subject to a demand condition given by exogenous market demand minus the supply of the other 'fringe' producers. This is clearly a simplistic notion of power which is essentially seen in terms of a producer's ability to determine price. But there is really little analysis of the process by which such power is established or explanation of what exactly allows the dominant firm to continue to exert such market power. Of course, mainstream theory has developed more sophisticated models to attempt to model firms' use of market power by examining strategic behaviour in a game theoretic setting. Nonetheless the conception of power remains similar.

An example of the attitude to 'power' adopted in modern mainstream theory is given in Skaperdas (1992) where it is commented that 'an agent's equilibrium win probability (or the share of total product) represents a clear index of the agent's power'.

> [Power is ...] however, a notoriously difficult concept to define and investigate. When it is defined, it is frequently viewed as an exogenous parameter with unspecified determinants (Skaperdas, 1992, p.721).

This indicates both the view of power typically adopted in mainstream analysis and the scepticism involved in trying to incorporate it into the analysis in a more general way. It is essentially a one dimensional view of power, and therefore, although specific and analytically useful, it is too narrow to capture other dimensions of power relations. This is generally true of the type of 'power' discussed in mainstream game theory, which whilst bringing 'power' to a more prominent position has severely restricted its dimensions.

One issue in game theory which is of importance for considering the role of power is what is usually known as 'cheap talk', i.e., any communication which takes place between players prior to the beginning of a particular game which incurs no cost to any of the players. This is often 'disallowed' on the grounds that if it were permitted it would give rise to an unmanageable number of potential outcomes. (The possible equilibria would clearly be significantly expanded.) This is not to say that some games do not take account of cheap talk, less still that the outcomes are influenced by cheap talk, but once we allow such pre-play communication there is no possibility of guaranteeing that an agreement/solution can be reached, or of predicting what the outcome might be. However, the pre-game environment and inter-play between the players is of great significance in that the initial conditions are crucial to the games solution. Moreover, consideration of the pre-game stage may give rise to a two dimensional view of power. (Lukes' category 2).

One obvious problem of analysing this within a standard game theoretic framework is that we can always imagine a prior game to the game being specified and therefore something qualitatively different has to be offered in order to find some alternative explanation of the initial conditions and the environment of the game under analysis. This would be a problem (although clearly not so severe) even in the absence of cheap talk given that the outcome of games is generally sensitive to the initial conditions. That game theory is characterised by multiple equilibria, suggests in itself that something more needs to be said about the environmental, institutional and historical conditions in which the game takes place which might limit the plausible solutions and outcomes.

Another feature of game theory where 'power' is important involves the fact that the solution to certain games appeal to some 'folk theorem'. These involve the following idea. If we consider a repeated game in general, then any feasible expected payoff can be sustained in equilibrium as long as each player's expected payoffs are greater than or equal to the payoff which that player is guaranteed if all the other players were to 'gang-up' on him or her. If this is so, then if a player is told by the other players to stick to an agreement under threat of all the other players 'ganging-up', then no single player has any incentive to deviate and a Nash equilibrium can be sustained. (On this see, e.g., Kreps, 1990). Now this idea clearly must involve some conception of power. How else are we to interpret the threat of players continuing to force a player to conform to an agreement? But although such threats seem to involve a simple one-dimensional view of power it is far from clear what form such power may take. Is it just a version of market power? Even if it is, the crux of the problem for neoclassical theory is that it does not really have a full theory of market or monopoly power. It has a theory of monopoly of course, but this is quite different. That no complete theory of monopoly power exists is acknowledged by some mainstream theorists. For example, Kreps (1990) sums up the situation by commenting that a firm's ability to stick to a monopoly price involves a fundamental problem of credibility and reputation, and that:

> [...] as long as we avoid [...] institutional details, it is hard to say much about whether a monopoly can muster credibility (p.317).

There is clearly scope therefore for a two dimensional view of power within mainstream theory, but the nature of such power would be limited by the assumptions made regarding the nature of agency. That is to say, the standard assumption that agents are rational instrumental utilitarians influences the nature and outcome of the game. It is also possible in principle that some type of three dimensional view of power might be possible within a broad neoclassical framework, although here there are much greater problems. There has been much work in recent years attempting to consider the problem of enforcement within organisations and firms endogenously but that has fallen short of considering endogenous preferences as well. Of course the possibility of endogenous preferences poses severe problems for neoclassical analysis.

As we shall discuss further in a later section, the idea of endogenous preferences is subvertive of the welfare basis of mainstream theory and calls into question the foundational assumptions needed to generate virtually all the results of mainstream economics[1]. This is not to say that such an approach is necessarily incorrect (much less that it is not worthwhile) but it does emphasise that mainstream theory adopts a particular perspective which may not be the most useful. It may actually be the case that it is not correct to treat preferences as exogenous and make that the basis of demand theory. Similarly neoclassical production theory may be severely limited by excluding the social relations of production. It would also be the case that the types of neoclassical solution to situations involving one and two dimensional views of power would be undermined. However, it would be possible to a degree to introduce the endogeneity of preferences into a framework which adopts views of agency and equilibrium characteristic of neoclassical analysis.

The prominence of power in Austrian economics is quite different to its role in mainstream theory. Austrian writers almost invariably dismissed the idea that power is inherent in 'free' market economies. This does not mean that there is no reference to or discussion of power in Austrian theory. On the contrary, there have been a number of discussions and comments on power by most prominent Austrians, but all have been in an attempt to deny its importance. Although it is not feasible here to consider the Austrians' views on power in depth, the main ideas and issues of contention may be illustrated by considering the main lines of thought which have influenced contemporary views. There are a number of different approaches within Austrian economics, which reach similar conclusions regarding the issue of power but for importantly different reasons. An early example of the dismissal of 'power' is Böhm-Bawerk's well known essay on 'Control or economic law' (1962/1914). The main thesis of this work is that although power or control[2] may be important in influencing the broader environment, economic laws still apply to market transactions. By this it is meant, for example, that the 'laws' determining price behaviour will apply even in cases of monopoly. This is entirely a neoclassical position. It is important to note that Böhm-Bawerk explicitly excluded cases of robbery, extortion and slavery from his discussion believing that these belong to a different category of economic problems.

The term power does appear in the Austrian literature even before this time, indeed 'power' quite frequently appears in Menger's Grundsätze (1950, 1871)[3]. As noted by Vaughn (1990), for example, Menger generally uses the term in the sense of power over resources or enabling powers rather than power relations between individual agents. This is similar to the aforementioned uses by Böhm-Bawerk, but it should be noted that Menger was certainly concerned with the exercise of economic power which threatened the proper functioning of the market. There are examples in the Grundsätze where Menger is critical of situations in which power is exercised over certain resources and land (see Young, 1992). This concern however, is again largely similar to neoclassical concerns regarding market power. It is important to emphasise however, the concern for the issue of 'power' particularly in the case of Böhm-Bawerk, who considered it to be threatening to his version of economic theory. This view has remained important in Austrian economics, but as indicated there are different views as to why power should be expunged from economic theory. To explain these we may briefly consider the main propositions relating to the ideas of Hayek, Mises and Rothbard.

In Hayek (1960, and most notably 1944) there is a clear reliance on the notion of competitive capitalism when discussing power and coercion. Virtually all of Hayek's claims about the absence of power from market capitalism are with reference to a competitive market. For example, in Hayek (1944) in arguing his central thesis that it is the state which wields power and that this is an 'evil' which is to be contained he writes:

> [...] to believe that power which is thus conferred on the state is merely transferred to it from others is erroneous. It is a power which is newly created and which in a *competitive* society nobody possesses. So long as property is divided among many owners[4], none of them acting independently has exclusive power to determine the income and position of particular people — nobody is tied to him except by the fact that he may offer better terms than anybody else. (Hayek 1944, p.77; emphasis added)

The idea that there is no power relation inherent in voluntary exchanges is crucial and runs throughout Austrian literature. However, given the reliance on competitive competition in dismissing the importance of power, we then must consider cases where there is some degree of monopoly over resources or source of employment which, it might be argued, is often found in practice. Obviously such cases are of concern in mainstream theory, but the Austrian line generally is to argue that exchange (contracts) is still voluntary in such situations. The problem here for the Hayek view is that when considering certain 'extreme' cases he appears to draw back from the strong subjectivist liberal argument and introduces rather ad hoc utilitarian ideas. Hayek (1960) for instance, gives a number of cases where government intervention is justified or where the 'normal' principles of the market are modified (e.g., in the case of compulsory purchase orders when the national interest is at stake, or a doctor providing free service to a dying person). Once such 'modifications' or qualifications are introduced of course, then we are entitled to question the wholly voluntary nature of exchange.

The Misean position is somewhat different, reflecting perhaps the methodological differences which exist between Mises and other Austrian theorists[5]. Broadly, the position which is articulated in Mises (1949) is that power is connected with the state and is generally absent from free market economies. This gives rise to the well-known policy view that the state should retreat from economic interventions. Mises however did develop a view of monopoly power based on the exclusive ownership of natural resources and limited-space monopoly (amongst several other conditions) which has been criticised by Austrians of a more radical subjectivist position on the grounds that even in these cases consumer sovereignty is not infringed (see O'Driscoll, 1982).

One proponent of this strong subjectivist line is Rothbard, whose approach is given in detail in Rothbard (1962). Rothbard (1970) develops these views with specific reference to power, again indicating the long-standing antipathy of Austrians to the intrusion of power into economic analysis. Rothbard defines 'economic power' as 'simply the right under freedom to refuse to make an exchange. Every man has this power. Every man has the same right to refuse to make a preferred exchange.' (1970, p.229). The state on the other hand wields political power and at various points Rothbard refers to 'violent' state intervention and to the 'coercive monopoly' position of state enterprises. Thus, as with Hayek and Mises, exchange is wholly voluntary and the problem of 'power' and monopoly originate with state intervention. In elaborating these claims Rothbard emphasises the distinction between 'power over nature' and 'power over man', which parallels and perhaps extends the distinction between economic and political power. Power over nature, it is argued, is essential for the advancement of mankind where as the power of one person over another does not contribute to progress.

Although Rothbard's views are clearly related to the ideas expressed by Mises (particularly in Mises, 1949), there would appear to be a critical difference between the two on the precise role of power[6]. As indicated, Rothbard (1970) effectively dismisses the importance of power to market transactions, but he is prepared to admit that there may be some coercive behaviour by individuals. This, however, is outside the scope of market transactions; it might involve for example, acts of violence or threats of violence by one agent on another and such problems are subject to legal restraint and not part of the economic domain. This however is *not* the view which is taken by Mises (1949). Mises denies the relevance of 'power' not by restricting it to another (non-economic) domain but by arguing that it is of no particular significance *why* an agent decides to transact at a particular price. That is to say, even if 'power' takes the form of coercion and such coercion is employed by one agent over another in determining the price of a particular transaction, it is of no relevance for a theory of prices. In Misean terminology the motives are of no significance for catallactics. This view however is difficult to sustain given that we would generally consider assumptions regarding the nature of agents' behaviour as an important determinant of economic outcomes (see Hollis, 1987). Similarly, a view which limits all aspects of power to wholly non-economic domains may be regarded as a less than satisfactory approach to market interactions.

In contrast to neo-liberal approaches, Marxist or 'radical' theorists have always emphasised the importance of power in economic and social theory and have offered a distinctive view of the meaning and role of power. Again, it is impossible to consider all aspects of the Marxist view of power here, but some of the main perspectives may be indicated. The idea that power is of great significance in economic life was recognised in early Marxist thought including many aspects of the works of Marx and Engels (e.g. Marx and Engels, 1846). Generally speaking, modern Marxian and radical theorists have tried to develop certain aspects of their approach. This has involved the perception of power as a broader and more multi-dimensional concept than in mainstream analysis. Indeed, it should be recalled that the Lukes type categorisation which has been adopted here is in itself an attempt to put forward a broader more 'radical' view of power.

An illuminating example of this more radical conception of power is contained in Tucker (1980) who contrasts the work of C.B. MacPherson with the liberal tradition. MacPherson regards power as the ability to exercise human capacities. This involves much more than the standard approach of liberal writers who in their concern for freedom and choice typically deal with a narrower conception involving an 'absence of constraints imposed by others' (Tucker, 1980, p. 112). Tucker notes that although liberal writers have often acknowledged wider aspects of power they have normally failed to include these in their own analyses. This would certainly seem to be true of mainstream economists.

As Tucker points out however there is a tricky problem with MacPherson's view in that the ability to do something might refer either to the manifestation of power or a pre-condition for the exercise of power. Following Tucker (1980) however, we might regard power as being less 'passive' than ability. Power involves the ability to *change* prevailing conditions. In this context economic actors may be viewed as fulfilling strategic rather than passive roles. This is in contradistinction to the view of agency adopted in traditional neoclassical analysis (and still applies to the competitive model) and also in Austrian theory where an agent's behaviour (somewhat ironically perhaps) is of a passive manner not unlike individual agents under conditions of perfect competition.

As with other schools of thought there are of course a number of divisions within Marxist inspired theory and the precise meaning and role of power may differ not unsubstantially. For example, structuralist Marxist approaches differ in important respects from modern radical economic approaches. The structural approach to power is exemplified by Poulantzas (1986) who treats power as 'the capacity of a social class to realise its specific objective interests'. As Lukes (1986) notes 'for Poulantzas, power identifies the ways in which the system (the ensemble of structures) effects the relations of practices of the various classes in conflict'. In this view class becomes not only a locus but the only locus of power operating through individuals (the 'bearers' or 'supports' of the structure) and its effects are understood solely in terms of the pursuit of class interests' (p. 4). As is well known, structuralist (and functionalist) Marxist theories have been much criticised, not least for their particular view of individual agency. In this context the structuralist view imposes a very specific interpretation of all dimensions of power.

Other radical approaches have been less emphatically concerned with notions of power which relate specifically and only to class struggle (at least in a structuralist interpretation). For example, some radical economists have been concerned to develop theories involving endogenous preferences in an attempt to move towards an analysis which considers the social relations of production. Contributions to this development notably include work by Bowles and Gintis who have provided new arguments in favour of the 'radical' contention that even competitive capitalism involves a particular set of power relations. In doing so, they adopt a definition of power which concerns 'the capacity of some agents to influence the behaviour of others to their advantage through the threat of imposing sanctions' (Bowles and Gintis, 1992, p. 325).

The claim that there is an unequal relationship between capital and labour in the production process is of course a central Marxian position which distinguishes it from mainstream theory and which gives rise to a completely different welfare view of competitive capitalism. In this sense, Bowles and Gintis and indeed other modern radicals are following in a Marxian tradition, but they are departing from the traditional Marxian view in certain important respects. For example, the emphasis on the nature of *class* relations is less pronounced and most certainly the historical character of these radical critiques is more muted or sometimes absent. (This may be less so with regard to Marglin [1984] though here too substantial criticisms of the historical character of such an approach have been made.)

Whatever the particular style and emphasis of Marxian and radical analyses it is clear that the role of power is more significant, wide-reaching and fundamental than in all forms of neo-liberal theory. In general, radicals would include all four categories of power outlined previously in their analysis of power relations. It should be recalled however that our purpose here is to illuminate and compare different approaches to power in different economic theories and no attempt has been made to assess the superiority of one approach over any other. Therefore, the fact that power often plays what seems to be a more significant role in Marxian theory than in mainstream or Austrian theories does not, of itself, invite the conclusion of its superiority.

CONCLUSION

The general proposition of this chapter is that all the types of economic theory which we have dealt with take a particular view of power either explicitly or implicitly, and that the recognition and discussion of this will furnish a better understanding of the principles/foundations of different economic theories and the ways in which they generate their conclusions.

Our deliberations have shown that the type of 'power' considered in mainstream and Austrian theories has in the main been of a one dimensional type whereas those within a radical/Marxian framework have included two and three dimensional views of power. This is, of course, to be expected. The discussion of power by Lukes on which the three dimensions are based is itself a radical analysis. But, this approach has been helpful in distinguishing between different types of theory and moreover, it appears that there is scope within mainstream analysis for moving towards a two-dimensional (and in a particular/limited manner three-dimensional) view of power.

It may be suggested therefore that mainstream theory could be improved by making the particular view of power which is adopted more explicit and by considering wider dimensions of the concept of power. In doing so of course it would not be necessary to move towards a Marxian position of power. It is clearly possible to maintain an essentially individualist approach whilst accepting, for example, a two-dimensional view of power. If however more radical ideas such as the endogeneity of preferences are embraced by the mainstream then the current formulation of the neoclassical approach would be undermined and a greater similarity with some modern radical approaches would ensue. Here again however, the fundamental conflict between individualist and class-based analysis remains. With regard to Austrian theories, there seems less scope for developing multi-dimensional views of power although it may be argued that in an attempt to deny the importance of power, the Austrians have in fact demonstrated its potential significance. Indeed, overall, power appears to be of considerable significance with regard to the behavioural foundations of most economic theories. An explicit analysis of it's dimensions may therefore be useful in constructing more convincing theories, including those attempting to explain the evolution of institutions.

NOTES

1. Stiglitz (1993) argues that mainstream theory has long recognised certain aspects of endogenous preferences, particularly with respect to advertising and 'subjective utility theory', but there has never been a general acceptance of the idea of endogenously formed preferences and it is clearly the case that all of neoclassical welfare economics is based on exogenous preferences.
2. The original title is 'Macht oder ökonomishes Gesetz'. Macht clearly means power, so although control is seen as more appropriate in a certain sense there is little doubt as to Böhm-Bawerk's meaning.
3. Menger's work is usually regarded as the origin of Austrian economics, and, though some of his ideas were developed along neoclassical lines Menger's work

is distinctively different to neoclassical theorists in some important respects and has not been regarded as adopting so neoclassical a position as Böhm-Bawerk.
4. It should be noted that by a wide distribution of property rights Hayek is not advocating an equal distribution across individuals throughout the economy. His arguments elsewhere, make clear his view that great inequality may at times be consistent with a competitive market economy in which differentials between individuals are necessary from a motivational/incentive standpoint.
5. Philosophically Mises adopted a neo-Kantian position (see Parsons, 1990) whilst Menger had explicitly tried to develop an Aristotelian position. Hayek, though clearly influenced by both, attempted what he believed to be a classical liberal approach.
6. This point is developed in some detail in Young (1993).

REFERENCES

Böhm-Bawerk, E. (1914), 'Macht oder Ökonomisches Gesetz?', *Zeitschrift für Volkswirtschaft, Socialpolitik und Verwaltung,* vol. 23, no. 3–4, pp. 205–71. (Translated into English as 'Control or Economic Law', *Shorter Classics of Böhm-Bawerk,* Libertarian Press, 1962.)

Bowles, S. and H. Gintis (1992), 'Power and Wealth in a Competitive Capitalist Economy', *Philosophy and Public Affairs,* Fall.

Dahl, R. (1957), 'The Concept of Power', *Behavioural Science,* 2.

Hayek, F. von (1944), *The Road to Serfdom,* Routledge, London.

Hayek, F. von (1960), *The Constitution of Liberty,* Routledge, London.

Hollis, J.M. (1987), *The Cunning of Reason,* C.U.P., Cambridge.

Kreps, D. (1990), *Microeconomic Theory,* Harvester, Wheatsheaf.

Lukes, S. (1974), *Power: A Radical View,* Macmillan, London.

Lukes, S. (ed.) (1986), *Power,* Basil Blackwell, Oxford.

Marglin, S. (1984), 'Knowledge and Power' in F. Stephen (ed.), *The Economics of Organisation and Labour,*

Marx, K. and F. Engels (1964) [1846] *The German Ideology,* Moscow,

Menger, C. (1871), *Grundsätze der Volkswirtschaftslehre,* Braumülter, Vienna. (Reprinted 1968 in von Hayek, F.A. (ed.), Menger, Gesammelte werke, Volume I, Tübingen: Mohr. English translation 1950: Dingwall, J. and Hoselitz, B.F. *Principles of Economics,* Free Press, Glencoe, Ill.)

Mises, L. von (1949): *Human Action. A Treatise on Economics,* Yale University Press, New Haven. (Based on Mises, L. von 1940: *Nationalökonomie. Theorie des Handelns und Wrschaftens,* Editions Union, Geneva. Reprinted 1980, Philosophia Verlag, Munich.)

O'Driscoll, G. (1982), 'Monopoly in Theory and Practice' in I. Kirzner (ed.), *Method, Process and Austrian Economics,* Lesington Books, Washington.

Parsons, S. (1990), 'The Philosophical Roots of Modern Austrian Economies: Past Problems and Future Prospects', *History of Political Economy,* Vol. 22, No. 2.

Poulantzas, N. (1986), 'Class Power' in S. Lukes (ed.), *Power,* Basil Blackwell, Oxford.

Rothbard, M. (1962), *Man, Economy and State,* vol. 1 and 2. Van Nostrand Reinhold, Princeton NJ.

Rothbard, M. (1970), *Power and Market,* Sheed Andrews and McNeel, Kansas City.

Rothschild, K. (1971), *Power in Economics,* Penguin, Harmondsworth.

Samuels, W. (Ed.) (1979), *The Economy as a System of Power,* Transaction Books, New Jersey.

Skaperdas, S. (1992), 'Cooperation, Conflict and Power in the Absence of Property Rights', *American Economic Review*, vol. 82, no. 4, September.

Stiglitz, J. (1993), 'Post Walrasian and Post Marxian Economics', *Journal of Economic Perpspectives*, vol. 7, no. 1.

Tucker, D.F.B. (1980), *Marxism and Individualism*, Basil Blackwell, Oxford.

Vaughn, K. (1990), 'The Mengerian Roots of the Austrian Revival,' *History of Political Economy*, vol. 22.

Young, D. (1992), 'Austrian Views on Monopoly: Insights and Problems', *Review of Political Economy*, vol. 4, no. 2.

Young, D. (1993), *Power and Austrian Economics*, Mimeo, Department of Economics, University of Manchester.

6. Towards an Evolutionary Perspective of Institutional Crisis

Christos Pitelis

INTRODUCTION

The aim of this chapter is to propose an evolutionary theory of institutional crisis. The focus is on the three major institutions for the division of labour and the allocation of resources under capitalism; the price mechanism (market), the firm, including the transnational corporation (TNC) and the state[1]. The term evolutionary is used in Veblen's sense of a process, that is, as an unfolding sequence.

From the two arguably dominant perspectives in (political) economics, the neoclassical and the Marxist, the former has recently recognized the importance of 'institutions' and has entered a lively debate on 'markets and hierarchies'. As the emphasis here is on the efficiency of the market system, little consideration is given to the possibility of systemic institutional failures. In the Marxist theories, however, very substantial effort has been spent on the analysis of 'crises' in capitalism. However, even the two approaches most in need for institutions in this perspective (the 'social structure of accumulation' and 'regulation school', see below) have arguably failed to seriously analyse the importance of institutions and institutional change. In this chapter I try to show that both approaches tend to be static and inadequately informed by historical insight.

This chapter attempts to move towards providing an explicitly institutions based, evolutionary theory of crisis. Following this Introduction, the next section compares and contrasts the mainstream and Marxist approaches to institutions and crisis. Having pointed to the limitations of both theories, in particular their static approach, the following section provides an explicitly institutional and evolutionary account of capitalist crisis. This synthesizes in a non-eclectic manner some of the major insights of mainstream and Marxian economics, but also breaks new ground. The main claim is that capitalist institutional crisis can be derived evolutionarily within a general framework of principals' (capitalists') attempts to further their interests through achieving a more efficient (from their point of view) exploitation of (the division of) labour. The process involves transaction costs economizing (the main focus of the neoclassical mainstream economics), but also attempts to cut production (including labour) costs.

The overall tendency which emerges from this is seen to be for an increasing profit share, which gives rise to a tendency towards a realization failure, and (in part) to internationalized production. Along with, and in part because of, internationalization, realization crises also lead to fiscal crises, and thus overall to a failure of the three major capitalist institutions: the private sector of firms and markets and the public sector (the state). The need for a new regulation regime arises, in the modern epoch the tendency being for an 'austerity consensus'; a direct result of the dominance of international capital over labour and the erosion of the relative autonomy of the nation state *vis-à-vis* capital. Some important tenets of the propositions developed here are tested in the fourth section. Concluding Remarks are in the final, fifth, section.

MAINSTREAM PERSPECTIVES ON INSTITUTIONS AND CRISES

The analysis of institutions has traditionally not been a topic of much interest in mainstream neoclassical economics. In essence neoclassical economics is a mono-institutional world, where the *market* (price mechanism) is the only institution for resource allocation. Where other institutions are seen to exist, for example the state, this is explained in terms of various *instances* of *market failures*. Similarly, the issue of institutional failures or crises has not traditionally preoccupied neoclassical economists. The possibility of endogenous crises is denied, while the business cycle is almost exclusively attributed to external factors, see Sherman (1990).

Marxian economic orthodoxy instead has always emphasized both the importance of institutions and that of (endogenous) economic crises under capitalism. However, Marxist theory arguably falls short of providing a coherent conceptual framework for analyzing the nature and role of capitalist institutions, notably the market, the firm and the state, (see below). The analysis of crisis and crises tendencies has been a major field of enquiry within Marxism. However, Marxist analyses have arguably failed to link conceptual ideas on crises to their institutional setting and to analyse the possibility of institutional failure-crises.

A reason for the failure to take institutions seriously by both perspectives is that they are both essentially static and ahistorical. This is obviously not to deny the existence of legions of historical studies both by neoclassical and Marxist economic historians. Rather it is claimed below that existing mainstream perspectives on institutions and crises have failed to put their conceptual analyses within the framework of a historically informed 'dynamic analysis'. Since the world we live in is both historical and evolutionary, it is our intention to adopt such a perspective in this chapter. First, we provide a very short account of the two perspectives on institutions and crises. A fuller account is in Pitelis (1991a).

The first and lasting attack on the neoclassical mono-institutional world has been Coase's (1937) classic article on the firm. Coase's contribution was the claim that the firm which was based on entrepreneurial direction was essentially dissimilar to the price mechanism which was based on voluntary transactions between equals. The firm supersedes (internalizes) the market for efficiency-related reasons, namely the inherently expensive nature of market transactions, related to obtaining information on prices and contracting. Williamson (1975, 1986) has elaborated on this view by claiming that high transaction costs of markets (which also include costs of measurement, negotiating, policing and enforcing agreements) can be explained by the coexistence of bounded rationality, opportunism and asset specificity. He went on to provide an explanation of firms' integration strategies and internal organization (the adoption of the multidivisional/M-form structure) in terms of this transaction costs related reasoning.

A similar type of a general explanation of the state has been proposed by Coase (1960) and Arrow (1970). Coase's explanation of the state is, in effect, in terms of high transaction costs of the private sector (firm, market), while Arrow provided a generalization of instances of market failures, such as externalities, public goods and imperfect competition in terms of transaction costs.

Despite such concern with institutions, there has been very little in neoclassical theory to address the issue of (institutional) crises. General Equilibrium theory is in effect institutions-free (excepting the market) and also crisis-free, given the assumed absence of market failure. Theories and explanations of the business cycle and of the great depression are normally in terms of exogenous factors and/or aggregate market failures (the

Keynesian perspective) or aggregate government failures (the monetarist and neoliberal perspective). The transaction costs approach can provide a link between micro and macro market and government failures, but also the possibility of institutional failures, in terms of simultaneous failure of all three major capitalist institutions, the firm, the market and the state. As noted, the possibility of firms and government failures is well within the logic of the transaction costs perspective, so along with market failures it can provide reasons for the *possibility of institutional failures*, see Pitelis (1993).

There are two essential reasons why neoclassical theory cannot (and does not wish to) go beyond possibilities. First, its essentially static and ahistorical nature and second its focus on self-correcting institutional failures (firms solving market failures, the state solving private sector failures, and the private sector solving state failures). This latter focus is flatly rejected by the Marxist framework, in which explicit factors leading to crises are being discussed. First, we outline Marxist economic approaches to institutions, particularly the firm and the state.

The two best known Marxist-type perspectives on economic institutions are those of Hymer, in Cohen et al. (1979), and Marglin (1974). Marglin's attempt was to explain the historical emergence of the factory system from the putting-out system. He claimed that this was not due to any technological superiority of the former but rather it was the result of the fact that in the factory system the capitalist boss could increase control over labour and (thus) profits. Accordingly, the factory system was the result of control and distribution not efficiency (although efficiency gains due to increased productivity could result from the enhanced control over labour). Hymer, on the other hand, viewed the market and the firm as two devices for the division of labour and examined the historical evolution of firms, from the small owner managed and controlled establishments of the nineteenth century, through the joint-stock company and the M-form organization to the multinational firm. He attributed this dramatic increase in the size of firms primarily to market power (structural market failure) reasons, as opposed to transaction costs type reasons (albeit he also provided arguments strongly reminiscent of transaction costs-type theorizing, see Pitelis and Sugden, 1991).

Marxian politico-economic theory has a long tradition in attempting to explain the capitalist state. There are three main perspectives here, the 'instrumentalist', the 'structuralist' and the 'capital logic' one. The first regards the state as an instrument of domination of the capitalist class over labour, see Miliband (1969). The structuralist school instead considers that there are structural factors (e.g., capitalist control over the accumulation process) which can explain the partisan pro-capitalist nature of the state which, however, is quasi-autonomous from specific capitalist interests and (thus) operates as a factor of cohesion of the capitalist class as a whole, see for example Poulantzas (1969). The capital logic school starts from the observations that the previously considered perspectives fail to address the question 'why state coercion' (as opposed to direct capitalist coercion), i.e., why does the state exist at all as a (quasi-) autonomous entity under capitalism. Their answer has three strands, first the apparent coincidence of capitalist and labour interest at the process of exchange, second competition between capitalists and third, the existence of direct control of capital over labour within the production process under capitalism, which removes this need from the state. The latter can just take on the 'higher' role of delineating and enforcing the overall rules of the game, see Holloway and Picciotto (1978). Some similarities with the neoclassical perspective can be seen here, excepting the focus on production (capitalist control) as opposed to the contractual process envisaged by the neoclassicals (see Pitelis 1991a for a further discussion on this theme).

Despite existing attempts to provide an analysis (however elementary) of some capitalist institutions, Marxian economic theory of crises has failed, so far, to incorporate such insights into their framework. In brief, early Marxian theories of crises can be divided in three categories; the organic composition/declining profit rate, the underconsumption/realization crisis and the 'increasing militancy of labour' approach. The first asserts the existence of a tendency for an increasing organic composition of capital (the capital to labour ratio in price terms) which results from labour-saving technological development, itself the result of competition among capitalists to reduce unit costs. As labour is the only source of 'surplus value' (potential profit), an increase in the organic composition tends to reduce the rate of profit, thus leading to crisis.

In the underconsumption–realization crisis story, there are many versions. In the best known, by Baran and Sweezy (1966), monopolization of markets tends to lead to an increasing 'surplus' (surplus value plus wasteful expenditures such as armaments) which restricts consumption and thus *ceteris paribus* induces a lack of effective demand. Here the reduction in actual profits and profit ratio comes about from their potential tendency to increase and it is initially at least manifesting itself in the form of excess capacity. Lastly, in the 'increasing militancy of labour' theory, it is asserted in one version that militant British workers have led to increased wages, thus reduced profits in Britain, Glyn and Sutcliffe (1972). In a cyclical version labour militancy increases in the boom, which leads to reduced profit rates, thus to the downturn, see Botty and Crotty (1975). It can be suggested that the secular versions of all three theories are compatible and synthesizable, see Pitelis (1991a). However, even if this is accepted, it is the case that these approaches to crisis are very crude in their treatment of institutions, while they are effectively history-free. Capitalist (firms) and markets are taken as *data*, while the state is normally seen as the *deus ex machina*, which interferes (usually in favour of capitalists) to solve the problem of crisis.

A more elaborate Marxist approach to crisis is that of the French 'regulation school', see for example Agglietta (1979), and the 'social structure of accumulation (SSA) school, for example, Bowles et al. (1983). Both suggest the existence of different 'regulation regimes' or SSAs, which are broadly capitalist quasi-stable institutional configurations, which allow profitable accumulation of capital. However, internal and external pressures to such 'regimes' can lead from time to time to a crisis of the 'regime' or the SSA, which can only be overcome through the establishment of a new regime. As Boyer (1986) has noted already in an excellent review of regulation theory, despite acknowledgement of, and reference to, institutions, these theories also take institutions as data and fail to provide an analysis of their nature and role. Boyer himself points to the potential usefulness of trying to incorporate Marglin and Poulantzas-type insights into the analysis, but makes no such attempt himself.

Alternative perspectives to the mainstream neoclassical and Marxist include the 'Austrian' and 'game theoretic' approaches, (see for example Hayek (1978), Schotter (1981), for respective treatments). At the risk of oversimplification, these tend to focus on contractual means of the emergence of institutions (as in Coase) but now from a state of no-institutions in individuals' efforts to coordinate their activities. This goes beyond the Coasian *market-failure*-based perspective. The Austrian perspective is retained in the 'public choice' literature, (see for example Mueller (1989)), where, however, the possibility of (post-contractual) predation is recognized through the assertion of self-interest maximizing agents of any type, for example state officers, bureaucrats etc. All these perspectives are also largely conceptual and pay scant attention to the possibility of the historically specificity of institutions.

A most interesting and largely *sui-generis* more recent case is that of North (1981, 1990). North has moved from an efficiency-based to a largely predation-based view of institutions, which views principals' (or rulers) utility maximizing objectives as the driving force behind institutions and institutional change. This perspective is claimed to be capable in explaining persistent inefficient property rights structures in much of economic history. This focus brings North near to the 'public choice' and more notably the Marxist perspective, as he himself acknowledges, (North (1990)). North applied his conceptual perspective to much of known history. It is not my objective to assess this grand design here. Worth pointing out, however, is that there is a need to derive North's conceptual framework from first principles and to analyse the possibility that ruler-principal driven institutions and institutional changes could be history specific, i.e., not characterize the whole of societal development (including the future).

Having said this, we share with North the focus on principals being the crucial agents in the emergence of *capitalist* institutions (see Pitelis, 1991a). In that light, the approach pursued in the next section explains the emergence, role, interrelationships and possible failures, of capitalist institutions as driven by the attempts by principals (the merchant-capitalist often in collaboration with the sovereigns) to further their interests, by attempting to remove constraints in realizing their objectives. This is a predation-based perspective which, however, allows for the possibility of contractual *ex-ante* emergence of institutions and the *ex-post* appearance of predation, as well as the possibility of coexisting efficiency *and* inefficiency (derived from power-control-distribution-type reasons), see below.

TOWARDS AN EVOLUTIONARY PERSPECTIVE ON INSTITUTIONAL FAILURE

Drawing on our earlier account, our starting point here is that we can regard the price mechanism (market), the firm (private hierarchy) and the state ('public' hierarchy) as three complementary capitalist institutional devices for the exploitation of specialization, the division of labour and team work, aiming at furthering the interests of the principals, see Pitelis (1991a) and North (1981) for a similar perspective. Historically, the early *capitalist* institutional device through which division of labour was performed was the price mechanism. Through it the emerging capitalists, the merchants, were able to profit by the simple act of buying and selling, by turning products into commodities, or use values into exchange values. Product availability in often remote markets and (thus) demand and supply considerations were the means through which a source of revenue was generated for the merchants in the process of exchange[2].

The use of the price mechanism was an inherently uncertain and (thus) imperfect means of satisfying the merchants interests: profit and (thus) power. Neither the availability of producers nor the price of products and commodities-to-be could be guaranteed for the merchants. Alternatively, such availability could only be guaranteed at the price of excessive market transaction costs; that is, the costs of finding producers, negotiating with them, contracting with them and policing such agreements. Such costs could endanger the very existence of a (satisfactory) profit. In this sense, the price mechanism was failing to deliver the goods to the merchants. The firm was the way out. In its earliest form, the putting-out system, the merchant-manufacturer replaced the price mechanism with an employment relation, where labourers worked for the merchant-manufacturer for a compensation, a wage, initially at their own place (and pace) and by making use of their own capital equipment[3].

* Within the capitalist logic of profit generation for the principals, the employment relation is transactionally superior to the price mechanism, and thus a more efficient means of labour division. In this sense the transactional properties of firms are not *per se* the reason for market failure; the reason is the transactional properties needed for capitalist control to be established. Such control is easier under the employment relation, which renders the latter transactionally superior from the capitalist point of view. Given this, (transactional) efficiency cannot in itself explain the existence of firms; the principals' objectives (thus control and distribution) also need to be considered. Efficiency and control distribution are inseparable, as are existence and objectives. This need not necessarily imply that firms are *not* Pareto efficient *ex post*. Given efficiency gains, from tighter control and reduced transaction costs, the opposite is more likely, at least from a pure pecuniary point of view. In a historical context, moreover, whether labourers to be preferred the status of labourer to (the uncertainty of) being free peasants is a thorny question, leaving unanswered the question of whether the firm was Pareto efficient or not *ex ante* too. Important, however, in my context is that the driving force has been efficiency for profit (control-distribution) and not efficiency for efficiency's sake (economizing) as the Coase-Williamson neoclassical institutionalism suggests.

The emergence of the employment relation does not remove the market *in toto*. It replaces the use of the price mechanism with a hierarchical device, for a particular type of transaction relating to the employment of labour. Outside this relation, the price mechanism remains. Going further, it can be said that the firm emerges *for* (the production of commodities for sale in) the market. The replacement of putting-out by the factory system, which initially at least brings together labourers in one site under the direct control of the capitalist, who now owns the means of production too, further enhances efficiency for profit, by solving two problems of imperfect control (and thus transaction costs) associated with putting-out: imperfect supervision of labour and imperfect control over organizational knowledge, which would allow some labourers to join the ranks of capitalists, given their ownership of capital. The factory system both solves these problems and fully frees labour from property[4]. It may also bring about benefits from team work. From the point of view of the capitalist, the factory system represents a further efficiency gain. Whether it is Pareto efficient is doubtful. *Vis-à-vis* the putting-out system, labourers lose control over their lives, for an uncertain increase in their wage, as their share in the efficiency gain.

In the above framework, the price mechanism and the firm complement each other in the principals' efforts to further their profits by achieving a more efficient division of labour[5]. The price mechanism in itself is an imperfect and insufficient means of achieving this aim because of the excessive transaction costs associated with its inherent reliance on voluntary exchanges. The private hierarchy, the firm, solves some these problems, but not all. The availability of labourers to be (the freeing of the peasants from their feudal lords) and the enforcement of the labour contract necessitate substantial expenses and suffer from public goods characteristics, and thus from potential free-riding. No individual capitalist may be willing or able to undertake the role of providing such goods. In this sense the firm (and the market, thus the private sector) fails.

A third party, the public hierarchy or state, can be the way out. This undertakes the provision of goods necessary for capital to achieve its aims, for a share in the resulting benefits. Transactional difficulties associated with capitalists trying to establish a private means of creating free labour and enforcing contracts at the aggregate level (containing labour unrests) are one reason for private sector failures to control labour directly, as capital *per se*. Historically, the pre-existence of a feudal state, with a ready army and, initially at least, on better terms with nobles than merchants, led to an alliance between the merchants and the crown, so as to share in the profit generated by the merchants; an alliance based on community of interest. In this sense, merchants and the crown can be seen as the principals in the early stages of capitalism[6]. A state 'instrument', living symbiotically with capital, was instrumental in creating the proletariat and establishing the 'rules of the game' allowing capitalism to function; that is, protection of (capitalist) property rights and freedom in exchange of commodities, including the one commodity *par excellence*, labour power. The control of labour at the workplace in the factory system rendered direct intervention by the state in production unnecessary, and provided a reason for the apparent *autonomous* form of the capitalist state.

The apparent community of interest between capital and labour, as income receivers, allows for the *possibility* of the autonomous form of the state. From the point of view of capital, the emergence of the capitalist state represented a transaction costs gain and thus enhanced efficiency. Again whether the capitalist state was also Pareto efficient is an open issue, considering the existing alternative, the feudal state, it might well have been. However, the driving force was efficiency gains for control-distributional gains, much in line with the case of the firm. The issue, once more, is not efficiency versus conrol-distribution, but efficiency versus efficiency for control-distribution. While the capitalist state saves private sector transaction costs for the principals, it has costs of its own, partly arising from the need to derive an agreement among the principals (initially the merchants and the crown) on how to distribute the profits. Such problems of 'opportunism', to use conventional language, but also the inefficiency of state functionaries (for example, because of bounded rationality) establish the possibility of state failures too. The possibility of the co-existence of private sector and state failures allows for the case of an institutional failure (crisis) which can be seen as a variant and extension of the neoclassical institutional approach; but one that derives efficiency for distribution, not for efficiency's sake.

Transactional problems related to the control of labour are one of the forces explaining institutions and their forms. The more basic underlying reason is the extraction of more output from given number of labourers, by increasing the productivity of labour (degree of exploitation). For every individual capitalist (firm) this introduces the additional (and related) need of technological improvements, as well as improvements in their organizational forms, designed to achieve the joint aim of extracting more profit. The existence of capital in the form of many capitals (firms) introduces a further element of competition, besides conflict between capital in general and labour in general; namely, competition between firms (rivalry) to distribute the profit derived from the exploitation of (the division of) labour and team work. This rivalry renders the conflict between capital and labour a means through which competitive advantages can be gained. Increasing efficiency in the exploitation of labour (division), but also in every other conceivable form, becomes a matter of life and death. In the competitive struggle the more efficient, talented and innovative firms will survive. Much of this, however, involves the application of this ingenuity in achieving a more efficient exploitation of the source of more profits: labour power.

Conflict with labour and rivalry with other firms become the *economic* driving force of capitalist accumulation, the reason why profit derivation and realization is not the simple expression of a sociological need for power, recognition or a religious ethic, but rather a condition of survival. Conflict with labour necessitates technological and organizational improvements, which, ideally, achieve the simultaneous enhancement of control over labour and of the degree of exploitation, work intensity and (thus) productivity of labour. Competition with rivals (rivalry) necessitates a reduction in unit costs, so that competitive advantages are gained. *Ceteris paribus*, the need to increase control over labour and simultaneously gain competitive edges over rivals tends to favour labour-saving technical changes. Both capital-saving and labour-saving changes can achieve reductions in unit costs, but 'machines do not strike'. The very threat of the introduction of labour-saving changes can be a powerful discipline device for the workforce. This creates the demand for such changes. Once the supply is there all the incentives are also there for the threat to be realized. To the extent that this happens a tendency towards a rising organic composition (ROC) of capital and (thus) a declining profit rate manifests itself. Given that one of the main reasons for the introduction of labour-saving technical changes is the control of labour and (thus) an increase in the degree of labour exploitation, the tendency towards a declining profit rate will, initially at least, be expressed in and thwarted by an increasing profit share.

Conflict with labour and rivalry with other firms also tends to increase the concentration and centralization of capital. In the competitive struggle, the fittest will survive. Fitness is measured in terms of exploitation of technical and transactional economies and labour, in order to reduce unit costs and increase profits. The attempts to minimize unit costs from all sources, so as to increase long-term profits, becomes each firm's objective. Under uncertainty, it is achieved through the pursuit of growth, both internal and external mergers. The attempts by firms to remove constraints in growing, such as financial, organizational and managerial constraints, can explain firms' evolution and organizational changes, such as the socialization of capital ownership in the form of the joint-stock company, the managerial and pension funds revolutions, and the M-form organization. Firms successful in introducing and exploiting such innovations are the winners in the competitive struggle; the others are taken over, disappear, become a competitive fringe serving the successful, or work directly for the successful, through, for example, subcontracting or licensing. This process introduces a tendency towards increasing concentration and centralization of capital which *ceteris paribus* tends to increase the profit share and thus the profit rate. This tendency also counteracts the tendency towards declining profit rates through ROC.

The emergence and growth of capitalist firms is tantamount to the emergence and growth of (the strength of) labour. Increasing monopolization facilitates the organization and power of labour against capital. This tends to counteract the ability of firms to increase the degree of exploitation in the production process and, to the extent that labour opposes labour-saving technical changes, it tends to thwart the tendency towards ROC. Monopolization through growth becomes the *sine qua non* of capitalist success. Giant firms can satisfy labour's demands by granting higher wage rates than smaller firms, by shifting increasing costs to consumers through increased prices. Monopolization and increasing wage rates for the monopoly sector's labour can therefore go hand in hand with increasing economy-wide unemployment as smaller firms go bankrupt and labour in the competitive sector (less well organized) is laid off. Thus increasing monopolization gives rise to increasing labour strength over wage rates, but simultaneously reduced levels of employment. In this sense increasing labour strength is perfectly compatible with increasing profit shares, despite increasing wage rates.

Overall, the dynamics of capitalist evolution imply a tendency towards increasing profit shares; through increased labour exploitation of the early phases of capitalist development (*laissez-faire* or competitive phase) and through reduced employment as the economy moves towards the next (monopoly) stage. This tends to counteract the tendency towards declining profit rates through ROC and increasing labour strength. Increasing prices and increased socialization of capital ownership enhance this tendency at the monopoly stage (Cowling, 1982; Pitelis, 1987). Monopoly pricing in the monopoly stage achieves what supply of labour does at the competitive stage; namely, the maintenance of the overall wage share at near subsistence (socially defined) levels. As wage rates tend to diverge from subsistence because of rising labour strength, but also interfirm rivalry, monopoly pricing becomes an alternative means of surplus value derivation, this time in the process of exchange.

Taxation by the state is a similar means of surplus value derivation. In the early phase of capitalism near subsistence wage rates imply that all taxation is paid by capital. This is a reason for the *laissez-faire* attitude of the state in this period, as its role is limited to sharing the surplus produced in production by firms. State autonomy in this phase is only in the state's *form* — autonomy in the sense of existing independently of (but symbiotically with) capital. Divergence of wage rates from subsistence imply the possibility of surplus value derivation from labour in exchange through taxation. This renders the state's relative autonomy more substantive; it enjoys relative autonomy from capital. This induces a 'preference' by the state for high employment levels, a source of taxation.

It is also an incentive for the undertaking of direct productive activities by the state to produce surplus value, which is state-monopoly capitalism. Such functions by the state are, to differing degrees and depending on the particular activity, beneficial to both capital and labour: to capital because of the socialization of the cost of, for example, infrastructure; to labour because of the security of employment in nationalized industries or increased welfare expenditures, such as unemployment and sickness benefits. The state (functionaries), capital and labour all favour increased state participation in the economy, to start with. However, such participation tends gradually to erode the power of capital *vis-a-vis* (and thus) the state, and to decrease the profit rate, given that certain state functions, such as welfare contributions, can only realize and not produce surplus value, at least not directly (Gouph, 1979). This, the increased share of surplus value going to state functionaries as a result, and the increased confidence of labour resulting from the removal of the potency of the threat of the sack, gradually generate capital's disenchantment with the state's increased participation in the economy. Demands for a return to *laissez-faire* capitalism are the 'natural' reaction of capital.

The increasing participation of the state in the economy in the monopoly phase of capitalism tends to reduce the profit rate in two ways: through its 'unproductive' expenditures but also through increased employment levels, thus wage shares, thus reduced profit shares. While these tend to enhance the realization of profit for capital through increased aggregate demand, they undermine the control of capital over investments and labour. Along with declining profit rates tendencies, this suggests capital's eventual 'disenchantment' with state interventionism, particularly when alternative forms of profit realization are available; internally (innovations) and externally (foreign markets). Given capital's control of a substantial part of production, and thus the threat of *domestic* investment strikes, which in a capitalist economy would harm all stakeholders, in particular the state and labour, the continuation needs of the system ensure the existence of an upper limit to the economic role of the state under capitalism. This itself creates the need for an increasing ideological role of the state, in part to justify to labour the maintenance of the system, given the evident *possibility* of the state undertaking an increasingly higher share of productive activities, turning itself into a socialist state, or a 'national socialist' one.

The tendency towards increasing monopolization puts constraints on the state's autonomy, both instrumental (increased wealth of firms, etc.) and structural (increased control of few private actors of investment decisions, etc.). The practical expression of this is a tendency towards favourable tax treatment of (retained) profits, and thus a facilitation by the state of the tendency towards increasing profit shares in the monopoly and state-monopolist stages of capitalism.

The tendency towards increasing monopolization and (through the) socialization of capital ownership, generates a tendency towards increasing profit shares, which exists alongside the tendency towards declining profit rates through ROC of capital and rising labour strength. The last two, as already suggested, tend to be offset by the increased degree of labour exploitation and increased unemployment, thus allowing the tendency towards increasing profit shares to dominate under monopoly capitalism. State policies favouring (retained) profits tend to ensure the prevalence of the tendency even when counter-tendencies (increased ROC, rising labour strength) are strong enough to offset the (pre-tax) tendency. After-tax profit shares therefore tend to increase under monopoly and state monopoly capitalism. Given that all such tendencies can be explained by exclusive focus on production level (conflict between capital in general and labour in general, leading to capital introducing labour-saving technical changes), it can be suggested that the ROC-TRPF notion is more fundamental than the alternatives. This need not mean that it is inconsistent with, or even that it prevails over, such alternatives. Indeed my claim is that the tendency towards increasing profit share is prevalent (albeit in a sense derivative), particularly at the (state) monopoly capitalism stage.

Capital is strengthened *vis-à-vis* labour and the state by its ability to undertake overseas operations. These operations cushion firms from the adverse impact on them of, for example, 'investment strikes' domestically. Such strikes can take the form of choosing to operate overseas (and not domestically). Monopolization and organizational forms such as the M-form make such operations possible. Conflict with labour and rivalry with other firms (domestic *and* overseas) make them necessary, as suggested by Hymer (in Cohen et al., 1979). This is a supply-side motive for transnational corporations (TNCs) to appear. The possibility or threat of a 'capital flight' tends to enhance the power of domestic monopolies *vis-à-vis* labour and the state.

The benefits from the exploitation of the factors leading to increased monopolization (capital abundance, advanced technology, etc.) create oligopolistic advantages to domestic firms, which initially tend to facilitate the conditions for an export-oriented improvement of the domestic standard of living. International competitiveness at this stage becomes the reason for the possibility of the establishment of a stable social structure of accumulation or regulation system. All this means is that the benefits to all (the nation) through exploitation of competitive advantages over foreigners are such that they allow an accord of capital and labour. This allows uninterrupted growth and accumulation. Countries that enjoy the advantage of earlier development also reap its benefits in terms of conditions allowing a focus on growth *given* distribution. What is good for the monopolists is good for the nation here as well, a statement which is for some time much more than a legitimizing slogan.

Crisis and international operations of firms through direct foreign investment (DFI) put an end to the euphoria and undermine the conditions of the regulation regime. Crisis is the apparent direct product of the tendency towards increasing after-tax profit shares. Such increases tend to reduce the ratio of consumers' expenditure to private sector disposable income through two mainly overlapping routes: smaller propensities to save wages than profits, and/or imperfect substitutability between corporate retained profits and personal savings (see Pitelis, 1987 for a detailed discussion). In oligopolistic industries operating below the full capacity level of output, reduced consumer spending will tend to lead to reductions in output not prices (Rowthorn, 1981). As a result, consumers' expenditure will reduce demand for consumer goods industries, and *ceteris paribus* the output and capacity utilization in such industries and the economy as a whole. Increases in excess capacity will tend to reduce the rate of profit, offsetting the tendency for an increasing profit rate owing to increasing profit shares. This tends to reinforce the similar tendency operating through ROC and increased unemployment owing to increasing labour strength. To the extent that capacity utilization decreases also adversely affect individual firms' decisions to invest (expand capacity), underconsumption will be reflected as excess capacity and, through the effects of the latter (itself an element of the profit rate, one of the most important determinants of investment), will tend to give rise to a 'realization crisis'.

Reduced effective demand, the manifestation of the realization crisis, tends to increase unemployment and provides a demand-side incentive for firms to become TNCs. The existence of financial capital in the hands of giant firms in the form of retained profits will facilitate this tendency from the demand side. Both factors will tend to relieve the firm's pressures on profitability. Unemployment reduces labour's confidence, and thus wage rates, and so does firms' DFI. All these tend to increase the profit rate and investment. However, investment need not take place domestically now; not unless wage rates (weighted appropriately to account for infra-structure, political risks and other such factors) are globally competitive. If not, domestic TNCs can invest abroad and foreign TNCs not choose a particular country. When unemployment and (or because of) TNCs' non-preference for a particular country coincide, the conditions for a stable social structure of accumulation are undermined. Monopolies fail to persuade on the coincidence of their interests with labour's. The state cannot satisfy both capital and labour, in great part because of the ability of TNCs to 'un-nationalize' themselves for tax purposes, by registering in tax havens. The effect is labour discontent arising from the failure of both the private sector and the state to deliver the goods. In this sense, internationalization of production allows the undermining of the SSA and leads to an apparent private sector failure and a fiscal crisis. Both together lead to an economic *and* a fiscal crisis; a failure of the three major capitalist institutions, the market, the firm and the state. As far as the state is concerned, this is expressed as a failure to deliver the goods to the 'citizens', and (thus) a legitimization crisis.

A new international division of labour emerges as a result, in which each country's relative attractiveness to international capital, in terms of what it has to offer, becomes the determining factor of the quantity and type of operations undertaken by TNCs in it. Early industrial countries, the 'homelands' of TNCs, become the headquarters, because of the availability of appropriately skilled personnel, but also for what they offer in terms of cultural and other activities to the top executives. Manufacturing is undertaken in or subcontracted to the low cost, high labour exploitation, countries and distributed to the rest of the globe. De-industrialization of early industrialized countries is in part the result of these tendencies. The result is a *dependent* industrialization of some less developed countries. This, does not exclude the possibility of independent industrialization in some cases, subject to the economic conditions and the will of the local bourgeoisie, people and state, as well as the articulation of their interactions.

The crisis and the internationalization of production contain the seeds of inflationary tendencies in de-industrializing developed countries, from three major sources, capital, labour and the state: the monopoly sector of capital through monopoly pricing; small capital (the competitive sector) through increased borrowing from the financial sector, which pushes up interest rates, mortgage rates and the general price level; labour (consumers) through increased demands for high wages to offset inflationary losses, and increased borrowing to re-establish (in the short run at least) their habitual standard of living; the state also through borrowing and spending, in part at least to satisfy the demands of both capital and labour, but also to satisfy its own needs, including the incumbent government's re-election. The co-existence of inflationary tendencies, of both cost push and demand pull type, and increasing unemployment owing to the crisis gives rise to the familiar stagflation. Engineered recessions by the state can exacerbate the unemployment tendencies. Such state actions can often be the only available policy capable of re-establishing competitiveness, and thus making the country more attractive than its rivals to TNCs.

The new transnational phase of capital establishes capital's control over labour and undermines the nation state's relative autonomy. There is a tendency for a new social structure of accumulation, a new regulation regime, based on an *'austerity consensus'* that labour has to understand that success and growth relative to rivals is through TNCs, and thus austerity is part and parcel of the package required to attract TNCs away from 'foreigner'. Austerity consensus is seen as the means through which *we* (e.g., British labour) become 'better' than *them* (e.g., German labour). Nationalism wins over international solidarity of labour. The tendency is enhanced by the economic success of some countries, such as Japan and West Germany. The success of these, in part due to a history — and policy-induced capital nationalism, can apparently be competed away by less successful rivals only through an austerity consensus. Thus both success and failure breed austerity, the new social structure of accumulation of advanced capitalism *and* the world as a whole[7].

I have tried in this short account to derive capitalist institutional failure evolutionarily. In part such evolution has been attributed to transaction costs, but other costs, particularly labour, are included, within a general framework of principals' efforts to further their interests by achieving a more efficient exploitation of (the division of) labour and the benefits of team work. The tendency from this type of behaviour is seen to be for an increasing profit share, which gives rise to a tendency towards a realization failure, and (in part) to internationalized production. Along with, and in part because of, internationalization, realization crises also lead to fiscal crises, and thus overall to a failure of the three major capitalist institutions the private sector of firms and market and the public sector (the state). The need for a new regulation regime arises, in the modern epoch the tendency being for an austerity consensus; a direct result of the dominance of international capital over labour and the erosion of the relative autonomy of the nation state *vis-à-vis* capital.

Two issues are worth emphasis here. First, my focus on increasing profit shares is not incompatible with the declining rate of profit tendency predicted from the ROC-TRPF theory or the rising labour strength theory. Indeed the tendencies can operate simultaneously, but be expressed as a rising profit share giving rise to excess capacity, reduced investment and a realization crisis. Second, it is at least implicit in my account that the rising profit share tendency becomes particularly evident in the monopoly phase of capitalism, and even more so in the state monopoly capitalism epoch, with a high degree of internationalized production and TNC activities. This last factor becomes instrumental in the rise and fall of the social structure of accumulation or the monopoly regulation regime.

SOME EVIDENCE

To test empirically every single theoretical proposition made in the last section would be a nearly impossible task, for well known reasons: data availability and reliability, their compatibility with theoretical categories, general problems associated with empirical–econometric work, time constraints — and often sheer lack of interest in so doing! Theory with no evidence however is just speculation (but see note 2). My means of balancing these two contrasting considerations is to focus on four major links proposed in my theoretical account and to discuss existing evidence or provide new evidence on them. These links are: first, a tendency towards an increasing after-tax profit share; second, the impact of increasing profit shares on consumers' expenditure; third, the effects of excess capacity on individual firms' decisions to invest; finally, the link between investment and firms' realized profits. To the extent that after-tax profit shares are increasing, that such increases reduce consumption, that (resulting) excess capacity reduces investment and that investment is positively linked with realized profits (implying that the latter decrease when investment expenditure does), I can claim that there is empirical support for the four major propositions of the theoretical account.

I have examined the first two links in detail elsewhere (Pitelis, 1987) for the cases of the USA and the UK. In both cases the after-tax gross profit share of gross private sector disposable income was steadily increasing in the whole post war period: from 12.42 per cent in 1945–9 to 14.79 per cent in 1980–4 in the USA and from 17.56 per cent in 1946–50 to 24.31 per cent in 1981–4 in the UK. The only exceptions were 1970–4 for the USA and 1961–5 for the UK, when small declines *vis-à-vis* the previous periods were observed. This evidence is in line with my theory. It suggests that existing evidence in favour of declining profit shares is the result of exclusive focus on pre-tax data (as in Weisskopf, 1979), on only one sector of the economy, such as manufacturing (as in Glyn and Sutcliffe, 1972), or on operating rates of return (both studies mentioned above), as opposed to the Kaleckian (and Marxian) measure, which also includes rent, interest and income from self-employment. As my measure is post tax economy wide gross (i.e., it includes profit, rent, interest and self employment income) profit share, it is, I believe, a more reliable one, at least for my purposes here. Room for disagreements obviously exists, and it would take a separate study to compare and contrast different measures of the profit share. All I claim here is that once the state is accounted for, as Weisskopf himself thought necessary but did not do, and a gross (Kaleckian-Marxian) measure is adopted, the US and UK evidence does support the claim of an increasing profit share.

In the period under examination consumer expenditure shares declined: from 82.64 per cent in 1945–9 to 81.39 per cent in 1980–4 in the USA and dramatically from 88.23 per cent in 1946–50 to 74.73 per cent in 1981–4

in the UK. Evidence on the effects of different income types on consumers' expenditure indicate that this decline was in part due to the
increase in the profit share. When corporate retained earnings and
pensions funds wealth shares are examined, it is found that both these
were on the increase in the post-war USA and UK and their degree of
substitutability with personal sector saving was minimal. This supports the
socialization of capital through shareholding (discretionary and compulsory through occupational pensions) leading to reduced consumers'
expenditure hypothesis. The issues and evidence are further discussed in
Pitelis (1987). Suffice it to point out here that through the two in part
substitute and in part complementary ways (increasing profit shares and
increasing compulsory saving owing to the socialization of capital), a
tendency towards decreasing consumer expenditure shares did manifest
itself in both the USA and the UK after the Second World War.

As already noted, it is widely believed that decreases in consumers'
expenditure will tend to result in increasing excess capacity through
reductions in output, and that this in turn will affect negatively firms'
decisions to invest. I have elsewhere reported some evidence pointing to a
coincidence between reduced consumers' expenditure, increasing excess
capacity and relatively stagnant manufacturing investment shares for the
USA and the UK (Pitelis, 1987). This *does not test* the link between
reduced capacity utilization and firms' decisions to invest, or aggregate
investment. At the aggregate level, there is some evidence in line with the
existence of this link; see Cowling (1982) and Stafford (1986) for surveys.
The microeconomic relationship is less explored. However, in a study on
the Western European chemical industry, Paraskevopoulos and Pitelis
(1990) report econometric results in line with the idea that capacity
utilization has a positive and significant impact on firms' capacity expansion programmes. Moreover, this effect is independent of the effects of a
multitude of other micro-level explanatory variables, such as the capacity
expansions of rivals, the firms' market share, the minimum efficient scale of
output, absolute capital requirements etc. This evidence supports the
existing evidence for the relationship at the aggregate level. It points to
the conclusion that capacity utilization reductions are in part at least
responsible for stagnant or declining investment expenditure shares.

Reductions in investment may in their turn have a negative impact on
aggregate realized profits, and the profit share and profit rate, thus turning
the underconsumptionist tendency to a full blown realization crisis. The
alleged positive link between aggregate investment and aggregate profits

has been proposed and tested by Kalecki (1971) as far back as 1934 with US data. Since then, there has been no empirical study to test this hypothesis, to my knowledge, save for a study by the present author (Pitelis, 1991b). In this study 1955–80 time series data for the UK have confirmed the hypothesis that aggregate realized profits are positively and significantly affected by aggregate investment. Moreover, the effect was independent of other explanatory variables, such as advertising expenditure.

A more important relationship, perhaps, is that between aggregate investment and the realized profit rate. The reason is that realized profit rate is widely acknowledged to be the major determinant of firms' decisions to invest, as already pointed out. Some evidence in line with this idea comes from studies testing the relationship between investment and capacity utilization, given that the latter is one of the constituent parts of the profit rate (Paraskevopoulos and Pitelis, 1990). That investment expenditure may be positively linked with the profit rate is a hypothesis never tested so far, to my knowledge.

The profit rate can be written as

$$\pi/K = \pi/W \cdot W/K$$

Given this, changes in π/W are directly reflected in changes in the profit rate π/K. We can, therefore, avoid the notorious problem of measuring the capital stock, and focus on π/W to test the link between investment expenditure and realized profit rates. If this is positive, then we have a scenario of cumulative reduction in investment arising from reduced capacity utilization, to start with, and (thus) reduced realized profit rates subsequently.

The data I used were UK time series for the 1955–80 period. They are explained in Pitelis (1991b), although the focus there is different. Only one equation was run, expressing changes in π/W as a function of changes in investment expenditure, the previous year's change in investment expenditure, the change in advertising expenditure and also the change in the previous year's π/W. This equation was obtained by using a Koyck transformation to the simpler static relationship

$$\Delta\,(\pi/W) = f(\Delta I, \Delta A)$$

where ∂ denotes the first difference, π, gross after tax profits, W wage income, I investment expenditure and A advertising expenditure, itself a form of investment expenditure.

A constant term, assuming the character of a time trend, was also included in the regression, which on estimate gave

$$\Delta(\pi/W) = -0.20^* + 0.000015^{**}\ \Delta I_t + 0.00034^*\ \Delta A_t$$
$$\quad\quad (2.68)\quad\quad (1.92)\quad\quad\quad\quad (4.05)$$

$$+ 0.00010\Delta I^*{}_{t-1} -0.50^*\ \Delta(\pi/W)_{t-1}$$
$$\quad\quad (2.83)\quad\quad\quad (2.87)$$

$R^2 = 0.6006, DW = 1.737,$ * significant at 5% level, ** significant at 10% level.

The lagged investment term and lagged dependent variable are the result of the adoption of the Koyck transformation and the assumption that investment affects π/W contemporaneously, while advertising does so with a geometrically declining lag. Justification for this treatment and the exact mechanics of the equation are discussed in Pitelis (1991b). Suffice it to note here that these two variables could also be included in the absence of the Koyck transformation; for example, for the sake of testing their effect by including them in the simple equation referred to above.

It can be seen from the regression that investment expenditure tends to affect positively and significantly π/W. This is also true of advertising expenditure. Past years' π/W, on the other hand, appear to affect negatively the current year's rate. Given the first differences form, the explanatory power of the equation is satisfactory. Multicollinearity does not appear to be a problem, judging from the low standard errors. However, autocorrelation's presence could not be excluded given the DW's bias towards indicating no autocorrelation, in the presence of the lagged dependent variable. Subject to this qualification, the equation seems to support the idea that investment expenditure increases the realized π/W and (thus) *ceteris paribus* the rate of profit. Given the rate of profit's positive link with planned investment, the overall effect is a cumulative decline in investment, resulting from and reinforcing the tendency towards reduced consumers' expenditure, and thus a realization crisis. This itself tends to reduce the income available to the state through taxation, thus tending to exacerbate the tendency towards a fiscal crisis.

The limited evidence discussed and provided here is broadly in line with the predictions of the theoretical analysis. Evidently, my theoretical points have not all been tested, nor could it be claimed that no other alternative interpretations could be made of the evidence[8]. All I wish to claim here is that the major economic and political institutions of capitalism need to be analysed in more detail, in a more synthetic non-dogmatic way and also dynamically, evolutionarily and historically. Such an approach was attempted here for three major institutions, the firm, the market and the state. I believe this approach provides useful insights on the existence, evolution and crisis of these institutions and, to a certain extent, capitalism as a whole. More research needs to be done; both in the direction taken here and towards incorporating more socio-political, psychological and ecological aspects in the analysis of capitalist institutions and the capitalist institutional crisis.

CONCLUDING REMARKS

It has been suggested that an explicitly evolutionary, historically informed perspective can provide useful insights on the issue of capitalist institutional failures–crises. This has been seen to accommodate concerns from neoclassical, Marxist and new-right perspectives in a non-eclectic manner and to provide interesting insights on the (articulation of) issues such as crises, internationalization and 'regulation'.

There are obviously numerous limitations in the previous account, including its rather non-dramatic final resort to near conventional realization failure-type arguments[9]. Although I am not sure this is in itself a limitation, one cannot fail but observe that we need a long way to go for a fuller analysis of institutional failure-crisis ideas. I hope this early attempt will be just a starting point for me and hopefully for others.

NOTES

1. The definition of institutions is elusive and contested in economic theory, as it is the identification of (any) differences between institutions, organizations, norms, rules, customs, etc. Existing definitions are often highly assertive and subjective and are not drawn from a general theoretical framework based on some sort of first principles. To fully address this problem there would be a need for a treatise on these definitional issues. Our purposes here are more modest. They are to analyse some aspects of the nature, role, interrelationships, failures and impact on economic performance of some (widely recognized as such) institutional or organizational devices for resource allocation and/or the division of labour under capitalism; that is, the market (or price mechanism), the firm and the state.

   For a notable (yet contestable, in this author's view) attempt to define institutions and distinguish them from organizations, see North (1981, 1990). He sees institutions as 'the rules of the game in a society, or, more formally, are the humanly devised constraints that shape human interaction' (p. 3). Organizations are 'groups of individuals bound by some common purpose to achieve objectives' (p. 5). From North's previous works these 'rules of the game' include rules, compliance procedures, moral and ethical behavioural norms which constrain individual behaviour for the purpose of furthering the maximizing objectives of 'principals'. I consider the focus on institutions as constraining (rather than constraining *and* enabling), the emphasis on predation, or principals (as opposed to both predation and contract) limiting, and the separation between institutions and organizations as at least given above, as questionable. However, I have taken a similar line to North's (Pitelis, 1991a) in starting from the merchant-capitalists' attempts to further their interests through trying to remove constraints to the realization of their objectives, in an attempt to explain the *evolution* of the *capitalist* firm and state. This focus is retained here. However, it is seen as historically specific, not a general basis for explaining the emergence, evolution and failure of institutions.

2. Note that these statements do not necessarily reject the classical 'labour theory of value' or accept the general historical *pre-existence* of the market as the institution par-excellence whose failure is required for the emergence of others. Indeed, as is often observed, (and patently shown in our framework here, which is historically specific) market operations presuppose other types of institutions, at the very least property rights or produced goods.

3. Based on the observation that in the putting-out system control was lying with the merchant manufacturers, I define the putting-out system as an early form of a (Coase–Marglin-type) firm, see Pitelis (1993) for more on this.

4. For the role of organizational knowledge as a 'barrier to entry' in Marglin's account of the 'rise of the factory', see Pitelis (1991b).

5. This in the dual sense of division of tasks and 'divide and rule'-type division of labour.

6. For a more detailed analysis of the role and nature of the capitalist state, see Pitelis (1994).

7. The *ceteris paribus* aspect of this statement should be emphasized here. Evidently more successful products, processes, organizational forms, strategic management, economic policies, etc. can all influence a country's relative success in the race. As, these are imitated by rivals, however, *austerity* tends to resume importance.

8. This tends to be a general problem with empirical work, which in our framework should be seen as not rejecting (which is not the same as confirming) the predictions of our analysis.

9. On the positive side, our analysis points to the possibility that some predictions derived from theories which ignore the role of institutions need not be inaccurate. However, richness of analysis is improved and new insights are found when institutions are considered. This could support the concept of 'completeness' as a criterion for economic methodology.

REFERENCES

Agglietta, M. (1979), *A Theory of Capitalist Regulation*, New Left Books, London.

Arrow, K. (1970), 'The Organization of Economic Activity: Issues Pertinent to the Choice of Market Versus Non-Market Allocation', in R. H. Haveman and J. Margolis (eds.), *Public Expenditure and Policy Analysis*, Markham, Chicago.

Baran, P. and P. Sweezy (1966), *Monopoly Capital*, Pelican, Harmondsworth.
Botty, R. and J.R. Crotty, (1975), 'Class Conflict and Macro Policy', *Review of Radical Political Economics*, vol. 7, no. 4, pp. 1–19.
Bowles, S., D.M. Gordon, and T.E. Weisskopf, (1983), *Beyond the Wasteland: a Democratic Alternative to Decline*, Anchor Doubleday, New York.
Boyer, R. (1986), *La Theory de la Regulation*, La Découverte, Paris.
Coase, R.H. (1937), 'The Nature of the Firm', *Economica*, vol. 4, pp. 386–405.
Coase, R.H. (1960), 'The Problem of Social Cost', *Journal of Law and Economics*, vol. 3, no. 1, pp. 1–44.
Cohen, R.B. et al. (eds.) (1979), 'The Multinational Corporation: a Radical Approach', *Papers by Stephen Herbert Hymer*, Cambridge University Press, Cambridge.
Cowling, K. (1982), *Monopoly Capitalism*, Macmillan, London.
Glyn, A. and B. Sutcliffe (1972), *British Capitalism, Workers and the Profits Squeeze*, Penguin, Harmonsworth.
Gouph, I. (1979), *The Political Economy of the Welfare State*, Macmillan Educational, London.
Hayek, F.A. (1978), *New Studies in Philosophy, Politics and the History of Ideas*, Routledge, London.
Holloway, J. and S. Picciotto (1978), *State and Capital: a Marxist Debate*, Edward Arnold, London.
Kalecki, M. (1971), *Dynamics of the Capitalist Economy*, Cambridge University Press, Cambridge.
Marglin, S. (1974), 'What do Bosses do? The Origins and Functions of Hierarchy in Capitalist Production', *Review of Radical Political Economics*, vol. 6, pp. 60–112.
Miliband, R. (1969), *The State in Capitalist Society*, Quarter Books, London.
Mueller, D.C. (1989), *Public Choice II. A Revised Edition of Public Choice*, Cambridge University Press, Cambridge.
North, D.C. (1981), *Structure and Change in Economic History*, Norton, New York.
North, D.C. (1990), *Institutions, Institutional Change and Economic Performance*, Cambridge University Press, Cambridge.
Paraskevopoulos, D. and C. Pitelis (1990), 'Capacity Expansion, Pre-emption and Strategy Signalling', Presented at the Royal Economic Society Conference, Nottingham, April.
Pitelis, C.N. (1987), *Corporate Capital: Control Ownership, Saving and Crisis*, Cambridge University Press, Cambridge.
Pitelis, C.N. (1991a), *Market and Non-Market Hierarchies*, Blackwell, Oxford.
Pitelis, C.N. (1991b), 'The Effects of Advertising (and) Investment on Aggregate Profits', *Scottish Journal of Political Economy*, vol. 38(1), pp. 32–40.
Pitelis, C.N. (ed.), (1993) *Transaction Costs, Markets and Hierarchies*, Blackwell, Oxford.
Pitelis, C.N. (1994), 'On the Nature of the Capitalist State', *Review of Political Economy*, vol. 6, no. 1.
Pitelis, C.N. and R. Sugden (eds.) (1991), *The Nature of the Transnational Firm*, Routledge, London.
Poulantzas, N. (1969), *Political Power and Social Class*, New Left Books, London.
Rowthorn, B. (1981), 'Demand, Real Wages and Economic Growth', *Thames Papers in Political Economy*, Thames Polytechnic, London.
Schotter, A. (1981), *The Economic Theory of Social Institutions*, Cambridge University Press, Cambridge.
Sherman, H. (1990), *The Business Cycle: Growth and Crisis under Capitalism*, University Press, Princeton.

Stafford, B. (1986), 'Theories of Decline', in Coates, D. and J. Hillard (eds.), *The Economic Decline of Modern Britain*, Wheatsheaf, Brighton.

Weisskopf, T.E. (1979), 'Marxian Crisis Theory and the Rate of Profit in the Post-War US Economy', *Cambridge Journal of Economics*, vol. 3, no. 4, pp. 341–78.

Williamson, O.E. (1975), *Markets and Hierarchies*, Free Press, New York.

Williamson, O.E. (1986), *Economic Organisation: Firms, Markets and Policy Control*, Wheatsheaf, Brighton.

7. Institutional Aspects of Regulating the Private Sector

Jonathan Michie[1]

INTRODUCTION

Privatisation has become a global phenomenon, with far-reaching implications not only for those sectors of the economy transferred into the private sector, but also for firms already in the private sector. First, such private businesses may for the first time be able to tender for work previously reserved for public sector firms. Second, firms which previously dealt with public sector customers, suppliers or collaborators may now find that these have been transferred to the private sector. And third, private sector firms may find themselves faced with new competitors as firms which were previously in the public sector have their former operating restrictions lifted. In addition, privatisation has led to a significant increase in the State's regulatory activities over private business. While the new regulatory bodies are designed primarily to oversee the operation of enterprises formerly in the public sector, their regulatory activities necessarily impinge on private sector businesses, whether these be private sector firms now operating in regulated areas where they previously could not — such as the newly licensed telecommunications operators — or simply private sector customers whose dealings with, say, British Telecom (BT) are now regulated, including on price.

In the economy of the future, business will therefore have to be conducted increasingly within regulated sectors, doing business with (and against) firms whose operations — and profit levels — are tightly regulated. The outputs of regulated industries may be traded internationally or at least have an impact on trade; air travel, airports, financial services, gas and electricity are examples. As a result, regulation in one country may interact with that in others, and this in turn will create the possibility of co-operation and/or conflict between national regulatory authorities, and the opportunity — or need — for contractual relations between them.

The institutional use of contracts to regulate the newly privatised sectors of the economy is being analysed in an ESRC research programme in the UK launched in 1994, building on the 'Contracts and Competition' programme established in 1992. This research programme aims, amongst other things, to shed new light on the choice of internalisation, market transactions or other institutional arrangements facing firms, and to consider how state regulators can influence these decisions where the outcome would otherwise be considered harmful (have negative externalities) when the wider effects on the economy and society are considered. The present chapter presents some of the background to these research questions in terms of the experience of privatisation and regulation in Britain and discusses some of the resulting issues.

ECONOMIC THEORY

Economic theory would suggest a number of reasons for the private business sector having to be regulated, quite apart from the standard arguments concerning problems of monopoly power or unfair trading. The competitive advantage of any given company, for example, will depend crucially on long term 'relational contracts' between the firm and its suppliers, customers, financiers, employees and others, which tend to reduce the uncertainty involved in market transactions[2]. It has been argued, for example by Gibson and Tsakalotos (1993), that these relational contracts are restricted to some extent in Britain by the financial structure of the 'City of London', being highly market-oriented in contrast to the more institutional approach adopted in countries like Germany and Japan. One aim of the regulatory bodies in Britain might therefore be not only to prevent the newly privatised companies from unduly exercising their market power but also to foster confidence amongst those who should be establishing 'relational contracts' with these enterprises that the regulated enterprises will indeed continue to operate in the future, neither having their markets swamped by new licensees nor having their future profits 'taxed' away by punitive price regulations.

There is a rather separate literature on globalisation, much of which would imply that in the economy of the future international business, far from having to face up to these national regulatory regimes, will on the contrary sweep such regulation aside as global operations bypass national governments, making any attempts at regulation futile. We have argued elsewhere that such claims regarding globalisation tend to be over-generalised and that increased international trade and investment can actually magnify the impact of national policies — whether regulatory or industrial — rather than negate them[3].

PRIVATISATION AND REGULATION IN BRITAIN

The privatisation process in Britain during the 1980s and 1990s created a number of regulatory bodies such as Oftel, for telecommunications, Ofgas, for the gas industry, Offer, for electricity, and Ofwat, for water, with vital areas of the economy now in the private regulated sector. These regulators can rule on the type of commercial contracts to be agreed between enterprises. Where competitive forces do not deliver the desired outcome, that outcome can be decreed, through in effect a regulatory contract between the regulator and regulated. There has thus been a significant increase in the number, scope and complexity of contractual relations, as relations which were previously internal to publicly owned industries are now the subject of market contracts between private firms, or of 'contracts' between regulator and provider. Vertical relationships — for example between electricity supply and distribution companies — have thus become far more complex, and the contracts will have to be far more specified than any which may have been used under the previous arrangements.

There was an expectation held by some that the new regulatory agencies would have a relatively short life, their task being to oversee the transfer of the industry from the public to the private sector, after which free market competition could be allowed to govern; (see, for example, Steven Littlechild, 1983, *Regulation of British Telecommunications Profitability*, London: HMSO). The experience has been quite different with 'free market competition' proving in many cases to be a rather difficult state to engineer. The importance of regulation has not in practice diminished; the existing regulators seem set to continue in operation for the foreseeable future, to be joined possibly by new bodies such as for the coal and rail industries. While the companies being regulated have, under British company law, a legal obligation to maximise the financial interests of their shareholders, the regulator may be charged with being the guarantor that the interests of wider stakeholders are taken into account[4].

Such regulators have, then, been charged with a mixture of the following tasks: introducing competition into the industry concerned, regulating the industry, and regulating the competition. These tasks are inextricably linked. The degree to which they are compliments or substitutes is not always clear.

Disputes have arisen between regulators and regulated over many of these issues, including over relations between the regulated and 'unregulated' firms (such as, for example, between the rival telecommunications operators BT and Mercury, and what sort of contracts BT should be obliged to agree with Mercury for carrying Mercury calls on BT's local networks). Other questions have also been subject to dispute, for instance over 'who should regulate the regulators?' (see the fifth section, below). These various difficulties reflect the, arguably, limited understanding of the processes involved, amongst practitioners and also with the academic community. Not even the nature of the 'regulatory contract' has yet been clearly established, either by practitioners or by academic research.

Yet in so far as the private sector has to do business with the newly privatised sectors — as customers, suppliers, collaborators, competitors and investors — a common understanding of the nature (and indeed of the precise terms) of the 'regulatory contract' may prove rather important for the economy of the future. Indeed, the extent to which the private sector is able to do business successfully with the newly privatised sector will depend in part on the extent to which such an understanding is achieved. One part — perhaps one half — of the 'regulatory contract' is for the regulator to guarantee the conditions for a sufficiently profitable operation of the regulated sector in the future to justify current investment. Thus, on the one hand regulation is required to prevent the enterprises concerned from abusing their monopoly (or monopsonist or oligopolistic) power, and to ensure that some necessary level of service or output provision is made at an acceptably low price, if necessary at a quality which also has to be regulated. The quid pro quo is that the regulator guarantees not to 'tax' away future profits which derive from current investments being made on precisely this understanding.

But as these regulated enterprises become increasingly entwined in the functioning of international business, then to that extent the 'guaranteed' levels of profitability and so on for the regulated firms will come to play an increasingly important role in the operation of private sector firms who were never in the public sector, and who are not subject to regulation, but yet may have a keen interest in the likely operation, behaviour, performance and profitability of the regulated firms, as these firms come to be suppliers, customers, partners, competitors and possible investment outlets (this last being either through Joint Ventures or simply through the regulated firm being seen as a potential home for arms length investments of reserve funds seeking a profitable return). Presumably with this in mind, the UK's gas regulator put forward draft proposals in September 1993 to 'ring-fence' British Gas's profits which arise from supplying household customers, to protect this profit from any costs associated with high-risk overseas projects.

British Gas has invested £1.5 billion in other countries since its privatisation in 1986 and plans to spend a similar amount over the next few years. Indeed, following the Monopolies and Mergers Commission report published in September 1993 which recommended that British Gas sell off its trading arm by 1997 and lose its monopoly over household supply by 2002, the company had stated that this would force it to put greater emphasis on its overseas interests. However, the regulator's plan to split British Gas's profits in this way was reported as being likely to curtail this overseas expansion programme, as such 'non ring-fenced' business would need to be funded to a greater degree on a project finance basis which could involve having to take on more debt[5].

Actual outcomes of regulation, such as profit rates, therefore require further analytical investigation. There have been several studies performed on the behaviour of privatised and regulated sectors in the sense of how service/output levels have changed quantitatively and qualitatively, what has happened to pricing and profitability and so on (for a study of *British Electricity Prices since Privatisation* see Yarrow (1992) who finds a surprisingly high increase in prices). But what is also needed are studies to draw up accounting frameworks able to delineate the effects of different measures, and to develop appropriate mechanisms for deriving justifiable rates of return for what are in many cases still fairly dominant enterprises within their industry. This requires some agreement (or at least decision) on the valuation to be made of the assets on which the rate of return is to be calculated, the assessment to be made of the riskiness of the return from investment in regulated utilities and hence the level at which this rate of return needs to be set, and so on.

While the above discussion has focused on the regulation of what might be thought of as the business or market sector of the economy, there has also been — particularly, again, in Britain — an increasing use of business-style regulation of Welfare State functions such as in the National

Health Service, education and other local and national government activities (for a detailed analysis of which, see Taylor-Gooby and Lawson, 1993[6]). These developments are also, though, of broader relevance throughout the economy since one of the aims of the process has been precisely to contract work out to the business sector; the role played by professionalism and managerialism in the British private and public sectors has also undergone policy-induced change as Government introduces these increasing degrees of privatisation and commercialisation into the public sector[7].

The effects of all this on the quality of professionals' service delivery will depend on the impact it has on factors such as trust: will the fact that service delivery is specified in contracts increase the trust which customers/patients/parents have that such services will be well provided, or will the formalisation of previously unwritten rules of behaviour lead to a 'bottom line' approach where only that contracted for is delivered, while previously there may have been relations of trust between professionals — as well as between professionals and the service consumers — which ensured that certain professional standards would be maintained regardless of contractual obligations.

Evidence from the ESRC's 'Contracts and Competition' programme (Hughes, 1993) suggests that public sector quasi-markets — such as created by the National Health Service reforms — depend for their survival on continual government intervention:

> Monitoring and regulation become major resource-consuming activities, as well as generating difficult problems of accountability and philosophical coherence. The market may survive, but at this stage its much vaunted efficiency advantages over the welfare bureaucracy will have all but disappeared. (Hughes, 1993)

It has also been argued more generally (for example by Laughlin and Broadbent, 1992) that the introduction of accounting-dominated regulatory law can go beyond acceptable levels, creating 'juridification' ('legal pollution' or 'overregulation'):

> [...] juridification does not merely mean proliferation of law; it signifies a process in which the interventionist social state produces a new type of law, regulatory law. Only when both elements — materialization and the intention of the social state — are taken together can we understand the precise nature of the contemporary phenomenon of juridification. (Teubner, 1987, p. 18)[8]

Faced with this 'juridification' the need is then to reverse the spread of such regulation rather than to develop it further. It may be that the only feasible way of avoiding this new generation of regulatory activity is by avoiding — or reversing — the very privatisation which spawned it; yet this option would appear to be ruled out on political grounds for the foreseeable future, regardless of the possible balance of economic or even political advantages of such a course. Rather, the present level of regulatory activity seems set to continue, with all the potential problems which are associated with the public regulation of private sector business. Thus the succession of Conservative governments in the UK from 1979, although elected on a promise, amongst other things, of cutting back the number of unelected regulatory bodies — the so-called *'quangos'*[9] — have, as a result of privatisation, done the exact opposite, overseeing a huge increase in resources devoted to regulatory activities[10].

THE NEW RESEARCH AGENDA

The 'regulatory contract' between the regulator and the enterprises operating within that regulator's jurisdiction includes the key price cap formula (RPI-x) tied to certain performance measures. The price cap is preferred to a 'cost plus' pricing formula or a 'rate of return' rule because of the incentive effects involved (as well as the difficulty of determining true efficient costs). However, the distinction between these rules is not analytically clear-cut. The more often the price cap is revised, the closer the regulatory regime moves to a rate of return concept, with all the potential incentive problems (such as the regulated enterprise boosting the capital intensity of their operations in order to translate a given rate of return into higher absolute profit levels). And fundamentally the regulator is trying to guess what costs would be if the enterprise were operating efficiently, so as to allow a 'cost plus' operating profit.

In practice, then, the regulatory practices pursued represent ever-changing combinations of the above three approaches rather than a choice of one and a rejection of the other two. Research is needed into how the balance of incentive mechanisms alter as new mixes are considered.

In regulating individual enterprises (such as Oftel over BT), there are complex theoretical as well as practical problems in defining and discovering costs. These problems include how to allocate overheads between different operations, problems of joint and common costs and so on. The decision made on these issues can in turn have incentive effects

recorder standards (which according to many, resulted in the 'worse' system being adopted), and on the other hand there are examples such as HDTV standards at present, on which the CEC is actively trying to promote a 'European' standard[14].

Telecommunications is perhaps the most important area of utility regulation as far as the economy of the future is concerned. Hagedoorn and Schakenraad (1990, 1992, 1993) for example show that the lion's share of the explosion of new cooperative business arrangements in the 1980s was accounted for by information and communication technology.

THE INTERNATIONAL TELECOMMUNICATIONS MARKET

According to Dr Robin Mansell of SPRU, telecommunication regulatory institutions are not coping with the technical changes occurring in telematics services such as electronic data interchange (EDI) and radical ways of regulating the supply of public telecommunication services are urgently needed, both to overcome the above failing and also to ensure continued universal access in an era when private operators will be seeking profitable business openings rather than undertaking public service obligations:

> In telecommunication, competition has been chosen as the pathway toward achieving equity and efficiency goals. But co-operation is essential too, and this requires agreements on the rules of the market. As with the railways, inter-operability and network access are necessary. Most suppliers, customers and regulators recognise the need for co-operation on numbering plans, infrastructure capacity where this proves cost effective, and technical information required to establish standards and plan the roll out of new networks. Co-operation is essential to competition in the new telematics environment. But as we have learned from studies of innovation, firms have a history, and this affects their willingness to co-operate. In telecommunications, this is particularly important because of the weight of older institutions. Even if BT's domestic market share were to slip to 70 percent by the year 2000, this company will have a strong base upon which to protect its market. Regulation, imperfect as it is, will continue to play a crucial role in monitoring, guiding and sometimes controlling, decisions by the main players in the market. But it is here, I suggest, that we see very few signs of radical regulatory innovation. (Mansell, 1993, p. 10)

The need to force public service obligations on telecommunications operators (basically, of universal access) requires public ownership or public regulation. Private operators may choose not to subsidise connection and access charges to the degree desirable (or even at all), even though such subsidies may make economic sense for society. The benefits to society come from the positive network externalities, whereby existing network subscribers benefit from additional subscribers joining the network[15]. This is one of the reasons why governments want to subsidise connection charges and line rental charges (to encourage people to join and then to stay on the network) and why Oftel has so far refused to allow BT to phase out these cross-subsidies.

It may even be in the operator's own interests to subsidise connection and rental charges, if the resulting traffic is profitable. But if that traffic could be lost to rival operators then this expectation of a private gain in profits may not be certain enough to justify the investment. Thus, for example, the French Télétel service (often referred to as Minitel after the name of its terminals) proved profitable to France Télécom despite the terminals having been distributed free, due to the additional telephone traffic. But this commercial success was only possible on the basis of a monopoly of telecommunications by France Télécom[16]. In the absence of monopoly, such outcomes would have to be engineered by regulatory means if they are to be achieved.

Thus while the pressure from international business will be for lower call charges and greater investment in the routes most used by the firms concerned, it is not necessarily in the best interests of international business itself for telecommunications networks to shrink as market solutions impose themselves, whether this takes the form of rising connection and rental charges referred to above, or of allowing investment to go disproportionately into those sections of the network of most immediate use to international business to the detriment of the network as a whole, or of simply failing to keep regulatory developments in line with technological advances to ensure that new areas are only allowed to develop along unregulated lines by conscious decision not simply by default:

> In summary, regulatory institutions are not coping with technical change, at least not very well. Some telematics services do need to be all-pervasive. The supercarriers are becoming less and less interested in public or universal service goals as they turn their strategic vision to the global market. To cope with disparities in access to the public network, there must be regulatory innovation. Structural changes in domestic markets are needed to control supplier power. A radical reorientation of regulation is also needed to ensure access to a planned set of 'universal' telematics services. This is one way of averting a tragedy — namely, the demise of the common public network. (Mansell, 1993, p. 14)

CONCLUSIONS

There are major theoretical issues which are still unresolved in the area of firm behaviour, inter-firm behaviour, inter-firm networking and so-called 'globalisation'[17]. In the economy of the future, it is going to be necessary to deal with increasing contractual complexities as new managerial methods and business structures emerge, with firms concentrating on their 'core' activities and contracting out activities previously conducted within the firm. And as business becomes more international, increasing numbers of international suppliers, customers and collaborators are having to be dealt with. One particular phenomenon within this is the need to deal with enterprises which are newly regulated — previously in public ownership and now transferred to the private sector but unable to operate (for whatever reason) without State regulation.

It is argued in this chapter that one lesson which can be learned from UK experience is that such regulation of private sector activities will not be the temporary operation — transferring assets from the private sector to the public sector and then withdrawing — which some had originally envisaged for it. On the contrary, State regulation seems to be here to stay in many sectors of the economy of the future. The 'regulatory contract' can be thought of as delivering to the consumers some guaranteed level of service at a regulated price, while delivering to the shareholders some guarantee against 'taxing' away future profit levels. Such 'regulatory contracts' will need increasingly to take account of international business on both 'sides' of such contracts — both as customers and as shareholders (or joint venture partners). Given the resulting complexities arising from the interaction of different national (or supranational) regulatory frameworks, such a conclusion, of course, raises more questions than it answers.

NOTES

1. Support of the UK's Economic and Social Research Council (ESRC) is gratefully acknowledged. The work is part of the ESRC Contracts and Competition Research Programme.
2. These processes are discussed in detail by, for example, John Kay (1993), *Foundations of Corporate Success*, Oxford: Oxford University Press.
3. See Daniele Archibugi and Jonathan Michie (1995), 'The Globalisation of Technology: A New Taxonomy', *Cambridge Journal of Economics*, and Jonathan Michie (1994a), 'Global Shocks and 'Social Corporatism'', in R.

Delorme and K. Dopfer (editors), *Political Economy of Complexity: Evolutionary Approaches to Economic Order and Disorder*, Aldershot: Edward Elgar.

4. Indeed, it has been argued that the structure of British company law — along with the pressures on companies for short-term financial returns which are said to emanate from the British stock exchange and financial systems — help create or at least exacerbate the disease of 'short-termism' often cited for undermining Britain's industrial development.

5. However, the director of competition and tariffs at Ofgas was reported as saying that the company had nothing to fear from the ring-fence proposals as long as its projects overseas were on a secure and viable footing (see the *Financial Times* of 3rd September 1993).

6. However, see Michie (1994a) for a review of this rather uncritical work.

7. The response of the professions to these developments has varied according to the structure of the sector. In the case of education, in the 'opted out' schools it has been the head teachers who have shifted their efforts away from teaching and teaching-related duties and towards management functions. In health, the GP contracts have resulted in the management duties being passed 'down' by the GPs to the clerical staff.

8. Cited and discussed in Richard Laughlin and Jane Broadbent (1992), *Accounting and the Law: Partners in the Juridification of the Public Sector in the UK?*, Sheffield University Management School Discussion Paper no. 92.2, p. 3.

9. Quasi-Autonomous Non-Governmental OrganisationS' — i.e., administrative bodies with financial support from and senior appointments made by the government but not controlled by the government.

10. 'It may seem strange that, thirteen years after the election of a Government in this country pledged to get government off the backs of British industry, we seem to have more government regulation or self-regulation within a governmental and statutory framework than ever.' Sir Gordon Borrie, QC (from Borrie, 1992, *Regulators, Self-Regulators and Their Accountability*, TSB Forum paper, p. 5). Sir Borrie was Director General of Fair Trading from 1976 to 1992.

11. See Martin Cave and Jonathan Michie (1992), 'Developing Competition in International Telephone Service', Chapter 1 of Franca Klaver and Paul Slaa (editors), *Telecommunications: New Signposts to Old Roads*, Amsterdam: IOS Press, p. 12, where this is analysed.

12. See, for example, Professor Surrey's comments in *The Observer* of 22nd August 1993.

13. See CEC (1987), *Towards a Dynamic European Economy. Green Paper on the Development of the Common Market for Telecommunications Services and Equipment*, COM(87) 290 final, and Nicholas Costello and Herbert Ungerer (1988), *Telecommunications in Europe*, Brussels: CEC. The present author worked as an Expert to the European Commission with Costello and Ungerer for two years between 1988 and 1990 on implementing regulatory reform in face of technological developments as well as the requirements of the 1992 programme; a key aim was to ensure compatible systems at the 'lowest' levels of the telecommunications infrastructure so as to assist the rapid development by business of 'higher' level services on the back of such 'electronic highways', even when, left to itself, the operation of international business would not necessarily deliver the necessary infrastructure. (See Costello and Ungerer, 1988, for a detailed discussion.)

14. For a discussion of the dilemma of wanting standardisation for connectivity, versus the danger of 'freezing' standards too early, see Christopher Freeman,

'The Economics of Technical Change', *Cambridge Journal of Economics*, volume 18, 1994.
15. In the jargon of neoclassical economics, utilities are interdependent. The utility of having a telephone is limited if no one else does.
16. For further details and discussion see Nicholas Costello, Jonathan Michie and Seumas Milne (1991), 'Industrial Restructuring and Public Intervention: Planning the Digital Economy', chapter 10 of Jonathan Michie (editor), *The Economics of Restructuring and Intervention*, Aldershot: Edward Elgar.
17. See Christopher Freeman, 'The Economics of Technical Change', *Cambridge Journal of Economics*, Volume 18, 1994, for a detailed discussion.

REFERENCES

Archibugi, Daniele and Jonathan Michie (1995), 'The Globalisation of Technology: A New Taxonomy', *Cambridge Journal of Economics*, vol. 19, no. 1, February.

Borrie, Gordon (1992), *Regulators, Self-Regulators and Their Accountability*, TSB Forum Paper, London.

Cave, Martin and Jonathan Michie (1992), 'Developing Competition in International Telephone Service', Chapter 1 of Franca Klaver and Paul Slaa (eds.), *Telecommunications: New Signposts to Old Roads*, IOS Press, Amsterdam.

Commission of the European Communities (CEC) (1987), *Towards a Dynamic European Economy. Green Paper on the Development of the Common Market for Telecommunications Services and Equipment*, COM(87) 290 final, CEC, Brussels.

Costello, Nicholas and Herbert Ungerer (1988), *Telecommunications in Europe*, CEC, Brussels.

Costello, Nicholas, Jonathan Michie and Seumas Milne (1991), 'Industrial Restructuring and Public Intervention: Planning the Digital Economy'. Chapter 10 of Jonathan Michie (ed.), *The Economics of Restructuring and Intervention*, Edward Elgar, Aldershot.

Freeman, Christopher (1994), 'The Economics of Technical Change', *Cambridge Journal of Economics*, vol. 18.

Gibson, Heather and Euclid Tsakalotos (1993), 'Getting Tough with the Traders', *New Economy*, Autumn, pp. 12–15, Academic Press, London.

Hagedoorn, J. and J. Schakenraad (1990), 'Strategic Partnering and Technological Cooperation', in Christopher Freeman and Luc Soete (eds.), *New Explorations in the Economics of Technical Change*, Frances Pinter, London.

Hagedoorn, J. and J. Schakenraad (1992), 'Leading Companies and Networks of Strategic Alliances in Information Technologies', *Research Policy*, vol. 21, no. 2, pp. 163–91.

Hagedoorn, J. and J. Schakenraad (1993), 'Strategic Technology Partnering and International Corporate Strategies', in Kirsty Hughes (ed.), *European Competitiveness*, Cambridge University Press, Cambridge.

Hughes, David (1993), 'Health Policy: Letting the Market Work?', in Robert Page and John Baldock (eds.), *Social Policy Review 5*, Social Policy Association, Canterbury.

Kay, John (1993), *Foundations of Corporate Success*, Oxford University Press, Oxford.

Laughlin, Richard and Jane Broadbent (1992), *Accounting and Law: Partners in the Juridification of the Public Sector in the UK?*, Discussion Paper no. 92.2, Sheffield University Management School, Sheffield.

Littlechild, Steven C. (1983), *Regulation of British Telecommunications Profitability*, HMSO, London.

Mansell, Robin (1993), *From Telephony to Telematics Services: Equity, Efficiency and Regulatory Innovation*, ESRC PICT Annual Lecture, May.

Michie, Jonathan (1994a), 'Global Shocks and Social Corporatism' in R. Delorme and K. Dopfer (eds.), *The Political Economy of Complexity: Evolutionary Approaches to Economic Order and Disorder*, Edward Elgar, Aldershot.

Michie, Jonathan (1994b), 'Managing the Public Sector', *International Review of Applied Economics*, vol. 8, no. 3, September.

Taylor-Gooby, Peter and Robyn Lawson (eds.), (1993), *Markets and Managers: New Issues in the Delivery of Welfare*, Open University Press, Buckingham.

Teubner, G. (1987), 'Juridification: Concepts, Aspects, Limits, Solutions', Introduction to G. Teubner (ed.), *Juridification of Social Sciences*, Walter de Gruyter, Berlin.

Yarrow, George (1992), *British Electricity Prices since Privatisation*, Regulatory Policy Institute, Studies in Regulation no. 1.

8. Michael Porter's Inquiry into the Nature and Causes of the Wealth of Nations — a Challenge to Neoclassical Economics

Paul Auerbach and Peter Skott

INTRODUCTION

Michael Porter's recent book (1990)[1] poses an important challenge to the main stream of academic economics. Porter and others, all of whom are on the peripheries of academic economics, are in the midst of a debate about the nature and causes of the wealth of nations, a topic clearly central to the history of economic thought. Even when academic economists participate in this debate, their discourse often departs significantly from the rhetoric and argumentation of academic economics, and not merely for reasons of popularisation: their more 'legitimate' arguments have not dealt with the central issues of public concern in a convincing way.

The fact that much of this debate is taking place outside of the Academy is, we believe, a significant event. For many academic economists, the non-academic discussion is merely an indication of the profession's failure to communicate the inherent scientific validity of its approach to a broader audience, so that room has been left for intellectual demagogues to conduct this debate. We claim, on the contrary, that Porter and others have moved to the centre of this debate because orthodox economics has indeed failed to explain the nature and causes of the wealth of nations. The weaknesses in these more 'popular' approaches stem from a failure to confront orthodox explanations openly and thoroughly, so that these approaches and their critique of orthodoxy appear to be imprecise. They also share with orthodoxy a lack of historical perspective from which the current changes in the world economy can be viewed. Furthermore, in some areas, most especially in dealing with questions

142

surrounding human and societal development, the break from orthodoxy is not severe enough.

We proceed as follows. In the first section we examine the failures of neoclassical growth theory in its old and new forms. In the second section we consider the challenge posed, explicitly and implicitly, to academic economics by Porter and others and set out the limitations of these critiques. A conclusion follows.

THE FAILURE OF ACADEMIC ORTHODOXY

Theories of economic growth

In the 1950s and 1960s, academic economists actively pursued the question of the determinants of economic growth at both a theoretical and empirical level. The dominant approach, and the immediate predecessor of the contemporary orthodox theory, was the neoclassical theory of economic growth (Solow, 1956; Swan, 1956).

According to this theory, *the economy's per capita rate of growth is uncontingent on its rate of investment* in the long run. This prediction has been largely a source of embarrassment for orthodoxy. As a matter of logic, all possible relationships between the rate of saving and economic growth are possible. Underconsumptionist models, for instance, predict a negative relationship (see Steindl, 1976), but by far the most popular presumption, reinforced perhaps by the contemporary Japanese experience, has been the 'old-fashioned' notion to be found in the growth models of Harrod and Domar that there exists a positive relationship between the rate of saving and economic growth, a proposition which even Solow (1993) suggests has a self-evident veracity.

A second conclusion of a traditional neoclassical approach is the notion that *one sector is as good as another — there is no such thing as a priority sector*. This conclusion is a corollary of two premises. The first is *fungibility*: in a world of ubiquitous markets, in which resources (including capital) can be freely shifted from one use to another, the rational strategy for a nation is to 'follow the market' and maximise returns. Thus, if a nation is rich in raw materials, it would be irrational to interfere with the operation of the market by the setting up of a priority sector (e.g., in manufacturing), since the option of costlessly shifting resources to any such priority sector at a later date always remains open. The second premise is the universal absence of *non-convexities* in all sectors, including manufacturing. This presumption is crucial. Non-convexities are incompatible with the conditions of the fundamental welfare theorem and will typically give rise to multiple equilibria and the possibility of lock-in. Growth strategies linked to notions of priority sectors in manufacturing are therefore often centred, explicitly or implicitly on the presence of scale economies in these sectors.

Associated with these central conclusions are three related notions from the theory of international trade — the prediction that 'factor endowments' will determine what a nation will produce, and the normative prescriptions in favour of free trade and free investment internationally.

From a purely scientific point of view, these conclusions from the traditional theories of growth and international trade have come to appear increasingly questionable. The 'factor endowments' story came under early attack[2], and under contemporary conditions has become progressively irrelevant as a determinant of the international distribution of economic activity. Furthermore, the empirical evidence shows persistent international differences in growth rates, and these differences cannot be explained by a general tendency of convergence in per capita real incomes. Some previously low-income countries have grown rapidly; others have remained poor, and some previous leaders have fallen back. Econometric studies typically find no significant correlation between growth rates and initial income levels, and in many cases the coefficient on initial incomes even turns out to be positive.

Partly in response to these empirical observations the 'new' growth literature has exploded in the wake of the contributions by Romer, 1986 and Lucas, 1988. In this literature, the rate of growth is determined endogenously by the decisions to accumulate produced factors of productions. This endogenous determination requires that there is non-decreasing returns to the set of factors that can be produced and accumulated or, alternatively, that factors which cannot be accumulated are in perfectly elastic supply. The second condition is satisfied in Harrod's analysis of growth under Keynesian conditions of unemployment (as well as in models of dual economies) but new growth theory shares with traditional neoclassical theory the assumption of full employment, thus ruling out this possibility[3]. Instead, new growth theory relies on non-decreasing returns to the factors that can be accumulated. If other factors — e.g., simple labour — enter as inputs into the production of basic commodities (in Sraffa's sense), this assumption implies the existence of non-convexities in the production possibility set. The existence of non-convexities, in turn, is inconsistent with perfect competition unless the non-convexities are external to the individual producers. Changes in the scale assumptions thus have implications for other aspects of the model, and the new models require a combination of externalities and imperfect competition[4].

There can be no doubt that new growth theory presents an advance over the traditional neoclassical theory. But it should be clear also that the main ideas have a long history: increasing returns to scale figured prominently in the work of, among others, Adam Smith and Karl Marx. More recently, Gunnar Myrdal and Nicholas Kaldor viewed increasing returns to scale as a central element in a theory of economic growth and development and criticised conventional 'equilibrium economics' precisely for its unwarranted assumptions of convexity and perfect competition. These earlier writers, furthermore, were well aware that increasing returns to scale could generate persistent differences in growth rates and invalidate the conventional policy recommendations of free trade and international capital mobility[5]. An explanation of the current popularity of the new theory may therefore be incomplete without consideration of the socio-political background.

Arguably, the reasons for the engendering of the 'new' theory have as much to do with the situation emerging in the US in the 1980s as with objective scientific veracity. However useful the prescriptions of the traditional theory are in reinforcing policy directives from the IMF and other agencies to debtor nations and others, there have been growing doubts in the US about the inviolability of notions of free trade and laissez faire: the 'stylised fact' of a link between industrial success and overall economic growth (OECD, 1992), coupled with stagnating real incomes and the disappearance of 'key' industries in the US has led to calls for 'something' to be done. The basic ideas of the theory may not be new but their time had come.

Romer (1989, p. 30) explains the profession's former reluctance to consider increasing returns by 'the technical constraints faced when they first tried to formulate equilibrium models'. But can there be any doubt that ways would have been found to solve or get around these technical difficulties *if* convex models had been seen to give seriously misleading conclusions for the country which dominates both the economics profession and the international economy? Models based on increasing returns and the centrality of the industrial sector gained widespread acceptance in the UK in the 1960s when Britain's relative decline became clear. American economists at the time were much less receptive to these ideas. Now, however, with fears about US relative decline, the same basic ideas (dressed up in models of greater mathematical complexity) receive a warm reception in the US.

It should be emphasised, finally, that these developments in orthodox growth theory have radical policy implications. Multiple equilibria, externalities and imperfect competition all imply that, in general, government policy will have an important role to play. Furthermore, although the existence of increasing returns to scale may raise the potential gains from international trade, the presumption that all countries automatically gain from free trade must be rejected, and 'managed trade' in some form may become attractive. The new theories undermine the righteous claims by rich nations of the efficacy for all participants of an international regime of free trade[6] as well as the diktat of laissez faire imposed upon developing countries by international agencies. The models can be used to show that in many cases deviations from the free market nostrums can be of benefit to poorer nations attempting to build a human and physical infrastructure to make up for their 'late start'.

Finally, the 'new' theory has essentially conceded to the critics of orthodoxy the whole argument surrounding the free flow of investment funds. Britain at the end of the nineteenth and the beginning of the twentieth centuries was investing substantial amounts of its financial capital in, for instance, American and Russian railway bonds. Critics of this practice, such as the famous MP Joseph Chamberlain, said that domestic industry was being run down. But advocates of free market orthodoxy asserted that if, indeed, the return on financial investment abroad was higher than that on domestic investment, to do anything but invest abroad would be irrational. The new growth theory now suggests that in order to reap the external benefits accruing to society from technological advance it might well be rational to ignore the signals of the free market. Domestic investment might be preferable to society as a whole, even if the financial returns to investment abroad are higher. Such a conclusion strikes at the heart of the traditional free market approach to investment, and emerges from what is now the main stream of orthodox growth theory.

Factors of production

Despite the insights of the new theory and the convergence of mainstream economics towards positions long advocated by their critics, important shortcomings remain. One set of problems — the ones we shall focus on in this chapter — concern the analysis of production.

In orthodox growth theory, old and new, growth is explained by the effect of factors — unskilled labour, human capital, capital equipment — with the implicit presumption that these factors are being used efficiently. To be sure, externalities or imperfect competition may lead to distortions in firms' choice of a point on the production possibility frontier and in the investment decisions of both households and firms with respect to human capital. Distortions of this kind are at the centre of the new theory, but it is maintained that production always takes place at the frontier.

This approach implies that a whole set of problems surrounding how best to organise resources is assumed away. It is implicitly presumed that the competitive process — 'the market' — has solved these problems by weeding out inefficient practices and producers. This presumption of microeconomic efficiency is, of course, standard in mainstream economics. It will be admitted that the assumption may not be fully accurate in a descriptive sense but, it is argued, assumptions of efficiency provide a good first approximation and the best theoretical starting point. Even critics of mainstream economics should, we believe, concede the strength of this argument: there are indeed many questions for which an assumption of microeconomic rationality and efficiency does provide a useful starting point. It is also true that the rationality approach is often carried to absurd extremes, but a methodological command which says 'don't ever assume rationality and efficiency' would be no more sensible than injunctions against theories that eschew the standard, mechanical optimisation approach. The real question therefore is whether there are good reasons to be suspicious of the efficiency assumption in the present context of economic growth. The answer, we believe, is yes.

The problem is that although productive efficiency may be a first approximation, the approximation may be poor and *differences in growth and other performance characteristics may be related precisely to differences in the goodness of fit*. Countries may perform well economically because their industries operate with less inefficiency than in other countries. A model which does not go beyond the first approximation of full efficiency cannot even address this possibility. By construction it must be blind to those organisational and institutional factors that could influence the degree of productive efficiency. Thus, the analytical structure of both the new and old theories of growth precludes consideration of what is perhaps the dominant view among contemporary economic historians that organisational innovation (or its absence) is decisive in shaping the growth trajectory of nations (Chandler, 1990; Elbaum and Lazonick, 1986).

As we shall see below in the case of the steel industry, Japanese success cannot be accounted for by their endowment of 'factors of production' or by technological innovation, but by their *superior organisation* of given resources and available technologies and their aggressively competitive *behaviour* as seen in the context of a dynamic approach to competition. More generally, many of the distinctive Japanese innovations to work practices, such as the *kan-ban* system, *make no use of high technology and could easily have been introduced at the turn of the century.*

As another example, consider the case of a developing country which seems to get low 'returns' in terms of economic growth on its investment in education. A critical question, most especially if we are to generalise this experience to other countries at comparable levels of development, is as follows: is this failure an intrinsic aspect (i.e., in terms of the nation's 'production function') of the inability of a country at this level of development to absorb and make productive use of educated individuals, or are these individuals being used inefficiently, because of corruption, race or caste discrimination? If the explanation is largely of the latter kind, the solution may take the form of political action on these matters, rather than giving up on education. Furthermore, if the low productivity in the country is rooted in such factors, rather than being an intrinsic aspect of the level of development, it may not be useful to generalise this experience as a 'law' which is widely applicable to other countries.

Technical change

In many of the new theories, the rate of growth is determined by the pace of technological innovation which, in turn, is produced endogenously in a separate R&D sector. This framework suggests that the R&D sector will be central to the growth performance of an economy. Following our earlier discussion, the existence of different degrees of inefficiency in the R&D sectors of otherwise identical economies could lead to variations in growth rates. However, the centrality given to technological innovation as the 'key' to national economic growth in the new growth theory may well be misplaced[7].

Purely 'national' technologies have receded in recent decades with the spread of multinational commercial activity and with the greater ease with which science, as opposed to craft-based technology is diffused (Nelson and Wright, 1992; Auerbach, 1988, ch.9)[8]. As a result the prize does not go solely (or even predominantly) to the nations engendering the new technologies, but to those capable of exploiting and adapting these technologies to commercial needs. Thus, in recent decades, nations with strong records in innovation (for example the US) have not had outstanding rates of growth, while the pace setters in economic growth such as Japan and South Korea have not in the past had outstanding records in fundamental technological innovation. A similar pattern could be observed during the period of US ascendency: until the post-World War II period the US lagged behind Western Europe in terms of research and technical innovation. What really distinguished US manufacturing was the size of the domestic market and the focus on mass production and mass distribution. Large scale production in turn was related to important organisational and managerial innovations in the US (Chandler, 1977; Nelson and Wright, 1992).

Nelson and Wright (1992) also suggest that the skills needed for the commercial adaptation of technology appear to be rather broad-based, including facility in production, marketing and finance rather than being exclusively focused on human capital's role in R&D work. At the firm level, this suggestion is confirmed by Teece (1992), who describes the many complementary capacities that are necessary if an innovating firm is to reap the commercial benefits of its innovation. The failure of EMI to profit from the creation of the body scanner is a classic example, while IBM's initial success with the PC shows that a product need not be technologically superior to be successful and to set the industry standard. Furthermore, geographical proximity to other producers in the whole 'chain' of activities involved in a particular sector may be important: specialisation and the use of 'markets' to the purchase of inputs from abroad may not always be an adequate substitute for the 'hands on' experience of interacting with suppliers in the making of new products:

> [...] sustained technological advance was not the result of one person or firm pushing things ahead, but involved many interacting people and firms [...] the success of new technical breakthroughs required that they mesh with prevailing complementary technologies, and that they fit into a complex chain of contingent production and exchange activities. (Nelson and Wright, 1992, pp. 1935–36)

This observation may help explain the disquiet widely felt over the fact that the US machine tool industry is now only one quarter the size of that in Japan (Baxter, 1992) — a fact of no significance in orthodox economic theory.

Finally, it should be noted that the emphasis on technological innovation in the new growth literature is associated with a bias in favour of discontinuous and technological achievements such as 'inventions' or patents over incremental improvements in technology and improvements in the 'ways of doing things' of a non-technological nature (e.g., a reorganisation of work practices)[9]. However, the most readily measurable manifestations of technological achievement — those from the development of patentable technology and from pure science — are often those which, under modern conditions of competition and international monitoring, are most easily copied and replicated by foreigners. Here, the 'public good' aspect is often international, and a primary focus on this kind of competitive advantage may be misleading.

Steel and the micro foundations of new growth theory

What is striking about the new economic growth is its lack of genuine 'micro foundations'. The latter phrase is usually taken to mean that the analytical structure under consideration has been built up from the axioms of choice. But here we are using the phrase — somewhat ironically — to suggest the lack of correspondence of orthodox growth theory with the well-known microeconomic histories of nations and sectors as they have tried to cope with the problems of economic growth.

The orthodox maximisation presumption is that all producers are operating on their cost frontiers: if they are not using 'optimal technology' given their factor prices, it is because the costs of acquiring this technology are too high. But this assumption is manifestly false, and there are endless examples from economic history. Japan in the 1960s made better use of existing technology to overwhelm rivals in the steel industry such as the US, even though much of this technology was even more relevant to the high labour cost US than to Japan[10]. Up to the 1960s, the steel industry was a series of national, relatively self-contained oligopolies. The Japanese industry descended upon the world like a shock. Japan was an unlikely candidate to create a revolution in this sector: not only was it without the requisite raw materials, but its low wage rates relative to other nations gave it little incentive (in neoclassical terms) to install capital intensive, 'best practice' technology. In fact, the dramatic results from Japan's use of the latest technologies such as continuous casting and the oxygen process (both of which had been invented in Europe) were a blatant demonstration that the industry world-wide had not been operating on the frontier of any 'production function' at all[11].

During the 1950s and 1960s, the Japanese steel industry received a great deal of help from government by way of both protective and promotion policies[12]. Preferential treatment was given to the steel industry with regard to foreign exchange allocations and a special licensing system for foreign technology encouraged the importation of technology. Some of the more important cases where this procedure aided the Japanese steel industry are in the importation of the operating technology for strip mills (1951), continuous casting technology (1954), and the basic oxygen converter process (1956). On the demand side, changes in the tariff system meant that the tariffs for steel products were high relative to the US and the European Coal and Steel Community, and this position remained until completion of the Kennedy Round GATT negotiations in 1967. Imports were effectively zero throughout that period. The 'visible hand' of government clearly had a decisive role to play in the critical period of the development of the industry.

The decisive innovations from the Japanese steel industry that brought it to world dominance and revolutionised the industry world-wide were not technological, but were concerned with the resourceful organisation of production and the assimilation of best practice technology developed abroad, the efficient use of material inputs and the realisation of hitherto underexploited scale economies. These innovations were almost exclusively managerial: the Japanese firm itself — 'the machine that changed the world' (as it has been referred to in the context of the automobile industry) and the managerial innovations associated with it have been the decisive aspect of Japanese economic success.

The supposedly exogenous changes which facilitated the development of the Japanese industry were to a great extent *brought about by actions consciously taken by the Japanese themselves*. Falling bulk transportation costs, for instance, were partially engendered by the industry's pioneering innovation of the giant bulk carrier for raw materials and the construction of steel plants in modern deep water port locations. Having established their industrial base, the Japanese then benefitted from a 'virtuous circle' of development, by which the high growth rate in the macro-economy and the government's long-term demand forecasts made the steel producers optimistic of continued increases in demand.

The competitive pressures and demonstration effects of Japanese success have subsequently led to dramatic changes in the behavioural patterns of steel producers (symbolised by, but not exclusively associated with the rise of the mini-mills), even in what had been the most notoriously laggard nations: thus, US firms are now in the forefront of current managerial innovation in the industry (see Dickson, 1991). As producers in the steel industry worldwide have become more aggressive, they have sought out overseas markets; this development is complemented by the increased tendency for purchasers of steel (e.g., in the car industry) to seek out the most economical (i.e., cost, delivery and quality) sources and not simply rely on local (i.e., national) producers.

The historical case of the steel industry is typical of the process by which differences in economic growth have emerged since the Second World War. In contradistinction to orthodox methodology, firms in the 1960s were not on the frontier of any 'production function'; the spectacular success of Japan was not linked to the presence of favourable factor endowments nor to the invention of new technology — 'competitive advantage' was created through the realisation of scale economies in the context of managerial innovation and imaginative adaptation of existing technologies; the very process of competition has dictated that the relationship of different firms and nations to the 'frontier' has shifted dramatically over time, and simple assumptions of constant degrees of productive efficiency are clearly irrelevant.

MICHAEL PORTER AS A CRITIC OF ORTHODOXY

Michael Porter's vast tome on the economic growth of nations (almost 900 pages and written with the help of an army of researchers) begins with four chapters outlining the approach and methodology, proceeds to analyse a host of industries worldwide, and gives the case histories of nine nations (of which only South Korea might qualify as being in the 'developing' category). It puts itself forth as a direct challenge to the approaches to economic growth in orthodox economics.

In fact, the approach taken by Porter is, in many ways, quite conventional. At first glance, it appears to be no more than an updating of the 'factor endowment-comparative advantage' approach of neoclassical theory, with the 'competitive advantages' replacing comparative advantage. Although cost advantages can be an aspect of competitive advantage, primary emphasis is placed on competitiveness with respect to different dimensions of 'quality'.

The competitive strength of the firms located in a nation will, it is claimed, depend on four major sets of influences: *factor conditions, demand conditions,* the presence or absence in the nation of *related and supporting industries* and the nature of domestic *competition* and the *strategy and structure* of its firms. Thus, traditional factor endowments appear as a minor determinant of the national environment which shape competitiveness. Instead, a nation's competitive advantages are based largely on the historical and institutional factors.

In its weakest aspects, Porter's competitive advantages (despite their claims to universality) are merely a set of generalisations derived from the experience of Japan and its great corporations in the previous few decades[13]. His work might thus be thought of as an updated version of John Kenneth Galbraith's *New Industrial State* of the 1960s, with its paean to General Motors, then perceived to be the way of the future for capitalism. At this level, Porter's work, like Galbraith's, is no more than an attempt at summarising the industrial development of the immediate past, but is no guide to future developments.

Despite weaknesses, however, Porter's analysis is highly stimulating. Embodied in his discussion are the germs of a critique of orthodox approaches to economic growth and intimations of a more useful approach. It is these elements of his work which we shall be emphasising below.

Factors of production

What primarily makes Porter interesting as a critic of orthodoxy is his approach to competition. As a management consultant, he strongly opposes the orthodox, academic view that competition automatically eliminates inefficient producers and that production takes place at a well-defined possibility frontier. On the contrary, competition is seen as a process which continuously forces producers to increase their efficiency. The factors of production therefore also appear in a different light:

> Competitive advantage from factors depends on *how efficiently and how effectively they are deployed.* [...] The mere availability of factors is not sufficient to explain competitive success; indeed, virtually all nations have some attractive factor pools that have not been deployed in appropriate industries or have been deployed poorly. (ibid., p. 76)

In fact, Porter becomes so exuberant about the central role in development of the organisation and deployment of resources that he comes close to dismissing altogether the significance of human and physical infrastructure:

> Many developing nations have [...] achieved a level of economic development
> that means that they too possess comparable endowments of many factors. Their
> workforces have the education and the basic skills necessary to work in many
> industries [...] Many other nations now have the basic infrastructure, such as
> telecommunications, road systems and ports, required for most manufacturing
> industries. (ibid., p. 14)

In a footnote, he claims that physical infrastructure can be built in decades,
as the examples of South Korea and Singapore (!) demonstrate.

Domestic demand and competition

Having played down the importance of both human and physical
infrastructure, Porter must find the main sources of competitive advantage
elsewhere. A key element, he argues, is the existence of domestic markets
that are capable of engendering and sustaining demand in the nation's
key sectors. In contrast to other management consultants (e.g., Ohmae,
1985) who focus on the performance of the 'big players' and on globalisation, Porter attempts to deal with the question of how a nation *develops* into an international competitor:

> It might seem that home demand would be rendered less significant by the
> globalisation of competition, but this is not the case. The home market has a
> disproportionate impact on the firm's ability to perceive and interpret buyer
> needs. (ibid., p. 86)

Furthermore, and in common with other management consultants, he is
capable of considering the subtle and qualitative aspects of such questions. The link between the home market and export potential is not simply
an issue of large home demand engendering scale economies (as in most
formal models of growth and international trade). It is the quality rather
than the quantity of home demand which determines competitive
advantage:

> Firms are better able to perceive, understand, and act on buyer needs in their
> home market and tend to be more confident in doing so. Understanding needs
> requires access to buyers, open communication between them and a firm's top
> technical and managerial personnel, and an intuitive grasp of buyers' circum-
> stances. This is hard enough with home buyers. It is extremely difficult to
> achieve, in practice, with foreign buyers because of distance from headquarters
> and because the firm is not truly an insider with full acceptance and access.
> (ibid., pp. 86–7)

Because of these informational aspects, competitive advantages develop when the special character of the home market gives local firms 'a clearer or earlier picture of buyer needs than foreign firms have' or when 'home buyers *pressure* local firms to innovate faster and achieve more sophisticated competitive advantages compared to foreign rivals' (ibid., p. 86).

Porter offers as another developmental principle the need for intense domestic competition between firms in those sectors which are to be internationally competitive. His approach, however, is not derived from orthodox efficiency analysis, but is related more to a behavioural, dynamic view of the competitive process:

> The presence of domestic rivals nullifies the types of advantage that come simply from being in the nation, such as factor costs [...] (by forcing) a nation's firms to seek *higher order* and ultimately more sustainable sources of competitive advantage. (ibid., p. 119)

Thus, for Porter competitive advantage *never* seems to come from monopolistic advantages and practices, nor from the presence of weaker pollution and child labour laws in the areas of operation. To coin a phrase, what is good for General Motors is good for the country, or so it seems from the consultant's vantage point. The argument is based on dynamic considerations, and is concerned with the *behaviour* of firms:

> Nowhere is the process of domestic rivalry more evident than in Japan, where it is all-out warfare in which many companies fail to achieve profitability. With goals that stress market share, Japanese companies engage in a continuing struggle to outdo each other. Shares fluctuate markedly. (ibid., p. 121)

But this kind of argument can come close to tautology. The question at issue is, precisely, how is such an aggressive, competitive environment *engendered*? Merely pointing out the existence of such an environment in Japan does not answer that question. Porter himself appears to suggest that the need for aggressive and innovative firms carries policy implications that are more or less in conformity with orthodox recommendations for developing countries' growth strategies:

> Among the strongest empirical findings from our research is the association between domestic rivalry and the creation and persistence of competitive advantage in an industry [...] We found [...] few 'national champions', or firms with virtually unrivalled domestic positions, that were internationally competitive. Instead, most were uncompetitive though often heavily subsidised and protected. (ibid., p. 117)

Porter's evidence, however, tells a different story. Even South Korea (p. 473), a nation in which the three largest *chaebol* (conglomerates) had sales equal to 36 percent of national product in 1984 (Amsden [1989], p. 116)[14], and 32 percent of total exports in 1988 (Porter, 1990, p. 472), is described as one of 'fierce and cutthroat rivalry' (p. 473)[15]. If Porter's description is an accurate one, it thus contradicts the traditional emphasis in industrial economics on market structure as the primary determinant of behaviour. On the other hand, it may simply indicate, in a tautological manner, that firms which act aggressively at home are likely to do so abroad as well.

Linkages and clusters

Arguably, Porter's most significant contribution is contained in the discussion concerned with non-market infrastructural and geographical links[16]. He claims that 'the basic unit of analysis for understanding competition is the industry' (ibid., p. 33), but it becomes clear that Porter's truly distinctive unit of analysis is the cluster, which consists of '[...] industries related by links of various kinds' (ibid., p. 131). He thus offers a broad conceptualisation of the unit of analysis relevant for industrial development, one which includes those firms supplying inputs for the industry and those making complementary products. The engendering of such infrastructures is seen as a key aspect of a strategy for emerging as an international competitor:

> As advantages (in a specific 'priority' sector) are developed [...] a national industry can achieve *remarkable rates of improvement and innovation* for a period of years or even decades. New domestic rivals spin off which open up new industry segments. Suppliers develop whose capabilities and resources allow more rapid improvement in process technology than firms themselves could support. Buyers with growing sophistication open up more new product avenues to pursue. (ibid., p. 161)

One may rightly complain that Porter's exposition here muddles up the virtues for national economic development of vertical integration, domestic rivalry and home market strength. The priorities among these different aspects of 'the cluster' are thus unclear for a nation seeking guidance on economic development. But despite these ambiguities, it is precisely in his discussion of forms of vertical connection considered at the level of the firm ('linkages') or within the nation ('clusters') that Porter's great strength is to be found. Following directly from the example of Japanese industry, these vertical connections are seen to have an efficacy far beyond their orthodox justification in terms of 'market failure' (see Williamson, 1975), and are part of the firm's and the nation's whole strategic positioning:

> Linkages not only connect activities inside a company but also create interdependencies between a firm and its suppliers and channels. A company can create competitive advantage by better optimising or co-ordinating these links to the outside [...] the opportunities for saving through coordinating with suppliers and channels go far beyond logistics and order processing, and encompass R&D, after-sale service, and many other activities [...] (pp. 42–3).

These vertical linkages have a dynamic aspect as well. Thus, for Italian jewelry makers, an advantage they possess in using Italian jewelry making equipment is their ready access to these cost effective inputs. But, for Porter:

> More significant than access to machinery or other inputs is the advantage that home-based suppliers provide in terms of ongoing coordination [...] Perhaps the most important benefit of home based suppliers, however, is in the *process of innovation and upgrading* [...] Suppliers help firms perceive new methods and opportunities to apply new technology. Firms gain quick access to information to new ideas and insights, and to supplier innovations. They have the opportunity to influence suppliers' technical efforts as well as to serve as test sites for development work. (ibid., p. 103)

Once again, it is impossible to deny the perspicacious nature of his observations: 'Pressuring local suppliers not to serve foreign competitors is ultimately self-defeating. 'Captive' suppliers dependent solely on a firm or the national industry, will provide less impetus to improve and upgrade' (ibid., p. 104). Porter's comments elucidate why IBM's 'captive' semiconductor division, selling exclusively to IBM was likely to fall behind its rivals, and probably tell us more about the failures of Soviet industry than most conventional explanations.

But in his analysis of infrastructure, as in other contexts, Porter's lack of precision contributes to ambiguity. Thus personal relationships through schooling and military service are factors that facilitate information flow within clusters by 'creating trust and mitigating perceived differences in economic interest between vertically and horizontally linked firms' (pp. 152–3). But, given his insistence on the necessity and significance of domestic rivalry, how should one balance the efficacious aspects of such factors with their clearly anticompetitive (see eg., Scherer, 1980, ch. 6) possibilities?

It should be emphasised, finally, that according to Porter it is not just vertical linkages that matter. The presence of related and supporting industries is also important because the pool of factors and the rate at which they are created are also shaped by them.

> Such industries possess or stimulate their own mechanisms for creating and upgrading specialised factors (and these) factors are usually transferable. (ibid., p. 135)

These arguments collectively form a powerful case against the inherent virtues of narrowly defined sectoral specialisation emerging from free trade, most especially in the context of developing nations (see as well Banuri, 1991). This is especially true for the last-named argument as it applies to the upgrading of human capital as a 'specialised factor'.

CONCLUSION

We have centred on a particular set of failures of orthodox growth theory. The resurgence of this literature in its 'new' forms has permitted the abandonment of some of the more unpalatable aspects of orthodoxy, most specifically, the conclusion that society's rate of investment was not linked to its long term rate of growth. Furthermore it is able to consider the role of human capital development in economic growth.

With these renewed aspects of relevance, orthodox growth theory has experienced a revival. But some of the fundamental failures of this approach remain present in the new doctrine. By implicitly assuming that 'the market' has generated an efficient use of factors of production, orthodoxy leaves little room for the effects of organisational structure and institutions on economic growth. The true 'micro foundations' of economic growth, as we have seen, are intrinsically linked to these factors.

Porter's book powerfully addresses these failures in the orthodox approach. As a management consultant, he inevitably finds it insufficient simply to leave decision making to 'the market', and he has forceful ideas about how an economy should be organised to best promote its competitive advantage. Of greater significance and originality, Porter's analysis also contains a strong developmental perspective. His extensive discussions of non-market infrastructural linkages of various kinds contain important aspects of a viable critique of orthodox growth models.

But Porter's analysis also suffers from serious weaknesses. His developmental perspective sits uncomfortably with the timeless, parametric nature of some of the competitive advantages he himself has described. Many 'facts' generating these advantages are discussed as if they have existed, and will exist for all time. Thus, for Porter:

> [...] the central question to be answered is why do firms based in particular nations achieve international success in distinct segments and industries? (ibid., p. 18)

With the present level of internationalisation of economic activity, this identification of a nation's economic viability with its competitive success internationally may be valid for most countries, but the transition in the nature of international economic activity — from foot race to warfare — is a recent phenomenon: the US rose to world economic supremacy almost exclusively through its industries being tested in the *domestic* arena (Chandler, 1990).

The detailed analysis of competitive advantage occasionally betrays the same lack of historical perspective. The discussion of domestic demand, for instance, centres on the important insight that sophisticated and demanding buyers pressure local firms to meet high standards in terms of product quality, features and service (cf. ibid., p. 89). But there's the rub. Porter's next sentence tells us that in Japan, for example, consumers are highly sophisticated and knowledgeable in purchasing audio equipment. Porter's 1990 perspective causes him to read history backwards. In the crucial period for the 'take off' of the Japanese audio industry, the 1960s, their domestic market was *incomparably* smaller than that of the US and demonstrably less sophisticated than that in either the US or the UK. Indeed, given these *obvious* truths, the question occupying decision makers in the poorer countries of the world remains — how did the Japanese do it? It will not do simply to project the present back onto the past, as Porter does.

In a similar way, the existence of low raw materials prices is described as if it were part of an inherent tendency of economic development. But the present trend in raw materials prices could easily reverse itself due to ecological constraints, or institutional change, such as the recreation of the cartels that until recently has dominated many raw materials prices[17]. Furthermore, the focus on present-day conditions for raw materials may contribute to Porter's general dismissal of low factor prices as part of an economic strategy for growth (e.g., pp. 49–50). This dismissal may be sensible advice, most especially for the world's advanced economies. But

South Korea's remarkable growth in the 1960s, which propelled it into the higher reaches of economic development, was fuelled precisely by a low wage strategy (Amsden, 1989, ch. 3)[18].

These examples point to three weaknesses in Porter's approach: we have in Porter the paradox of an analysis from a developmental standpoint juxtaposed with the absence of a notion of contingent development, a weak historical perspective and a focus on the problems and needs of the richer countries (despite the claims to the universality of his approach). These are weaknesses which Porter's approach shares with orthodox growth models.

None of the popular critics of orthodoxy has enunciated a full-fledged alternative view of the process of economic growth[19], and none has focused on its most important aspect — the problems of economic development for the poorer nations of the world. But they have succeeded in highlighting weaknesses in the orthodox literature and have made more difficult the claim that 'there is no alternative' to the prescriptions emanating from orthodoxy.

NOTES

1. All references to Michael Porter's writings will be to this source unless otherwise noted.
2. The tortuous history of the attempts to come to grips with the Leontief paradox illustrates the difficulty involved in testing predictions which 'in principle' should be readily testable.
3. It is not the introduction of a neoclassical production function which precludes this possibility. By itself, the existence of a smooth and well-behaved, aggregate production function would neither invalidate Harrod's analysis nor ensure that the choice of technique will be such that the warranted and natural growth rates coincide (see Skott, 1989, chapter 5).
4. The models differ in the way they deal with this issue. Romer (1986) and Lucas (1988), for instance, exclude non-convexities that are internal to the firm and retain the assumption of perfect competition while some later models, e.g., Romer (1990) and Grossman and Helpman (1991a, 1991b) introduce elements of imperfect competition.
5. See Skott and Auerbach (1994) for a discussion of the new theory from the perspective of heterodox theories of cumulative causation.
6. Of course a genuinely free international market, in which the goods of poor nations could be sold without discrimination in rich countries, would be a great improvement on the present international economic regime imposed by the rich nations. Such a market, however, is unlikely to be forthcoming.
7. See also Nelson and Winter (1982), Dosi *et al.* (1988) and Rosenberg *et al.* (1992) for a discussion of neoclassical and alternative conceptions of technical change.

8. We would note as well the relatively recent phenomenon of transnational technological collaboration (see, for example, Bradshaw, 1993).
9. In defense of this bias it could be argued that the discrete inventions lend themselves much better to 'objective' statistical measurement and thus provide a more solid foundation for the analysis. But we then have the odd situation of the development of policy prescriptions in favour of investment in 'technology' derived from a methodological predisposition for measurable manifestations of achievement.
10. Auerbach (1988, ch. 9) and Adams and Mueller (1982); we would like to thank Graeme Henley for additional material on the steel industry used here.
11. The high concentration in the US industry may well have encouraged X-inefficiency, but the even higher concentration in the Japanese industry — overseen furthermore by a MITI whose views on co-ordinated behaviour have been a good deal more benign than those of the US Justice Department — has been consistent with a tremendous dynamism.
12. The factual aspects of the discussion below on Japan largely follow Yamawaki (1988).
13. The influence on Porter of the phenomenon of Japan, with its tremendous success in specific industrial sectors juxtaposed with its relatively backward retailing and agricultural sectors, is evident in one of his most fundamental conflicts with the orthodox growth literature in which he emphasises the need for the development of key sectors and industries, as opposed to a focus on the measurement of overall productivity of factors in the economy.
14. This figure may somewhat overestimate the power of these companies, since it is a ratio of sales to national income, and the latter is a value added concept.
15. In fact, South Korea offers many counterexamples of the need to abjure the creation of 'national champions'. One of the most spectacular is POSCO, the state-owned steel company which is, in Porter's words, the exception that 'proves the rule' (p. 473), whatever that means. One of the keys to its success seems to have been the careful tutelage received by the national industry from Nippon Steel as part of Japan's war reparations (Amsden, 1989, chapter 12). Perhaps the true lesson to be learned from this case is that a good way for poorer nations to develop is to retain domestic ownership of industries, and for the richer nations to offer extensive financial and technical assistance of the kind given by Japan to the Korean steel industry. The process could begin with the US paying reparations in this form to Guatemala, El Salvador and Vietnam.
16. His analysis has close links with the literature on economic development, and in his examination of the role of supplier industries (to be discussed below), Porter gives reference to Hirschman (1958), perhaps not an everyday occurrence among management consultants.
17. The relative price of many raw materials might also rise as a result of techno-logical change: a wooden covering is, relatively speaking, far more expensive for a 1993 £99 CD player than its equivalent £599 CD player of 1986.
18. Similarly, Porter views *advanced factors*, which include modern digital communications infrastructure, graduate engineers and research institutes, as 'the most significant ones for comparative advantage' (p. 77). On the basis of this kind of analysis, can we expect a whole generation of leaders in developing countries to be bullied into reaching for the 'commanding heights' with the production of computer scientists and modern digital communications infra-structure at the expense of resources for nutrition, basic literacy and trams?
19. Of the well-known critics, Reich (1991) comes closest to a rounded view of economic development in his exposition of a 'virtuous circle' of economic

growth based around education and infrastructural development.

REFERENCES

Adams, W. and D. Mueller (1982), 'The Steel Industry', in Adams, W. (ed.), *The Structure of American Industry*, Macmillan, sixth edition, New York.
Amsden, A. (1989), *Asia's Next Giant South Korea and Late Industrialization*, Oxford University Press, Oxford.
Auerbach, P. (1988), *Competition*, Basil Blackwell, Oxford.
Banuri, T. (1991), *Economic Liberalization: No Panacea*, Oxford University Press, Oxford.
Baxter, A. (1992), 'The Machine Tool Industry', *Financial Times Survey*, vol. 6, May.
Bradshaw, D. (1993), 'Two Heads Are Better Than One', *Financial Times*, vol. 6, March.
Chandler, A. (1977), *The Visible Hand*, Belknap Press, Cambridge Mass.
Chandler, A. (1990), *Scale and Scope*, Belknap Press, Cambridge Mass.
Dickson, M. (1991) 'How Nucor is Stealing a March on the Big Mills', *Financial Times*, vol. 29, May.
Dosi, G., C. Freeman, R. Nelson, G. Silverberg and L. Soete, (1988), *Technical Change and Economic Theory*, Pinter Publishers, London.
Elbaum, B. and W. Lazonick (1986), *The Decline of the British Economy*, Clarendon Press, Oxford.
Galbraith, J.K. (1967), *The New Industrial State*, Penguin Books.
Grossman, G.M. and E. Helpman, (1991a), 'Endogenous Product Cycles', *Economic Journal*, vol. 101, pp. 1214–1229.
Grossman, G.M. and E. Helpman, (1991b), 'Quality Ladders and Product Cycles', *Quarterly Journal of Economics*, pp. 557–586.
Hirschman, A. (1958), *The Strategy of Economic Development*. Yale University Press, New Haven.
Lucas, R. (1988), 'On the Mechanics of Economic Development', *Journal of Monetary Economics*, vol. 22, pp. 3–42.
Nelson, R. and S. Winter (1982), *An Evolutionary Theory of Economic Change*, Belknap Press of Harvard University Press, Cambridge Mass.
Nelson, R. and G. Wright, (1992), 'The Rise and Fall of American Technological Leadership: the Postwar Era in Historical Perspective', *Journal of Economic Literature December*, 1931–64.
OECD (1992), 'Industrial Policy in OECD Countries', *Annual Review 1992*, OECD, Paris.
Ohmae, K. (1985), *Triad Power*, The Free Press, New York.
Porter, M. (1990), *Competitive Advantage of Nations*, Macmillan, London.
Reich, R. (1991), 'The Real Economy', *Atlantic*, vol. 267, no. 2, pp. 35–52.
Romer, P. (1986), 'Increasing Returns and Long-run Growth', *Journal of Political Economy*, vol. 94, pp. 1002–37.
Romer, P. (1989), 'Increasing Returns and New Developments in the Theory of Economic Growth', *NBER Working Paper*, 3098.
Romer, P. (1990), 'Endogenous Technical Change', *Journal of Political Economy*, pp. 71–102.
Rosenberg, N., R. Landau and D. Mowery (1992), *Technology and the Wealth of Nations*, Stanford University Press, Stanford CA.

Scherer, F.M. (1980), *Industrial Market Structure and Economic Performance*, Rand McNally, Chicago.

Skott, P. (1989), *Conflict and Effective Demand in Economic Growth*, Cambridge University Press, Cambridge.

Skott, P. and P. Auerbach (1994), 'Cumulative Causation and the 'New' Theories of Economic Growth', *Journal of Post Keynesian Economics*, forthcoming.

Solow, R.M. (1956), 'A Contribution to the Theory of Economic Growth', *Quarterly Journal of Economics*, vol. 70, pp. 65–94.

Solow, R.M. (1993), 'Dr. Rivlin's Diagnosis & Mr. Clinton's Remedy', *New York Review of Books*, vol. XL, no. 6, March 25.

Steindl, J. (1976), *Maturity and Stagnation in American Capitalism*, Monthly Review Press, Second edition, New York.

Swan, T.W. (1956), 'Economic Growth and Capital Accumulation', *Economic Record*, vol. 32, pp. 334–61.

Teece, D.J. (1992), 'Strategies for Capturing Financial Benefits from Technological Innovation', in Rosenberg et al., (ed.), *Technology and the Wealth of Nations*, Stanford University Press, Stanford CA.

Williamson, O. (1975), *Markets and Hierarchies*, Macmillan, New York.

Yamawaki, H. (1988), 'The Steel Industry', in Komiya, et al. (eds.), *Industrial Policy of Japan*, Academic Press, Tokyo.

9. Standards as Institutions. Problems with Creating All-European Standards for Terminal Equipment

Claes-Fredrik Helgesson, Staffan Hultén and Douglas J. Puffert

INTRODUCTION

It is widely recognised that standards are an essential part of the modern world. In this chapter the process where terminal standards change within the telecommunications sector in Europe is examined. In focus are the EC efforts to establish all-European terminal standards and the problems connected with realising this manifest goal. These activities are part of the larger institutional change often labelled deregulation of telecommunications which is taking place in many regions of the world. In short this deregulation could be described as a change where the principle of the 'invisible hand' is seen as more desirable than the old principle of the 'large visible hand' in coordinating the production of telecommunications equipment and services[1]. In the case of European terminal standards this transformation produces co-existence of, and competition between, three standard-setting regulatory regimes: the old national regulatory regime, the emerging market driven regulatory regime and the regulatory regime of the EC.

Stability and Change of Standards

> Throughout the scheme of life of that portion of mankind that clusters about the centres of modern culture the industrial process makes itself felt and enforces a degree of conformity to the canon of accurate quantitative measurement. There comes to prevail a degree of standardization and precise mechanical adjustment of the details of everyday life, which presumes a facile and unbroken working of all those processes that minister to these standardized human wants. (Veblen, 1904, p. 14)

164

The existence of standards facilitates coordination of humans and artifacts and thus increases the possible scale in production and the possible division of human activity. Standards can hence be seen as a somewhat arbitrary agreement on how to measure weight, how to define a telephone set and so on, where the established standard gives us a form of constructed stability. An interesting problem occurs when forces require a standard to change or when forces require new standards to be developed and adopted. These forces can be propelled by new technological developments revealing new and yet unstandardised dimensions, or new demands for increased compatibility between different already established standards. In such cases the prevailing stability gained is disturbed, leading the system into a process where old standards are redefined and/or new ones are created. The working of the system then becomes broken and complicated.

The EC and Telecommunication Terminal Standards

Regarding terminal standards, the EC tries to change the regulatory framework, to harmonise established national standards and to establish and promote new all-European standards for new telecommunications services. The focus is therefore both on handling old terminal standards ex post and to create and promote all-European terminal standards ex ante. In the first case the new harmonised standards will be an interim solution that will last until the emerging future telecommunications systems have spread over Europe. In the second case the new standard will be extremely costly to implement in the short run, and its implementation may produce technical choices that delimit the future development of the telecommunications industry.

The believed advantages of creating a Community-wide telecommunications terminal market are new opportunities, increased strength of the terminal industry and lower prices for the terminals (Richter, 1991). An additional advantage for the consumers will be the possibility of freely moving around in Europe with their terminals. The difficulties for the EC with creating this market are the problem with ex-post harmonising of existing national standards and the problem of enforcing new international standards. If standards are viewed as institutions, i.e., as diffused and shared rules for action, these two problems refer to either changing established institutions or rapidly creating new institutions.

Three sources of inertia in switching from one standard to another are technical restrictions, the users' reluctance to change equipment and the vested interests of the owners of the production equipment. The existence of different terminal standards creates both easily solvable problems and problems that are very difficult to solve. Problems caused by differences in the configuration of the dial plate or the design of the socket can, for instance, easily be mastered by simple measures like switching the dial plate on the individual telephone set or the introduction of a standardised adapter for sockets. Other problems are much more difficult to solve, e.g., the inherent variety in national telecommunications signalling standards. These technical differences have hitherto effectively impeded the movement towards European standards for telecommunications terminals.

The users' willingness to change from one terminal to another or from one system technology to another has varied from case to case. The most notable feature is that transitional standards have emerged that have captured significant shares of the markets for wireless and wired telecommunications. In the mobile telecommunications networks in Europe diverse standards have evolved. Before the introduction of GSM in 1992 a number of incompatible mobile telephone systems had more than 4 million subscribers. To some extent international roaming existed in some networks, e.g., in the NMT systems, and subscribers that belonged to the same system standard in different countries benefited from lower terminal prices due to economies of scale. At present no feasible European standard exists for mobile data networks. The heterogeneous mobile data system standards do not even permit the development of international terminal markets due to the usage of different frequency bands in different countries.

In the wired network the absence of all-European standards for analogue telecommunications services together with the difficulties in developing all-European standards for the new digital telecommunications technologies have effectively restricted the breakthrough for any new standardised terminal equipment. Private consumers and organisations do of course buy new terminals but the markets are still national.

Another large problem for the EC has been the long time taken to produce new all-European standards. This has caused much concern and has in some cases led to changes in the regulatory framework to speed the standardisation process by reducing the influence of vested interests. The rule of standard setting in Europe was for instance changed, from unanimous decisions in CEPT (Conference of European Postal and Telecommunications Administrations) to majority decisions in ETSI (European Telecommunications Standards Institute), to restrict the possibilities for an actor, or a small group of actors, to block the development of new standards.

PERSPECTIVES ON STANDARDS

Standardisation is, as Clark (1923) noted, one of the most pervasive terms in the lexicon of business. Chamberlin saw perfect product standardisation as the prerequisite for perfect competition. He further on stated that:

> Not only goods but sellers, must be 'standardized' under pure competition. Anything which makes buyers prefer one seller to another, be it personality, reputation, or [...] must be identical, otherwise individual sellers will have a degree of control over their individual prices'[2.] (Chamberlin, 1938)

From an economic point of view, standardisation provides benefits for users and vendors. Standards produce benefits through greater scale economies in production, enhanced competition among suppliers, net work externalities on the demand side (Farrell and Saloner, 1986), and reduced transaction costs by improved product recognition and decreased buyer dissatisfaction (Kindleberger, 1983). However, Abbott (1955) recognised that the effect of the enforcement of some standards destroys or diminishes quality competition, while other standards, e.g., of weight, enhance quality competition.

From a technological point of view standard has two meanings: that of a convention or code of practice, and that of the technology that comes to dominate (Arthur, 1988). Hence, this perspective primarily emphasizes that standards reduce the variety of practices and technologies.

Both the economic and the technological perspective overlook the importance of the institutional setting of the standard. They are delimited in both time and space. In industry, standardised production techniques and standardised products are generally confined to the production plant and its historical evolution. In a similar way standardisation of infra-structural systems evolved within and were delimited by the borders of the nation state. Later on, the strive towards international compatibility of infrastructural systems has gradually transformed the old national standards to a patchwork of national and international standards.

From an institutional point of view, standards are vehicles for facilitating coordination of economic activities. Instead of repeated coordination between actors, a standard solves a number of dilemmas for actors within the industrial system. A standard therefore diminishes the need for short-run coordination. On the other hand, there is an increased need for concerted action when standards are created or changed.

ON THE ECONOMICS OF STANDARDISATION

Research on the economics of standardisation has concentrated on four areas: (1) the economic value of standards and who gains from standards; (2) the timing of standardisation; (3) the lock-in of standards; and (4) the standard setting process.

The Economic Value of Standards

From an economic point of view standardisation is in itself desirable. If no uncertainty about the optimal standard exists, early standardisation removes the incentive to wait for the standard to settle down, and thus encourages early adoption of the technology (Farrell and Saloner, 1986). Unless a technical standard is based on patented processes, it is available simultaneously to all producers in the industry. This is the case of technical standards as public or collective goods (Kindleberger, 1983). In this case, firms independently or through collective activity choose the same technical standards for their products (Berg, 1989). If the standard is based on a patented process (ibid.) or if a firm sets a de facto standard (Farrell and Saloner, 1986), then the standard is a private good. When a standard is a private good, firms select different standards, and their products are more or less incompatible.

According to Farrell (1990), in information industries the users and the small vendors typically push for standards while dominant firms often resist or are reluctant. The large firms are less interested in making their products compatible with the smaller firms' products because they can lose more from giving away their competitive advantage than they can gain from the users increased willingness to pay, due to increased network externalities. Hence, when benefits and costs of standardisation are asymmetric, e.g., when small firms and users are winning and large firms are losing, a large firm can block standardisation (Katz and Shapiro, 1985).

The economic rationale of standards is that they produce benefits that are larger than the costs. Farrell and Saloner (1986) list three kinds of benefits through standardisation. First, standards allow different manufacturers to exploit economies of scale in production and distribution and they allow savings in the costs of learning how to use a good. Second, when a standard is set for a network technology positive effects evolve in the form of network externalities. 'A product may simply be more valuable to each buyer the more others have the product' (ibid.), and complementary products may be more readily or cheaply available as more people have the standardised product. Third, Farrell and Saloner (ibid.) claim that standardisation produces benefits through enhanced competition because (1) standardised products give direct competition in price and performance, (2) it commits producers to compete in an aftermarket in for instance spare and replacement parts, and (3) it reduces the importance of second-sourcing as a way to secure deliveries.

But standards also produce social costs. If variety is valuable in itself, or if it represents a better option than standardisation for innovation, then it is possible that a standard is less beneficial than a non-standard. Further on, if users value a differentiated supply then a standardised supply is less attractive than a non-standardised supply. The result of standardisation is a form of contest between the purchaser's preference and the producer's search for economical production (Clark, 1923). The beneficial effects of standards through enhanced competition are further restricted by the anti-competitive effects of dominant firm strategies (Berg, 1989). In principal, dominant firms can gain market power and reduce the demand for the competitors' products by refusing to ensure compatibility with competing standards and through predatory standard switching (Farrell and Saloner, 1986). Another possible social cost could occur if forced standardisation clusters the supply of products and thereby creates gaps in the chain of substitutes. Except for the institutional barriers erected, entrepreneurs would have golden opportunities to move into deserted product areas and earn excess profits (Abbott, 1955).

The Timing of Standardisation

Farell and Saloner (1986) write: 'Since standardisation itself is desirable, early standardisation is more desirable than late, if the same standard be set'. But a standard that is introduced later regularly benefits from advancements in technology. Consequently, a trade-off exists between exploiting the potential for technical change and the advantages of standardisation (Foray, 1990). 'To be more specific, for example, early standardisation of products may encourage innovation in complementary technologies and organisation, and it may promote subsequent incremental innovations designed to perfect the original technology. On the other hand, de facto standardisation may prematurely close off basic exploration of technological opportunities in a wide area' (David and Greenstein, 1990).

The Lock-in of Standards

The economic problem with a successful network technology standard is that it regularly deters entrepreneurs from launching a competing superior technology. Users are often unwilling to switch from an old to a new one because they are unsure about the benefits of the new standard and are unwilling to replace equipment that still functions (Farrell and Saloner, 1986). Besen (1992) has labelled this the consumers' fear of being 'stranded' with the wrong technology, if he makes an early purchase.

The problem of an installed base of users locked-in to a standard loses importance when the growth rate of the system is large enough. This was true for mobile telephony in Sweden from 1965–1992. The installed base of mobile telephones was 100 users in 1965 and from that time on, four new system standards were introduced as the number of subscribers increased with an average of 40% a year for more than 25 years.

Inertia to switch from an old to a new standard may also arise on the supply side. The producers' dilemma is in fact more fundamental than the users' dilemma. The latter only risks his investment in the equipment while the former may face bankruptcy if making the wrong choice. The producer is, however, in a better position to influence the future development of the industry. This is particularly evident in the committee work of ETSI where nearly all major telecommunications equipment producers and operators participate regularly, but only a few large telecommunications users.

The Standard-setting Process

The setting of a standard is basically a coordination problem. It can either be a sequential market driven process that creates a *de facto* standard or a process confined to a committee or a government agency that ends with the simultaneous introduction of de jure standard (Farrell and Saloner, 1986; David and Greenstein, 1990).

The effectiveness of the standard-setting is determined by the speed of the process, the technical optimality of the standard and the costs incurred during the process. Sometimes the market mechanism achieves rapid and effective coordination. But generally, committees are desirable if they work effectively and if the losses from product design mistakes are large compared to the costs of the committee (Farrell and Saloner, 1988).

STANDARDS AS INSTITUTIONS

Although research on the economics of standards and standardisation has illuminated several aspects of standards, they have nevertheless somewhat delimited the dynamic and contextual aspects of standards and standardisation. In this part, the perspective in these respects will therefore be expanded by viewing standards as institutions.

A network technology standard is in itself a device facilitating coordination at the primary level, but it requires a solution to other coordination problems in order to be established. The creation of the standard has to be coordinated to some degree, and subsequently the diffusion and widespread acceptance of the standard has to be coordinated. The existence of any standard is consequently the result of a transfer of the coordination problem from the primary level to the level of coordinating the creation and enforcement of the standard.

The establishment of a standard can be propelled by a market-mediated process or it can be driven by political processes taking place in agencies or committees (David and Greenstein, 1990). In this chapter, the label regulatory regime has been chosen to signify how this is coordinated for a particular standard. The very nature of standards presupposes the existence of some kind of regulatory regime for them to be established: 'A regime exists when interaction between the parties is not unconstrained or is not based on independent decision making' (Stein, 1982). Once established, vested interests and momentum arise in connection to the standard. These forces will influence future changes of the standard: Vested interests seeking to influence future development (Farrell, 1990), and the inertia created by the momentum of the installed base (Hughes, 1987), will both counteract radical change of the standard.

An established standard can therefore be seen as an institution. It is a widely accepted code facilitating coordination that is embedded in a regulatory regime. Vested interests and the momentum of the installed base enforce its further acceptance and conservation. This means that any given standard cannot be understood apart from the regulatory regime establishing and maintaining it[3].

In the case where there is a desire to replace old standards with new, as in the telecommunications terminal case, a large number of coordination problems have to be solved: (1) the regulatory regime may have to be altered, i.e., the coordination mechanism establishing and maintaining the old standard may not be suitable for creating the new standard; (2) the vested interests of the old standard may have to be coordinated or forced to promote the new standard; (3) the installed base may need to be induced to switch to the new standard. A change of standard is no less than an institutional change, demanding not only the standard itself to be changed, but also demanding other components connected to it to change.

Until the last few years, it was generally assumed that telecommunications standards were set formally and explicitly, by governments or monopolistic firms domestically and by the ITU internationally (Farrell, 1990). This structure for setting standards has now completely ruptured and has been replaced by a heterogeneous structure of competing regulatory regimes influencing the setting of standards on an international level. Three different kinds of regulatory regimes can be identified. These are: (1) the old kind of nation-oriented regulatory regimes; (2) the emerging regulatory regime driven by market actors within the industrial system; and (3) the formal regulatory regime developed within the EC.

THE REGULATORY REGIME OF NATIONAL TELECOMMUNICATIONS STANDARDS

The regulatory regimes establishing the earlier telecommunications standards were inward looking. The system building and subsequent transformation of the technological system principally aimed at keeping the local systems connected to the national system and avoiding sunk costs. Consequently the national systems showed a path-dependent development in which the early technical choices have come to influence technical decisions all the way until the present situation. The standards reflected: (1) the choices made by business enterprises; (2) the growth of the nation's GNP; (3) the country's geography; (4) the choices made by the country's neighbouring countries; (5) the time of the system building and (6) the national language. These sources of variety produced national telecommunications standards that to some degree were internationally incompatible. The lack of compatibility was particularly manifest for teleequipment that were adapted to local systems. The national tele-communications systems have acquired different technological styles[4].

The variety in telecommunications terminal standards is evident in many different aspects. Listed below are some examples where national standards for telephones differ:

1. The sockets used for connecting telephones to the network differ heavily between countries. Almost every European country has adapted their own standard for sockets.

2. The signalling system between telephone set and the local exchange differs between countries, e.g., in the number of pulses representing different digits or even the specified length of each pulse.

3. The amperage used by the telephone sets differs between countries. This means that telephones using a higher amperage than the national standard may disturb the transmission on other local lines.

4. The specifications for assessing speech quality of a telephone set differ between countries. It has been argued that this is a result of different languages requiring different specifications of good speech quality.

5. The procedures for testing an apparatus according to a national standard also differ between countries. The result is that the tests necessary for testing a specific aspect of an apparatus may differ even if the specification of that aspect happens to be the same.

The variety in the standards is, as the last example shows, not only a variety in the specifications as such but is also evident in how a particular aspect of the standard is tested, which probably is the result of institutionalised engineering practices. The regulatory regimes establishing these national standards have in essence been national and the variety created is obviously also reflected in national vested interests and inertia created by the momentum of the installed base. The national focus of the early regulatory regimes is consequently now reflected in nationally focused forces conserving the established national standards.

STANDARDS DRIVEN BY NETWORKS OF INDUSTRIAL ACTORS

The old nation-oriented regulatory regimes for setting standards are increasingly replaced by various actors and groups of actors within the industry that develop and seek to impose their standards on an international level. Actors co-operate and compete with other actors and together this forms an industrial network[5] within which several new and competing standards emerge. In this form of standard setting, the coordination takes place between various industrial actors and it produces a diverse set of standards.

This outcome is especially evident in the swift development of mobile communications. One explanation for the diversity of the standards is the mobile networks' rapid growth rate during the last 10–15 years. The number of subscribers in mobile telephone networks has increased from less than 1 million in 1981 to nearly 20 million in 1993. Mobile data networks emerged in the late 1980's and presently they have 500,000 to 1,000,000 users.

In the mobile telephone operation it took 30–40 years to go from regional systems within countries, over national systems and bilateral roaming agreements to a pan-European standard, GSM, in 1991 (Hultén and Mölleryd, 1993). Presently the installed base in analogue networks is 10–20 times larger than the installed base in the digital GSM networks and at the same time, new non-standard digital technologies are entering the market.

The digital mobile data networks are even more heterogeneous than the established analogue mobile telephone networks. The mobile data operators have not even been able to decide on using the same frequency bands for the same mobile system technology. Such deficiencies will effectively block movements towards international roaming agreements and the creation of international terminal markets. Further complications are: (1) that user needs are not well-known and (2) that system standards will develop according to the demands of the complementary computer industry.

Hence, in mobile communication operations, a path-dependent development is evident where feeble standards are being substituted by another set of feeble standards. The competing forces within the network of industrial actors effectively stall the development of sustainable standards.

THE ESTABLISHMENT OF EUROPEAN TERMINAL STANDARDS

In Europe, the European Community has sought to implement a common approach by the member states in the field of telecommunications since

1984 (Delcourt, 1991). Formally the European Community has moved forward, since then, with a number of directives that have laid the ground work for the future information technology and telecommunications infrastructure.

The lodestar for the EC has been the creation of an internationally competitive telecommunications infrastructure based on a more competitive supply of telecommunications equipment and services. This in turn has led to a desire to increase the element of competition within the industrial structure, so that the 'price-mechanism' could gain increased importance in the coordination of the industry.

The abundance of different standards in Europe came early into the focus of the EC regulators. The existence of many, often incompatible, standards for telecommunications terminals is, from an EC point of view, one of the impediments to the creation of an internationally competitive telecommunications infrastructure. It is certainly true that, e.g., different incompatible telecommunications telephone standards inhibit the free trade of telephones between European countries, and restrict competition in the European market for telephones. The EC therefore wants to gain some control over the standard setting process for future standards in the belief that this coordination cannot be left totally to the actors in the market.

In this struggle for decreasing the number of standards, the EC has come across the basic problem of standardisation: *ex ante* versus *ex post* standards. On the one hand, the EC wants to create new modern pan–European standards based on the latest technologies for different kinds of telecommunications terminals. On the other hand, the EC aims at rapidly increasing competition in the large existing equipment markets based on national standards and partly dated technologies. In order to succeed with both these objectives, the European Community has followed the parallel tracks of creating new standards based on modern telecommunications technology and into re-regulating the existing markets for telecommunications equipment.

Changing the regulatory regime for the established and diverse standards

The EC has taken two routes to increase competition in telecommunications terminal markets where national standards already exist. First, they have introduced a new harmonised approach to how manufacturers will get type approvals and the right to sell equipment in the different EC countries. Second, they seek to achieve a coherent standardisation policy and to harmonise the diverse national standards (Delcourt, 1991).

The new harmonised approach for type-approval procedures is meant to make it easier for manufacturers to gain access to different national markets. This effort became evident in 1984 when the EC commission concluded an agreement with CEPT to prepare common technical specifications for the approval of terminal equipment. Two years later CEPT presented the technical basis for the European norms for telecommunications when EC Directive 86/361 came into force (Richter, 1991). This directive placed a clear obligation on member states to allow connection of terminals to the public network on the basis of common conformity specifications. The Directive also envisaged the mutual recognition of type approval certificates for terminals, so called 'one-stop testing' (Delcourt, 1991). This step was taken with the telecommunications terminal Directive 91/263 that came into force in November 1992. The directive aims are:

1. To establish the final stage of the implementation of the single market for telecommunications terminal equipment based on essential requirements, which must be complied with and are legally enforceable.

2. To bring into force harmonised procedures for certification, testing, marketing, quality assurance and product surveillance of terminal equipment.

3. To guarantee the right to connect terminal equipment, legally placed on the market, to public telecommunications networks without further procedures (Richter, 1991).

Hence the procedures required for getting a type approval should be the same for all EC countries even if the national standards are different. With the requirements of the different national standards made public and with harmonised test procedures, a manufacturer can go to any accredited testhouse and test the firm's equipment for any EC country's standard.

The EC has also tried to harmonise the actual standards for different types of terminal equipment. It commissioned CEPT and after 1988 ETSI to work out a harmonised basic standard for normal telephones based on a compromise of the present national standards. This work has not produced any new harmonised pan-European standard and many observers believe it never will due to the technical diversity of the national standards. There are even problems in agreeing on how different aspects of a telephone standard should be measured.

Creating new all–European standards

The EC has given the introduction of new telecommunications services a large amount of interest. The idea is that by forcing on early standardisation, the new emerging telecommunications services will be based on pan-European standards, thus enhancing competition for the terminal equipment.

The process of creating a new all-European standard involves a number of organisations. The formal work with creating the standard is done within ETSI which is commissioned by the European commission to develop new standards and to develop technical specifications and procedures on how to test equipment. When the standard is completed, it is sent out for public comment for many weeks and is furthermore examined by three bodies within the EC: the European Commission itself, ACTE (the Approvals Council for Telecommunications Equipment), and TRAC (the Technical Recommendations Advisory Committee) (Healy, 1992). When a standard, a Common Technical Regulation (CTR)[6], for a specific terminal type is in place, it will be taken into effect by national statues in the member states[7].

When a CTR is in place, an apparatus only has to be tested and approved in one of the EC-countries to be approved in all the EC countries. The actual testing and approval of equipment will be performed by private organisations that are certified by the EC to perform these tasks[8]. The idea is that these will compete with each other and hence reduce the size of bureaucracy needed to handle this regulatory framework.

The framework for regulating the establishment of new all-European standards has come into place but it has proven to take considerable time to produce CTRs. When the telecommunications terminal Directive 91/263 went into effect in November 1992, there were still no Common Technical Regulations in place.

Difficulties in establishing EC standards

At the policy making level it has been simple to define the steps required to create a single European market for telecommunications terminal equipment. However, at the technical level it has not been easy to take these steps. Most particularly, it has not been easy to develop a complete set of technical standards that can be used throughout Europe. The reason for this is that each country's telecommunications infrastructure has developed independently for over 100 years. As a result, telephones, facsimile machines, modems and other terminal equipment may function imperfectly, or not at all, outside their home market, even though there are common international standards that apply to the primary functions of fax machines and modems.

The development of pan-European terminal equipment requires one of the following three steps: (1) the adoption of common standards throughout Europe; (2) the development of terminal equipment that can easily be adapted by the user to fit each national standard, or (3) the development of central-office equipment that can recognise and respond to terminal equipment based on new, pan-European standards, while continuing to support the installed base of terminal equipment using each country's standard.

Each of these alternatives poses substantial technical difficulties. (1) The adoption of common European standards would require a costly transition process. Much existing central-office and terminal equipment would no longer be usable, and it would be difficult to coordinate the process of conversion. (2) The development of multi-system terminal equipment would add substantially to the technical complexity, cost and bulkiness of the equipment. (3) The development of dual system central-office equipment would also be technically complex and costly. If such equipment can be developed, however, it would facilitate the gradual adoption of pan-European standards as older, national-standard terminal equipment is replaced over a period of several years.

The simplest transition to pan-European standards is taking place in cellular telephony. There are two reasons for this. First, there is already a demand for a new technology, digital cellular service, which is necessarily incompatible with each of the previous technical standards based on analogue technology. Second, adoption of the new technology does not require the immediate obsolescence of a large value of previous-generation equipment.

The cost of the installed base of cellular-radio equipment is much less than that of wireline equipment. In addition, it will be possible to offer analogue and digital service simultaneously for several years until analogue equipment is replaced. As we indicated earlier, this transition is made more complicated by the entry of new non-standard digital mobile networks in many European countries.

CONCLUSION: STANDARDISATION EX POST AND EX ANTE

It has not been our aim to evaluate the steps taken by the European Community to establish all-European standards. We have instead tried to depict the difficulties for the EC in establishing all-European standards using a framework based on current research on standards and on a notion of the institutional aspects of standards. Establishing all-European standards for telecommunications terminals is neither easy nor effortless. It is an effort that takes time and is attached to great costs irrespective of whether ex ante or ex post standardisation is chosen. The European Community has chosen both paths.

A new formal regulatory regime is established based on coordination in international committees and enforcement by EC and national legislation. But, as yet, little has happened in terms of established all-European standards. The ex post standardisation path has encountered several technical and institutional difficulties and there is no sign of any important ex post harmonised terminal standard being introduced in the near future. If substantial time passes before any of the established national standards are harmonised, still more resources will be invested in their future growth. The ex ante standardisation path has, in this respect, shown greater success and in the near future we will have a couple of new all-European standards. The installed base using these standards will, in most cases, be comparatively small in many years to come and they will, in many cases, have to compete with un-harmonised but widely spread national standards. In some cases the new transitional standards established outside the regulatory regime of EC will compete with the new all-European standards.

In the present transitional stage we can therefore identify three kinds of competing regulatory regimes, each having its own momentum. The new regulatory regime of the EC is contested in two ways by two other regulatory regimes. Regarding the efforts to harmonise old and diverse national standards, the regulatory regime of the EC is contested by the old nationally oriented regulatory regime conserved by a large installed base and vested interests connected to it. Regarding standards based on new technologies, the large effort of the EC to create new all-European standards is contested by industrial actors creating transitional standards outside the regulatory framework of the EC (see next page, Figure 9.1).

*Figure 9.1 Regulatory regimes and their momentum in the telecom-
munications sector*

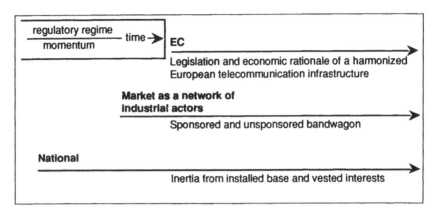

The EC's desire to create an all-Europe telecommunications infrastructure
is strong, leading among other things to immense efforts in creating all-
European standards for terminal equipment. However, the difficulties in
creating them are also mighty. It has been fairly simple to establish a new
formal regulatory regime, but the institutional change related to it is still in
its early beginning.

NOTES

1. See Cowhey (1990) for a good description and analysis of the general transformation of the international telecommunications regime that began a little more
   than a decade ago.
2. Chamberlin refuted the possibility that also the buyers must be standardised under
   pure competition. In his view, the utility of a product is the capacity to satisfy a
   want, and that remains the same regardless of the variety of uses to which it is
   applied. Veblen, on the other hand, saw that the standardisation imperative of the
   industrial system clearly would standardise the 'details of everyday life' as well;
   see quote at the beginning of this chapter.
3. Several examples from telecommunications indicate that the technological style
   (cf. Hughes, 1987) of the standard is dependent on the regulatory regime establishing and maintaining it.
4. See Hughes (1987) for a thorough discussion on possible sources for the
   development of different technological styles.
5. The notion of viewing industrial structures as industrial networks stems from the
   Swedish 'markets as networks' research tradition. For an overview of the main
   ideas in this tradition, see Axelsson and Easton (1992).
6. These CTRs will in most cases be restricted to what is labelled essential requirements, e.g., ensuring that the network will not be damaged. Requirements ensuring

that the terminal works end-to-end will only be included in special justified cases. The only justified cases identified today are: analogue telephony and telephony in GSM, DECT and ISDN.

7. It is also possible for EFTA countries to influence the standard-setting process to a certain extent and to use the completed standard.

8. The actual way a manufacturer obtains a type approval differs depending on whether or not it is certified according to ISO 9000/ISO 9001. In the first case, the manufacturer only needs an administrative decision from a notified body before the equipment is approved. In the two latter cases, the manufacturer must first have the equipment tested at an independent test-house that is a notified body before the equipment can be approved (Council Directive, 91/263/EEC).

REFERENCES

Abbott, L. (1955), *Quality and Competition, An Essay in Economic Theory*, Columbia University Press, New York.

Arthur, W.B. (1988), 'Competing Technologies: an Overview', In G. Dosi et al., *Technical Change and Economic Theory*, Pinter Publishers, London.

Axelsson, B. and G. Easton (eds.) (1992), *Industrial Networks: A New View of Reality*, Routledge, London.

Berg, S. (1989), 'The Production of Compatibility: Technical Standards as Collective Goods', *Kyklos*, vol. 42, pp. 361–83.

Besen, S. (1992), 'AM Versus FM: The Battle of Bands', *Industrial and Corporate Change*, vol. 1, no. 2, pp. 305–26.

Chamberlin, E.H. (1938), *The Theory of Monopolistic Competition: A Re-orientation of the Theory of Value*, Harvard University Press, Cambridge.

Clark, J.M. (1923), *Studies in the Economics of Overhead Costs*, The University of Chicago Press, Chicago.

Cowhey, P.F. (1990), 'The International Telecommunications Regime: The Political Roots of Regimes for High Technology', *International Organization*, vol. 44, no. 2, pp. 169–99.

David, P.A. and S. Greenstein (1990), 'The Economics of Compatibility Standards: An Introduction to Recent Research', *Economics of Innovation and New Technology*, vol. 1, pp. 3–41.

Delcourt, B. (1991), 'EC Decisions and Directives on Information Technology and Telecommunications', *Telecommunication Policy* (February), pp. 15–21.

Farrell, J. (1990), 'The Economics of Standardization: A Guide for Non-Economics', in J.L. Berg and H. Schumny (eds.), *An Analysis of the Information Technology Standardization Process*, North-Holland, Amsterdam.

Farrell, J. and G. Saloner (1986), 'Economic Issues in Standardisation', in J. Miller (ed.), *Telecommunications and Equity*, North-Holland, Amsterdam

Farrell, J. and G. Saloner (1988), 'Coordination Through Committees and Markets', *RAND Journal of Economics*, vol. 19, no. 2, pp. 235-52.

Foray, D. (1990), 'Exploitation of Network Externalities versus Evolution of Standards: Markets, Committees, and the Dilemma of Efficiency', Conference Paper presented at *8th ITS-conference*, Venice.

Healy, F. (1992), 'Disapproval for Approvals Process', *Communicationsweek International*, 17 February, C8.

Hughes, T.P. (1987), 'The Evolution of Large Technological Systems', in W. Bijker, T.P. Hughes and T. Pinch (eds.), *The Social Construction of Technological Systems*, MIT Press, Cambridge.

Hultén, S. and B. Mölleryd (1993), 'Cellular Telephony in Retrospect: Foundations of Success', *TELE* (English ed.), no. 1, pp. 2–7.
Katz, M. and C. Shapiro (1985), 'Network Externalities, Competition, and Compatibility', *The American Economic Review*, vol. 75, no. 3, pp. 424–40.
Kindleberger, C.P. (1983), 'Standards as Public, Collective and Private Goods', *Kyklos*, vol. 36, pp. 377–96.
Richter, J.A. (1991), *The 91/263 Directive: Background and Current Status*, Commission of the European Communities.
Stein, A.A. (1982), 'Coordination and collaboration: regimes in an anarchic world', *International Organization*, vol. 36, no. 2, pp. 299–324.
Veblen, T. (1904), *The Theory of Business Enterprise*, Charles Scribner's sons, New York.

10. Collective Action, Strategic Behaviour and Endogenous Growth

Patrizio Bianchi and Lee Miller

INTRODUCTION

Recent literature on development theory has stressed the role of local forces in driving processes of economic growth. Much attention has been paid to innovation, R & D, human resources, and technological change, calling the development sustained by these internal factors as endogenous growth[1]. We want to underline that these factors are relevant, but it is necessary to explore the social dynamics of economic behaviour. The thesis of this chapter is that a crucial aspect of endogenous growth is that it is not simply a technical problem of innovation, but rather a social and political problem of how a given group reacts to change. Therefore, the contributions of classical political economists who analyse economic dynamics as an evolutionary interaction of social forces need to be taken seriously[2].

The link between individual behaviour and institutional change, which is the key to endogenous growth, must be examined closely. Here we assume that social norms which are inextricably linked to local and national institutions shape individual behaviour[3]. Therefore, the social dynamics of economic behaviour refers to the fact that all behaviour takes place within, and/or among, groups and these groups have ways of doing things which govern economic behaviour. However, this is not to say that there is a one-way causal relationship. In fact, the influence can travel both ways. This becomes especially important when dealing with policy initiatives as shown in the final section of the chapter.

Economic behaviour, at least in developed countries, is characterized by competition. Those who compete effectively survive. The key to competing successfully is innovation. Change is necessary to gain, or maintain, competitive advantages. Successful incorporation of 'innovative' individual behaviour, implies the existence of collective mechanisms coordinating individual responses, that is, institutions which are sufficiently 'complex' to allow positive interaction among independent subjects. The trick, as we will see in more detail in the second and third sections of the chapter, is to be able to innovate without threatening the stability of the group.

Endogenous growth is a process of economic transformation generated by the interaction of a group of individuals. This group is situated in a larger social, institutional, and economic context which shapes it. Changes at the local level are sometimes imposed from the outside, for example, from regional and/or national institutions. These are 'top-down' policies. However, the focus of this chapter is on 'bottom-up' approaches. When faced with 'bottom-up' innovation, responses of others to any novel behaviour becomes more problematic as it does not already have the institutional legitimacy attributed to 'top-down' innovation[4]. It is our opinion that 'bottom-up' innovation is likely to be more productive as it speaks to specific local needs for change. It is the key to endogenous growth.

INNOVATION AS A COLLECTIVE PROCESS OF CHANGE

A rich and heterogeneous pool of literature[5] has recently noted that innovation may be defined as an action on the part of an individual that breaks away from the ordinary course of action. It is the moment when new routines emerge within the firm, within the market, and more extensively, within society as already established routines begin to lose their propulsive function.

Innovation, however, sometimes constitutes an abrupt break with the past that does not always facilitate adjustment. Both within the individual firm and within society at large, this rupture may provoke an overall imbalance in the homeostasis mechanism if there are not sufficient numbers of individuals interacting for selection to leave a sufficient number of them to maintain the institution.

SELECTION AND LEARNING

In a market context, i.e., in an institutional arrangement created by the free interaction of a multiplicity of independent individuals sometimes called a polyarchic social context, the innovation undertaken by a single firm has a positive effect on the whole social body if self-regulative mechanisms are activated to define paths of collective adjustment believed to lead to improved individual and collective efficiency.

In this case, a selective process may be set in motion which, in the presence of new entrants or of a rapid increase in positively selected subjects, regenerates the collectivity and thus re-establishes an institution on new social norms. This kind of behaviour can, however, have unexpected consequences when the change proposed by an individual or a group of individuals within a larger social group is such that there is the risk that the other individuals will be unable to respond by either generalizing the change or by counter-attacking with sanction-applying measures. This situation becomes more serious as the market becomes more institutionally closed, or when formal access to the market exists but there are no potential competitors who wish to enter. Therefore various 'negative' outcomes may result. The first case might be that the innovative behaviour by one individual induces the others to leave the market, thus creating a situation of monopoly.

It could equally happen, however, that the selection excludes too many subjects with respect to the size of the collectivity so that, instead of leaving, they establish a new coalition that seeks to apply institutional sanctions against the innovator. In this latter case of negative selection, which induces non-innovative subjects to form a new coalition with its own internal code, the social body creates a new institution which resists change both by applying collective sanctions to the innovator and by drawing up new general rules for the social group as a whole. In other words, in all the literature on social behaviour which draws its theoretical base from biology, there is a major emphasis on the positive effects of selection, and the assumption that the defeated (i.e., those negatively selected) will individually exit from the market and die off.

To refer to Hirschman's (1970) well-known thesis, it is the existence of an individual 'exit' option that gives credibility to the existence of a biological evolution where behavioural innovation by an individual activates a process that selects others on the basis of their ability to imitate such behaviour. There is also the possibility, however, that a change which the group regards as too rapid to be generalized will engender an aggregation of conservative subjects which, in the reiteration of collusive forms of behaviour generated by a common desire to oppose the innovator, will consolidate into a parallel structure. This will apply its own rules in order to oppose the pre-existing institution by inhibiting the innovative change. In other words, the 'voice' option may lead to sanction-applying behaviour which obstructs positive evolution.

An innovative development is therefore more successful the greater the number of individuals and the openness of the group; the more the social regulation of the group is closed and internally rigid, the greater the risk that innovative behaviour by an individual will either become monopolistic behaviour, with a substantial change in pre-existing social norms, or it will provoke a reaction by a coalition of potential losers who, instead of exiting individually and accepting the change brought by the innovation, will form a coalition which applies sanctions to the innovator in order to preserve the existing structure.

Therefore, the key to incorporating innovative individual behaviour which can then be successfully generalized by the collective is the existence of voice. When voice is present, a collective is stable enough to welcome change, even at the institutional level, without jeopardizing the system itself.

REGRESSIVE AND PROGRESSIVE COALITIONS

We use the term 'regressive coalition' to refer to an aggregation of individuals united by a common interest in opposing a negative selection process. This aggregation is not, however, capable of inducing alternative forms of the social division of labour. A regressive coalition therefore also unites actors who do not have interests in developing complementary specializations and thus requires a small level of effort since it is enough to oppose the innovator individually, but at the same time it is not able to develop any alternative paths toward a stable social aggregation.

We have a 'progressive coalition' if the process of aggregation of individuals induces a progressive transformation of the capacities and abilities of the individuals such that a relative complementarity of action among them is generated. This ability to adjust the division of labour allows a system to be stable, since the members are interdependent and complementary, without being rigid, since change is incorporated. Thus, a relationship exists between the presence of progressive coalitions and the relative specialization of individuals and, likewise, we can argue that there is a relationship between the formulation of regressive coalitions and the existence of a process of relative de-specialization among the individuals present in a collective.

Recalling Adam Smith's postulate will help us understand what these hypotheses mean. Smith (1776) assumes that the wealth of nations is tied to the capacity to develop 'skill, dexterity, and judgement' of labour and that these productive capacities are connected to the way in which collective labour is organized. Assuming the existence of an innate propensity to trade, that is toward collective action[6], Smith claims that this interaction among individuals leads to a process of productive integration, defined as division of labour, which by allowing each individual to specialize himself in a specific series of activities permits the individual to develop his own competencies to the utmost and allows the entire collectivity to realize greater and more articulated production. This division of labour, which allows the development of individual and collective competencies can become more specific as the number of individuals interacting in a group increases. Nevertheless, based on these considerations it appears evident that the process of development of the division of labour does not only require further specialization of complementary capacities and competencies. This mechanism can be found in a hierarchical structure as in a firm or a planned economy, or can be developed through an evolutionary mechanism which, through a process of progressive adjustment, induces the definition of complementary interests and capacities.

For Smith (ibid.) this mechanism can certainly be applied to the production of a specific good, but it may also be applied to the organization of an entire community. He develops a series of examples that demonstrate how in a small village there is not enough 'social' space in which to express specific productive specializations. Yet in Smith (ibid.) it is evident that on the social level this mechanism must be able to demand the existence of mechanisms of entrance and exit and, above all, some sort of institutional stability which favours the development of reciprocal complementarities. The widening of the extension of the market in Smith (ibid.) is directly tied to the affirmation of a society in which the number of those who can exert their own entitlements and their productive activity increases. Thus the example of the 'invisible hand,' which Smith takes from a noted metaphor derived from Newton, does not seem to correspond to the definition of an external force that moves the world, but is simply the demonstration that whatever the original impetus, the wealth of nations depends on free social interaction.

It is in this sense that a relationship between endogenous growth and progressive coalitions exists. In a stable institutional context, forms of interaction among individuals based on the development of reciprocal specializations may evolve. In this sense 'institutional context' simply means a situation in which there is a general conviction that all the participants in collective action, that is the members of the community, accept the basic rules, are willing to cooperate, and therefore are capable of communally sanctioning a possible transgressor or free-rider. In such a hypothesis it is just this development of conditions of complementarity which permits the adjustment mechanisms of institutional stability because the individual has already invested in activity which is non-recuperable (sunk) in the face of sharp variations in the rules of the game.

In the opposite scenario, that is in a situation of uncertainty, the tendency to specialize does not exist. If one does not know if there is the possibility of sanctioning free-riders, and cannot be relatively sure about how other members of the group will behave, one will not assume the risk of investing in sunk activity which would limit his strategic options.

Yet in a context in which there is less interest in relative specialization, there is also less interest on the part of individuals in participating in that group since there are no positive externalities resulting from operating in a context in which the productive forces of labour are developed. This starts a degenerative mechanism which, if it is not halted, leads to further social disaggregation or the reinforcing of regressive coalitions. Furthermore, a social context in which there are processes of monopolization, and social blocs based on exclusive rights to resources, the possiblity of developing progressive coalitions diminishes, and at the same time, the possibility of activating regressive coalitions which block change without offering alternative mechanisms of relative specialization increases.

SIZE AND OPENNESS

Innovative development is more likely to succeed when the population of interacting individuals is large and open. The more closed and intro-spective the social group, the higher the risk either that the innovative behaviour of an individual will translate into monopolizing behaviour with a substantial modification of the pre-existing social norms, or that it will result in a reaction on the part of a coalition of potential losers. Such a coalition, rather than exiting or adapting themselves individually and accepting the institutional changes, will group together regressively to sanction the innovator in the name of the preservation of the pre-existing institutions.

At first sight this seems to go against Olson's theory that the 'larger the group, the less it will further its own interests' (Olson, 1965, p. 36). However, later Olson explains that this is true only for exclusive groups. The distinction between exclusive and inclusive groups lies in the type of collective good the group is trying to procure. (The same group may be inclusive in some cases and exclusive in others.) When trying to gain a zero-sum good, the group members want to keep the group as small as possible to ensure that there is enough of the good to go around. This is the case of exclusive groups. On the other hand, when the good is not clearly divisible, as in the case of a new law, the group becomes inclusive since the more members helping to achieve the good the better (Olson, p. 39). It is the nature of the collective good that is crucial. In order to have an inclusive group the collective good must not be zero-sum.

Another characteristic of exclusive groups is that the members are more concerned about how the other group members will react in response to what they do. This is caused by the need for 100% cooperation in any type of collective action because of the threat of free-riding. Olson considers the market to be an exclusive group in which each member is not only a rival, but also a collaborator (Olson, p. 42).

A further distinction should be made. When speaking about the existence of a market, one needs to specify which market. For example, the market for a certain product, such as washing machines is a relatively stable market. A group of firms competing with each other to sell washing machines is an exclusive group. However, when considering a national, international, or world market in general we cannot use the concept of exclusive group. True, those who participate in these markets are interested in profit, but as they are all selling different goods they are not necessarily competing with each other, and 100% collaboration is certainly not required for collective action. The distinction becomes more clear if we divide the market into sectors. Within each sector, the profit is relatively zero-sum, unless new market niches are developed. Thus, sectors are exclusive groups. However, the market in general is an inclusive group.

It is helpful to turn once again to Adam Smith (1776). In the third chapter of *The Wealth of Nations*, he explains that the division of labour is limited to the extent of the market. The division of labour increases as the market increases, and so does the amount of work. It should be noted that for Smith the market means the power of exchanging within a nation, and therefore is an exclusive group. Social differentiation is fundamental

to economic policy and integration processes. The French sociologist
Emile Durkheim's idea was that 'social differentiation is the peaceful
solution to the struggle for survival.' In other words, through differentiation consensus may be achieved[7].

A NEW APPROACH TO INDUSTRIAL POLICY

These considerations are of particular importance in the formulation of
public policies. A policy designed to promote innovative behaviour must
be accompanied by social action aimed at regulating the openness of the
social body to ensure that the selection process thus activated does not
transform itself into 'negative' institutional changes which favor monopolizing solutions or conservative reactions.

One should ask oneself, therefore, what happens in cases where there
are not enough individuals interacting to a degree sufficient to activate an
evolutionary mechanism. This is the case, in fact, in those countries whose
economic backwardness manifests an 'underdevelopment' of relations
where rapid change may introduce, not social evolution, but institutional
breakdown and the creation of parallel institutions which form to counteract change. An example of this is provided by the EEC structural
policies in less-developed areas of Southern Europe or in developing
countries where, at the local level, either there are too few entrepreneurs or
those entrepreneurs that do exist are constrained by non-market relations
which cause rigidity in the system.

As the national systems of innovation are still very different throughout
Europe, the EEC decided in the late 1980s to reverse the convergence
process from top-down to bottom-up, by introducing programs which are
aimed at stimulating the creation of a network of innovators. This
approach was clearly influenced by the debate on industrial districts and
by the more general debate on innovation diffusion. It is based on the
possibility of favoring the aggregation of firms, research institutes, universities, framed in their own national contexts, but forced to cooperate in
producing innovation. The positive result is not limited to the innovation
'per se', such as a patent or a book, but it is the capacity to induce
individuals and institutions to modify the existing routines in order to
'work together' with individuals and institutions rooted in different frameworks.

This idea is clearly based on an evolutionary, neo-institutionalist approach: because the interaction among people creates norms for collective action which induce subjects rooted in different institutional contexts to come together to work on a specific project. It is clear that university systems in Europe cannot be driven to converge ('to become the same'), but it is possible to promote a scheme of compatibility among different countries, and in the meantime, to induce universities and firms to cooperate on specific projects.

This concept of convergence (not to be the same, but to be compatible) can be supported by the creation of funds to finance the creation of networks of research institutions and productive firms. There are a variety of programs which support research and industrial cooper-ation throughout Europe. In particular the SPRINT program is devoted entirely to developing networks of innovators, favoring aggregation of firms and institutions, taking into account both the territorial and the technological aspects of productive organization. These programs are structural policies, which are part of local systems of production, aimed at creating new relations of production among industrial leaders in order to make the industrial atmospheres (IAs)[8] of specific districts more innovative and to encourage a process of integration among them. In this sense, the new approach to industrial policy experienced by the EEC underlines two areas of intervention. On the one hand, there is the possibility of intervening in the costs of the relations themselves, divided into costs of information and costs of coordination. On the other, there is the possibility of intervention in those collective intangible assets that characterize the territory and the group of firms.

These considerations enlarge the normative relevance of this new approach, based on the possibilities of addressing the institutional framework and intervening on the social externalities provided by the common knowledge and collective norms of a group of firms and local institutions, and applying this approach in a variety of specific conditions. Inducing firms and institutions which are involved in local networks to work together on innovation means intervening in both the industrial relations and the specific competences of the different agents. Creating linkages between local leaders means encouraging compatibility among local networks and thereby increasing the possibility of redefining the division of labour and the specialization process in light of a wider context.

With regard to interventions in already existing districts experiencing periods of crisis, such as in the European textile districts, industrial policies must be aimed at renewing the IAs themselves by working backwards to rebuild the technological foundations of the firms and by lowering the costs of information and coordination. These interventions have to create new linkages between these local districts and new sources of innovation, and must establish connections between existing districts in order to develop relative specialization within Europe.

In the case of pre-existing districts, interventions such as the setting up of production service centers can become a means of carrying out the selection and promotion of leading agents operating in different areas and can serve to modify the existing productive relations. These may then transform the existing local system into a wider system under the leadership of a limited number of agents chosen by means of this selection process. These centers can be constituted at the local level by taking advantages of national systems of innovation. This means using the national research laboratories, the local universities, or private facilities that are well-established as technological leaders in their national frameworks. A variety of SPRINT interventions can be indentified as public policies aimed at redefining the IA framing the transnational network of innovators.

In the case of interventions in local systems, or in a group of firms, or institutions not characterized by a pre-existing IA such that it cannot already be considered as a network of innovators, the structural intervention will consist of several integrated actions:

1. Action aimed at making the system itself explicit, encouraging agents to see themselves as part of an integrated system.

2. Actions which give direction to the specializations of the agents in order to permit greater division of labour based on mutual reliability.

3. Action concerning costs of coordination, which can be shared by the creation of a 'collective project', even by means of public support.

Several experiences promoted by European programs could be analysed as policy aimed at favoring the creation of networks of innovators: the FAST experiences, and also the Human Capital and Mobility program, which is aimed at supporting research projects among European universities is based on the concept of creating networks of innovators.

In any case, the final aim of these policy actions is the acceleration of the innovation process, not by breaking the existing national and local networks, but rather by integrating them in a wider context. The goal is to allow the openness of the local systems without the dispersion of accumulated knowledge. In fact, this industrial policy leads to systemic adjustments that necessitate the integration of pre-existing agents with agents which have traditionally been outside the cultural and territorial area covered by the district.

In the end these actions will also change the national systems of innovation. This approach induces an integration process that moves from the bottom-up: it creates linkages between local leaders, which have to change their traditional procedures of interaction within their own national framework. The cooperation program establishes new procedures of relations between firms and public institutions that are compatible at the European level.

To conclude, public policy cannot be action merely aimed at encouraging technical innovation. It must be directed at guiding the processes of social organization to ensure the existence of the collective mechanisms needed to effectively handle and incorporate change which occurring on the local level. In this way, policies encouraging endogenous growth may be implemented.

NOTES

1. An assessment of this literature is in Boltho and Holtman, (1992); see also Scott, (1992).
2. Krugman (1992) has recently reconsidered the pioneering works on development theory in the 1950s and in the 1960s from Rosenstein-Rodan to Hirschman, assuming that these contributions were neglected for years simply because they were not acceptable to modern economists; to the English classical political economists, from Smith to Marshall.
3. Here 'social norms' include all rules governing behaviour, even economic behaviour . The 'social' refers to the nature of how the rules come about and how they are enforced, rather than their content.
4. We are grateful to Gilberto Antonelli (University of Bologna, Department of Economic Sciences) for helping us to identify this distinction.
5. For a review of this literature see Dosi (1988).
6. There is some ambiguity in the use of 'collective action' here. It is used to refer to two different situations. The first is collective action as a means to achieve a collective good. The group moves together (more or less) to reach a common goal — for example, any action on a national level like a war, or on the group level like a specific lobby group's efforts to change legislation. Note that this does not mean that such an action does not also indirectly further specific individual goals. The second refers to collective action which directly furthers individual goals. For instance, to further their own goals all take part in the market and play by the rules established by the collective. They certainly do not do so for the collective good, but rather to directly further individual interests. If they did so for the collective good we would no longer have to worry about problems like free riding and

monopoly. We use the second, and more general, definition. Here, the collective good is the web of social norms which governs both group and individual behaviour in a given collective. A helpful example of this is what Alfred Marshall (1920) termed the 'industrial atmosphere' surrounding aggregations of firms sharing the production process.
7. Durkheim (1947) takes the problem of size and the division of labour a step further. Although for Durkheim 'division of labor' refers to 'social differentiation', he lists three crucial variables: volume, material density, and moral density. By volume, Durkheim means the number of individuals. Material density means the number of individuals in a given space, and moral density means the intensity of interaction among these individuals. When these factors are present we have social differentiation of which the economic division of labour is a reflection.
8. Alfred Marshall's notion of 'industrial atmosphere' refers to the common knowledge and social norms which shape behaviour within a group of firms working together in a limited geographic area. See Marshall (1920).

REFERENCES

Boltho, A. and G. Holtman (1992), 'The Assessment: New Approaches to Economic Growth', in *Oxford Review of Economic Policy*, vol. 6, no. 4, pp. 1–14.
Dosi, G. (1988), 'Sources, Procedures and Microeconomic Effects of Innovation', *Journal of Economic Literature*, vol. 26, pp. 1120–71.
Durkheim, E. (1947), *The Division of Labour in Society*, trans. with introduction by G. Simpson, Macmillan, New York.
Hirschman, A. (1970), *Exit, Voice and Loyalty*, Harvard University Press, Cambridge Mass.
Krugman, P. (1992), 'Toward a Counter-counterrevolution in Development Theory', in *Proceedings of the World Bank Annual Conference on Development Economics*, pp. 15–62.
Marshall, A. (1920), *Principles of Economics*, VIII Edition, Macmillan, London.
Olson, M. (1965), *The Logic of Collective Action*, Harvard University Press, Cambridge Mass.
Scott, M. (1992), 'A New Theory of Endogenous Growth', *Oxford Review of Economic Policy*, vol. 6, no. 4, pp. 29–43.
Smith, A. (1776), 'An Inquiry into the Wealth of Nations', in R.H. Campbell and A.S. Skinner (eds.), *The Glasgow Edition of the Works and Correspondence of Adam Smith*, Clarendon Press, 1976.

11. Determinants of Supplier Dependence: An Empirical Study

Hans Berger, Niels G. Noorderhaven and Bart Nooteboom[1]

INTRODUCTION

According to transaction cost economics (TCE), as formulated by Oliver Williamson (1975, 1979, 1985, and 1991), the governance of vertical inter-firm relations is determined predominantly by the degree to which assets are specific to the transaction relation. In the absence of safeguards, asset specificity leads to vulnerability to opportunistic rent-seeking by the other party (Klein, Crawford and Alchian, 1978). Therefore the alignment of the level of asset specificity and the configuration of safeguards is important. The basic explanatory scheme of TCE is given in Figure 11.1.

Figure 11.1 A simple model based on TCE

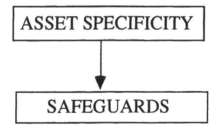

At low levels of asset specificity arms' length market relations are expected because in the absence of relation-specific assets that need to be protected, this governance structure is efficient and offers strong incentives. At high levels of asset specificity on the other hand, market relations break down because the firm incurring the specific investments finds insufficient protection. Therefore, integration of both firms under common

195

ownership and hierarchical control of transactions is to be expected.

At intermediate levels of asset specificity, full integration would not be efficient, but a governance structure offering more protection than a pure market relation will have to be erected. In this case the relationship is more durable and tight than the typical market relationship, but at the same time looser than the relationship between parts of one and the same firm, and can be called a 'hybrid', compared with the pure forms of market and hierarchy (Williamson, 1991).

The two most important mechanisms for safeguarding intermediate levels of asset specificity are legal ordering and private ordering. In the case of legal ordering detailed, legally enforceable long-term contracts are specified in which as many contingencies as possible are dealt with. However, no contract covering a transaction of some complexity and duration can ever be complete. Therefore in hybrid inter-firm relations, formal contracts are often replaced by or complemented with other arrangements, aimed at establishing a better balance between the vulnerabilities of both parties.

These other arrangements go under the name of 'private ordering', because their efficacy does not depend on the use of legal courts. An example of private ordering is an arrangement according to which the assets that are specific to the production for a certain buyer are paid for and owned by that buyer, so-called 'quasi-integration' (see Monteverde and Teece, 1982; and Blois, 1972). In this way the scope for opportunistic behaviour by the buyer in hybrid relationships is reduced.

In this chapter we focus on the market and hybrid relationships with suppliers of one particular buyer, a Dutch manufacturer of office equipment. The level of asset specificity may be assumed to vary between these relationships, and — following transaction cost reasoning — we expect parallel variations in supplier dependence and the kinds of safeguards (legal and private ordering) installed. Whereas most of the literature deals with a broadly defined market-hierarchy dichotomy or a market-hybrid-hierarchy trichotomy, we focus on the variation of specific safeguards within market and hybrid relationships.

PERCEIVED DEPENDENCE

In received TCE, the perception of managers is seen as relatively unimportant. The objective circumstances call for one or the other governance structure, and a manager who fails to interpret the signals correctly will bring his firm to bankruptcy.

In our view, received TCE does insufficient justice to the fundamental uncertainty managers of business firms face, and falls short of acknowledging the stringent boundaries to the rational capabilities of human decision makers. For instance, Williamson (1985) assumes that the sometimes very complex private ordering arrangements proposed by TCE are completely designed ex ante. A very high strain is put on the rational faculties of parties if they are to design the private order that is to discipline the relationship before the actual start of the transactions. While TCE ostensibly employs a bounded rationality assumption as proposed by Simon, the theory is also characterized by a 'strong commitment to intended rationality' (Williamson, 1985, p. 387).

However, there is no unambiguous information, nor a simple algorithm, for managers deciding on the optimal governance structure for inter-firm relations. Managers can only advance on the basis of their own imperfect perceptions, using trial-and-error, and making the most of an abundance of equivocal signs. Given the importance of these perceptions, they should explicitly be taken into account in a theory of inter-firm relations (cf. Dietrich, 1994).

The insertion of perception in the causal chain between asset specificity and governance structure has several implications. In the first place, perception may dampen the effect of changes in asset specificity. A supplier's asset specificity may grow over time (e.g., in the form of skills and knowledge) without the increase being perceived. Or a supplier may notice an increase of asset specificity, and perceive an increase in dependence, but nevertheless refrain from demanding a change in the governance structure. Threshold effects are likely to occur.

Secondly, the perception of dependence will not only be influenced by the level of asset specificity, but also by other factors. Some factors, like the proportion of total turnover made up by the sales to a particular buyer, will contribute positively to perceived dependence. Other factors, in particular those discussed in the following two subsections of this chapter, may have a negative effect on perceived dependence. In sum, the inclusion of perceived dependence in the model has the effect of opening up the analysis for factors not taken into consideration in received TCE.

Moreover, perceived dependence and governance structure may affect each other. A higher perceived dependence will cause a manager to demand more stringent safeguards, but once these safeguards have been installed, they have the effect of mitigating perceived dependence. Therefore the level of perceived dependence interpreted as independent from asset specificity and governance structure is hardly meaningful. In combination, however, these concepts can be very informative. To anticipate the discussion of the empirical investigation in the following sections, if for some reason or the other the governance structure is not adequately aligned with the level of asset specificity, this may result in a high level of perceived dependence on the part of the party that has incurred the investments in these assets. In this way perceived dependence can serve as a thermometer for the adequacy of the safeguards installed.

We will now turn to the discussion of the factors that should in our view be incorporated into a theory of vertical inter-firm relations.

NETWORK EMBEDDEDNESS

Parties in a particular transaction relation normally also maintain relations with many other firms. In some instances all these relationships may be completely self-contained. If this is the case a theory isolating a particular transaction relation from all other relations does not neglect valuable information. Most of the time, however, there will exist multiple relations between buying and selling firms in a certain industry and in a certain region. When this is the case, the focal relation is said to be 'embedded' in a network of social relations. The implications of this condition have to be taken into account (Granovetter, 1985, 1992).

Network embeddedness may influence the relationship between asset specificity and governance structure, leading to the installation of safeguards that on the face of it are either too weak or too strong. The direction of this influence depends on the relative network positions of the parties. Two cases with relatively straightforward implications will be reviewed here: 'positive' and 'negative' network embeddedness (as seen from the position of the supplier).

In the case of positive network embeddedness, the supplier uses inputs from several subcontractors that are in no direct relationship with the buying firm. This means that the supplier performs a coordinating function for the buyer. An example of this network configuration is the Japanese automobile industry, in which main suppliers coordinate the inputs of second and third tier subcontractors that are not directly in contact with the automobile manufacturers (cf. Asanuma, 1989).

In the opposite case of negative network embeddedness, the supplier does not only sell to a particular buyer directly, but also indirectly. That is, part of the total turnover of the supplier consists of deliveries to third firms, which use these inputs in their production for the same buyer firm. In this situation the supplier is more dependent, for not only the direct but also the indirect sales to the buyer firm are at risk in the case of a conflict. At least, this is the case if the buyer firm is assumed to be able to persuade the third firms to discontinue buying from the supplier in question.

In the case of positive network embeddedness the supplier can be somewhat less easily disposed of, for the buyer would also have to replace the network of contacts it maintains. Therefore, other things being equal, a supplier in a position of positive network embeddedness can be expected to demand less stringent safeguards and/or express a lesser sense of dependence. Negative network embeddedness, all other things equal, makes us expect more stringent safeguards, or a greater sense of dependence in their absence.

THE TIME DIMENSION

Transaction relations are not only embedded in networks of relationships, but also in time. Temporal embeddedness refers to the history of the transaction relationship, and to associated expectations with regard to future transactions. If two parties have been doing business together for a long time, and if this relationship is relatively satisfactory, the expectation grows that they will be doing business together in the future.

This expectation is not necessarily based in rational considerations, but may be largely unconscious. Repeated interactions lead to the forming of habits and the institutionalization of behaviour (Berger and Luckmann, 1966; Zucker, 1987). Both processes have as their effect that patterns of behaviour are shielded from rational decision-making in the pursuit of efficiency. Case study research has borne out that in industrial buying relations buyers display a strong tendency to persist in the use of existing suppliers (Woodside and Möller, 1992). This kind of inertia has to be reckoned with in a theory of vertical inter-firm relations.

Other things being equal, we expect that in a relationship that is temporally embedded, i.e., in which habitualization and institutionalization of interactions has taken place, a given level of asset specificity will lead to a lower perceived dependence. At least the risk associated with dependence will be smaller, as the relationship is assumed to continue indefinitely. The negative relationship between temporal embeddedness and perceived dependence will in turn, ceteris paribus, lead to less stringent safeguards.

TRUST

The third concept we propose to add to the analysis is trust. To 'trust' another party means to engage voluntarily in a course of action the outcome of which is contingent on choices made by that other party (Barber, 1983; Deutsch, 1973; Gambetta, 1988). The view on trust expounded here is consistent with our emphasis on bounded rationality. Trust is pre-eminently an expedient for reducing complexity (Luhmann, 1979). If one feels that the other party can be trusted to honour his or her part of the letter and the spirit of a deal, many thorny questions that might increase the dangers of opportunism regarding future developments can be avoided.

The urge to bring the concept of 'trust' into TCE stems from the finding in various empirical studies that trust is often the glue that keeps business partners together (Barber, 1983; Lorenz, 1988; Palay, 1984). However, incorporation of the concept of trust constitutes a breach with the explanatory strategy of received TCE[2].

Williamson assumes that 'some individuals are opportunistic some of the time and that differential trustworthiness is rarely transparent *ex ante*. As a consequence, *ex ante* screening efforts are made and *ex post* safeguards are created' (Williamson, 1985, p. 64). However, the main thrust of TCE is to explain existing safeguards in transaction relations as a response to the problems of opportunism. The possibility of screening successfully for opportunism and consequently of being able to renounce safeguards is hardly worked out. The line of reasoning is that if it is very difficult or impossible to recognize an opportunistic actor *ex ante*, those who design a governance form must reckon with opportunism all the time.

We propose that managers, at least in transaction relations of some duration, *can* successfully screen for opportunism. In the process of exchange, opportunities for opportunistic rent seeking will inevitably occur, and the behaviour of the other party can be monitored closely. Every time he renounces an opportunity for opportunism, trust grows.

Trust, just like temporal embeddedness, will tend to mitigate the perceived dependence stemming from asset specificity, or at least the perceived risk associated with this dependence. Therefore trust may be expected to lead to less stringent safeguards, other things being equal.

The three factors discussed above, both network and temporal embeddedness as well as trust, may under some circumstances be highly correlated. For one thing, as the development of trust takes time, higher levels of trust are to be expected in older relationships. Furthermore, if business relations are a part of a dense network, they will presumably on average be longer-lived, and are more likely to be governed by social norms. Consequently trust, temporal embeddedness and network embeddedness may in many cases come as a complex of variables rather than as isolated factors.

Figure 11.2 Model based on extended TCE

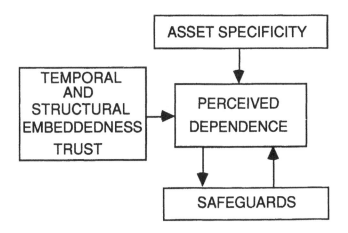

The model based on our version of TCE is represented in Figure 11.2. Perceived dependence can be measured independently, but can be interpreted only in the context of the independent variables and of the safeguards installed. Various tests of hypotheses based on received TCE and our changes and additions to the theory will be discussed in the next section.

DATA COLLECTION AND ANALYSIS SCHEMES

In order to test the hypotheses that can be derived from (our version of) TCE, we are conducting a series of empirical investigations. In the first study we analysed the supplier relations of one particular firm, a manufacturer of office equipment ('Buyer'). Buyer has a turnover of $1.4 billion and a net profit of $54 million, and employs 12 thousand people (1991).

In the first phase of this study, we interviewed the managers who were responsible for maintaining relationships with Buyer's suppliers, as well as their counterparts at 12 suppliers. The purpose of these interviews was the drafting and testing of a written questionnaire. In the second stage, we sent this questionnaire to 80 of Buyer's largest suppliers. The response was a total of 67 returned questionnaires (84%). For some suppliers, supplementary information relating to legal ordering was derived from internal Buyer sources.

Questions in the questionnaires pertained among other things to asset specificity as incurred by suppliers, legal and private order safeguards installed, perceived dependence of Buyer and supplier, trust, length of the supply history, the development of the supply relationship in terms of sales volume, and the occurrence of positive and negative network embeddedness of the supplier. Most items had the format of five-point Likert-type scales. On the basis of the individual items a number of additive scales have been constructed[3].

First, we attempted a direct test of the causal scheme of TCE, according to Figure 11.1. Here, asset specificity is seen as a (the?) cause of safeguards. Regressing different measures of safeguards on measures of specificity, we found no statistically significant results. But on second thought, we should see safeguards as being constructed into an integrated, coherent governance scheme, and perhaps it makes little sense to regress individual items of such a scheme on asset specificity. But it is not clear how individual items of governance should be combined to reflect the overall design, as tailored to each individual case. Thinking further, it seemed to make most sense not to look at safeguards as dependent variables, but at perceived dependence. Our causal scheme for this is given in Figure 11.2. Here, dependence is seen as providing the incentive to institute means of governance, and as resulting from measures already instituted.

Safeguards are instruments to reduce a dependence which results from causes such as asset specificity, enhanced or attenuated by embeddedness in networks and time, trust, percentage of sales involved in the transaction relation, etc. By taking perceived dependence as the dependent variable, we are looking at the crucial end result of the entire scheme, and we can test for all factors simultaneously. Hence, we focus on perceived dependence of suppliers, since in the present study of a large number of suppliers to a single buyer that is where interesting variation occurs.

Another reason for this focus of the analysis was the remarks made by purchasing managers from Buyer. According to these informants, standard contractual clauses were widely used. Whatever variation of contractual terms occurred was seen as coincidental rather than a meaningful parameter of relationships with suppliers. The same would be true for private ordering. Relation-specific tools were routinely paid for and owned by Buyer, and the provision of technical knowledge depended on the technical expertise of the supplier, and not on considerations of governance.

As a result, the variation in safeguards observed in our sample would at best very imperfectly reflect the risk of dependence incurred by suppliers that have invested in relation-specific assets. According to our restated model of Transaction Cost Economics (see Figure 11.2, p. 201), this would result in an increased net perceived dependence for these suppliers. The results of the regression analysis confirm this expectation (see Table 11.2, p. 207).

OPERATIONALIZATION OF VARIABLES

From the perspective of (TCE), the variables explaining dependence are asset specificity and safeguards. A scale of asset specificity was constructed by adding items pertaining to location specificity (one item), physical asset specificity (two items), dedicated capacity (four items), and knowledge specificity (two items)[4].

For the safeguards we require measures of legal and private ordering. With regard to legal ordering, five questions were answered by Buyer pertaining to the question of whether all transactions with the supplier in question were governed by a 'master contract'; the term of notice in the contract; whether or not security stocks of components of materials were specified; whether or not the terms of delivery on order diverged from the standard formulation; and whether or not the technical specifications of the products to be delivered diverged from the standard formulation.

On the basis of these variables we hoped to be able to construct a scale of contractual extensiveness, with taken-for-granted standard contracts on one extreme of the scale, and carefully negotiated contracts on the other.

Our premise was that parties seeking protection in legal ordering will spend more effort in negotiating and drafting the agreement, resulting in a non-standard contract. However, the correlations between the first two variables and the other three proved to be very low. Factor analysis on the five variables revealed two distinct factors, with master contract and term of notice loading high on one factor, and terms of delivery and technical specifications on the other. The fifth variable, security stocks, showed intermediate and opposite loadings on both factors.

On the basis of these observations it was decided to construct one additive scale of contract extensiveness on the basis of the items pertaining to terms of delivery, technical specifications, and security stocks only[5].

Two dichotomous items were considered for the measurement of private ordering. The first item pertained to the question of whether specific tools were paid for and owned by Buyer; the second item pertained to the question of whether Buyer provided technical knowledge to the supplier. Both arrangements can be seen as mitigating the risk of asset specificity borne by the supplier. If specific tools are paid for by the buying firm, the supplier has to incur lower specific investments. And if the buying firm provides technical knowledge, this helps create a balance of dependencies, for in case of opportunistic rent-seeking by the buying firm the supplier can now retaliate by using this technical knowledge in a way that would be harmful to the buyer[6]. The summative scale of the two items was rejected for a too low value of Cronbach's alpha. The first item was extremely skew: as almost all suppliers used tools owned by Buyer, the item does not discriminate. This left us with the second item as a sole measure of private ordering.

ON THE OPERATIONALIZATION OF ADDITIONAL VARIABLES

Two kinds of embeddedness were distinguished, both measured on a dichotomous scale: positive network embeddedness, if the supplier extensively used the input of third parties in the production for Buyer; and negative network embeddedness, if the supplier also delivered to Buyer indirectly.

The time dimension was included by constructing a variable measuring the number of years the supply relationship already existed. The natural logarithm of this number was used in the analysis, because the influence of this factor was assumed to be non-linear. Not only the age of the supply relationship, but also its development is important. Therefore another variable was added, reflecting the growth or decline of sales to Buyer during the past five years, on the hypothesis that growth might mitigate perceived dependence[7].

A scale was also constructed for the trust of the supplier in the goodwill of the buyer[8]. The sales of the supplier to Buyer as a percentage of its total turnover was considered as an additional determinant of dependence as perceived by the supplier. Annual total turnover of the supplier was also considered, on the basis of the hypothesis that larger firms are better able to handle risks and reduce transaction costs (Nooteboom, 1993).

For both variables the logarithm was taken on the assumption that the effect may be subject to diminishing returns. Means, standard deviations and intercorrelations of the various measures are printed in Table 11.1 below.

Table 11.1 Means, standard deviations and correlations

VARIABLES	MEANS	S.D.	1	2	3	4	5
1. Net perceived dependence by supplier	−1.86	1.46					
2. Supplier dependency perceived by supplier	2.07	1.14	+.746***				
3. Buyer dependency perceived by supplier	3.93	0.97	−.626***	+.052			
4. Asset Specificity	22.53	6.05	+.437***	+.557***	+.051		
5. Contractual extensiveness	3.79	1.09	+.106	+.097	.066	+.001	
6. Natural logarithm of length of supply history	2.48	0.54	+.114	+.237**	+.054	+.078	+.154
7. Growth of sales to buyer	11.39	2.41	+.159	+.221**	+.025	+.242**	+.111
8. Knowledge Exchange	1.29	0.46	−.114	−.226**	−.111	+.118	−.259**
9. Negative network embeddedness	1.71	0.46	+.273**	+.102	−.285**	−.030	−.167
10. Positive network embeddedness	2.35	0.69	−.062	−.171*	−.126	−.349***	−.390***
11. Trust in goodwill buyer	24.57	4.12	−.216*	−.185*	+.071	+.004	−.053
12. Trust in competence-buyer	8.81	1.37	−.104	−.068	+.091	+.030	−.103
13. Natural logarithm of total turnover supplier	7.82	1.49	−.343***	−.323***	+.170	−.032	+.146
14. Natural Logarithm of sales to buyer as % of total sales	1.75	1.10	+.376**	+.515***	+.031	+.180*	+.368***

VARIABLES	6	7	8	9	10	11	12	13
1. Net perceived dependence by supplier								
2. Supplier dependency perceived by supplier								
3. Buyer dependency perceived by supplier								
4. Asset Specificity								
5. Contractual extensiveness								
6. Natural logarithm of length of supply history								
7. Growth of sales to buyer	+.096							
8. Knowledge Exchange	−.205**	−.111						
9. Negative network embeddedness	−.056	+.163	−.039					
10. Positive network embeddedness	−.016	−.118	+.214**	+.079				
11. Trust in goodwill buyer	−.005	+.206*	−.024	−.166	+.086			
12. Trust in competence-buyer	+.177*	+.404***	+.118	−.141	+.073	+.558***		
13. Natural logarithm of total turnover supplier	−.277**	+.154	+.089	+.054	−.014	−.091	+.038	
14. Natural Logarithm of sales to buyer as % of total sales	+.242**	+.027	−.249**	−.275**	−.210*	+.008	−.099	.470**

*** $p < .01$
** $p < .05$
* $p < .10$

FINDINGS

Two approaches to the explanation of perceived dependence were used. One approach was to take the supplier's perceived dependence as the dependent variable, and to take the dependence of the buyer, as perceived by the supplier, as one of the explanatory variables (with the hypothesis of a negative effect). The alternative was to take net perceived dependence as the dependent variable, defined as the excess of the dependence the supplier perceives for himself over the dependency he perceives for the buyer. Our hypotheses are as follows:

1. There are positive effects on dependence from: asset specificity, percentage of total sales to buyer, negative network embeddedness.

2. There are negative effects on dependence from: contractual extensiveness, total turnover of the supplier (as a measure of firm size), positive network embeddedness, trust in goodwill of the buyer, information provided by the buyer to the supplier, length of supply history, growth of sales to buyer.

The empirical results are given in Table 11.2. The coefficients are stan-dardized regression coefficients, labelled beta[9]. For missing observations in explanatory variables means substitution was applied. Cases with missing variables in the dependent variable were deleted. The left column gives the results for net perceived dependence as the dependent variable (supplier dependence minus buyer dependence, both as perceived by the supplier). The right column gives the results for (gross) perceived supplier depen-dence. The results in the left column are based on fewer observations due to the policy to delete cases with missing values in the dependent variable (there are missing values in buyer dependence as perceived by supplier).

Table 11.2   Results of a regression analysis[a]

	Net Perceived Dependency by Supplier	Supplier Dependency Perceived by Supplier
Buyer Dependency Perceived by Supplier		.089664 (.3566)
Length of Supply History	−.073882 (.5417)	.015654 (.8761)
Trust in Goodwill Buyer	−.211940 (.1246)	−.238367 ** (.0317)
Asset Specificity	.444565 *** (.0008)	.490929 *** (.0000)
Contractual Extensiveness	.178780 (.1883)	.010070 (.9282)
Growth of Sales to Buyer	.106631 (.4146)	.091941 (.3937)
Knowledge Exchange	−.114951 (.3659)	−.202502 ** (.0486)
Total Turnover Supplier	−.306616 ** (.0316)	−.164452 (.1577)
Negative Network Embeddedness	.294782 ** (.0177)	.182140 * (.0790)
Positive Network Embeddedness	.195393 (.1354)	.127083 (.2340)
Sales to Buyer as % of Total Sales	.170351 (.2608)	.358378 *** (.0042)
Trust in Competence: Buyer	.081062 (.6033)	.081285 (.5030)
R Square	.47539	.58792
F-statistic	3.87191	6.30143
Significance F	.0005	.0000
N	59	66

[a]Coefficients are standardized. T-Significance in parentheses.
*** p< .01; ** p< .05; * p< .10

Table 11.2 shows that in both models the effect of asset specificity is highly significant, and in the expected direction. For both models negative network embeddedness has the expected positive effect, and this effect is fairly to moderately significant. In the model for net dependence the only additional variable with an expected significant effect is total turnover (firm size of supplier). This effect is not significant in the model for perceived dependence. But in that model we see significant expected effects for trust in goodwill buyer, knowledge exchange and percentage of total sales sold to buyer.

In neither model do we find expected effects for length of supply, contractual extensiveness and positive network embeddedness. Nor do we find the expected negative effect of buyer dependence on (gross) supplier dependence.

DISCUSSION

In this study no direct relationships between asset specificity and individual elements of governance structure are found. In retrospect this is reasonable. The findings of our study suggest that items of governance structure are composed into a coherent whole, in order to meet the specific configuration of conditions and requirements of a given situation. Significant results, which are to a large extent in accordance with our theoretical expectations, are found when we consider the joint, simultaneous effect on perceived dependence of causes and conditions of dependence, together with measures of governance taken to influence dependence.

The analysis of the net perceived dependence of suppliers (Table 11.2, column 1) indicates an incomplete alignment of asset specificity and safeguards; suppliers perceive themselves as more dependent on the Buyer than the other way around. Hence, no balance of dependence is achieved. However, the analysis of (gross) perceived dependence does not show any significant effect of perceived dependence of the other party (the buyer), which indicates that suppliers may not think in terms of a balance of dependence. We focus now on the results for the second model (gross dependence). Contractual extensiveness shows no effect, which is difficult to explain on the basis of the hypothesis that legal safeguards are used to neutralize (imbalanced) dependencies. However, if the degree of contractual extensiveness cannot be used to compensate for supplier dependence, or is unilaterally imposed by Buyer, this finding is understandable. Information exchange does show the expected effect, and this can be considered as an element of private ordering. As pointed out above, the effect of asset specificity is positive and highly significant, and thus confirms this aspect of TCE.

Negative embeddedness shows the expected effect. So does trust in goodwill of the buyer. These results confirm part of our extension to TCE. Also as expected, percentage of sales to buyer contributes to dependence, while firm size of the supplier reduces it. However, positive network embeddedness fails to show the expected effect. Neither of the two variables reflecting the temporal dimension of the transaction relation contributes significantly to the explanation of perceived dependence, and this contradicts our expectation. This could be taken as an indication that habitualization and institutionalization do not play an important role in the relationships investigated.

However, perhaps allowance should be made for the possibility that time reduces the probability of discontinuity of the relation, but increases the penalty incurred when discontinuity occurs, so that the net effect on dependence is ambiguous. Another consideration is that perhaps these two variables fail to reflect the most relevant aspects of the temporal dimension of transaction relations. For instance, perhaps the expectation of future exchange should be measured directly, instead of being inferred from the length of the supply history (cf. Heide and John, 1990; Heide and Miner, 1992). Habitualization and institutionalization could also be measured directly, using questions that probe the degree of conscious decision making in the context of a specific exchange relation, and the use of procedures and routines.

Our data refer to only one buying firm, and hence we must be modest in our conclusions. Specifically, with regard to factors like embeddedness and institutionalization of behaviour, firm and industry-specific factors may play a quite important role. Larger samples, encompassing several industries and many buyers, can help us to distinguish between general tendencies and firm-specific and industry-specific phenomena. Nevertheless, some conclusions can be drawn.

CONCLUSIONS

Our most important finding perhaps is the strong positive association between asset specificity and perceived dependence of suppliers. In the first place, this finding confirms that asset specificity is an important factor. Secondly, it endorses our suggestion that the perceptions of the parties to a transaction relation have to be included in the analysis. Inclusion of this variable allows us to apply transaction cost reasoning also in cases in which governance structure is more of a constant than a variable. It also opens up the analysis to factors that are excluded from received TCE, such as negative network embeddedness and trust. In this study these factors had significant effects. The dynamic dimension of transaction relations, represented in our analysis by the variables pertaining to the length of the supply history and the development of sales volume, did not make an interpretable contribution to the explanation of the dependent variables. There is an obvious limitation in including a time effect in a cross-sectional study. However, given this limitation, we still think that the time dimension can be captured more adequately. Suggestions for improvement have been made.

APPENDIX

Transaction cost economics and extensions of this theory guided the development of the scales employed in the study. Most items had the format of five-point Likert-type scales. Individual scale items were factor analysed and items with factor loadings exceeding 0.30 and contributing positively to each scale's reliability (Cronbach's alpha) became part of each construct. The Cronbach's alpha coefficients for the scales range from 0.59 to 0.82, which is satisfactory for exploratory research. A respondent's score for a particular construct was the sum of his response over the number of items from which the scale was constructed. For missing observations in independent variables; means substitution was applied. Cases with missing variables in the dependent variable were deleted.

NOTES

1. This chapter is a product of a research project sponsored by the Economics Research Foundation, which is part of the Netherlands' Organization for Scientific Research (NWO). Berger and Nooteboom work at the University of Groningen, Noorderhaven works at Tilburg University. The authors gratefully acknowledge valuable comments made by Celeste Wilderom.
2. This is worked out more systematically in Noorderhaven (1995).
3. The questionnaire items are available from the authors. The adequacy of the scales was tested by means of Cronbach's alpha, taken to be satisfactory when >0.5.
4. Cronbach's alpha for the asset specificity scale is .7493 However, it can be reasoned that the scale is formative rather than reflexive, and that Cronbach's

alpha is irrelevant.
5. Cronbach's alpha for this scale is .7329.
6. The fact that specific tools are owned by the buyer can also increase the vulnerability of the supplier, in the absence of other specificity (e.g., human asset specificity), as the buying firm can now more easily shift business to another firm (cf. Semlinger (1991)).
7. A scale was constructed (Cronbach's alpha .5918) from three five-point Likert items: (1) the relation between our firm and buyer has improved in the course of time; (2) the relation in the course of time has encompassed more areas, and (3) how has your sales to buyer evolved in the past five years?
8. The scale was constructed from six items, with a Cronbach alpha of .8246. An alternative dimension of trust considered in the study is trust of the supplier in the competence of the buyer. This was neither expected nor found to have a significant effect on perceived supplier dependence.
9. Regression coefficients multiplied by the ratio of the standard deviation of the independent variable to the standard deviation of the dependent variable results in a dimensionless coefficient. The beta coefficient is the slope of the least squares regression line when both dependent and independent variables are expressed as z scores (deviation from mean in standard deviations).

REFERENCES

Asanuma, B. (1989), 'Manufacturer-Supplier Relationships in Japan and the Concept of Relation-Specific Skill,' *Journal of the Japanese and International Economies*, vol. 3, pp. 1–30.

Barber, B. (1983), *The Logic and Limits of Trust*, Rutgers University Press, New Brunswick NJ.

Berger, P.L. and T. Luckmann (1966), *The Social Construction of Reality*, Doubleday, Garden City NY.

Blois, K.J. (1972), 'Vertical Quasi-Integration', *Journal of Industrial Economics*, vol. 20, pp. 253–72.

Deutsch, M. (1973), *The Resolution of Conflict; Constructive and Destructive Processes*, Yale University Press, New Haven.

Dietrich, M. (1994), The Economics of Quasi-Integration, *Review of Political Economy*, vol. 6, pp. 1 – 18.

Gambetta, D. (ed.) (1988), *Trust: Making and Breaking Cooperative Relations*, Basil Blackwell, Oxford

Granovetter, M. (1985), 'Economic Action and Social Structure: A Theory of Embeddedness', *American Journal of Sociology*, vol. 91, pp. 481–510.

Granovetter, M. (1992), 'Economic Institutions as Social Constructions: A Framework for Analysis', *Acta Sociologica*, vol. 35, pp. 3–11.

Heide, J.B. and G. John (1990), 'Alliances in Industrial Purchasing: The Determinants of Joint Venture Action in Buyer-Supplier Relationships', *Journal of Marketing Research*, vol. 27, pp. 24–36.

Heide, J.B. and A.S. Miner (1992), 'The Shadow of the Future: Effects of Anticipated Interaction and Frequency of Contact on Buyer–Seller Cooperation', *Academy of Management Journal*, vol. 35, pp. 265–91.

Klein, B., R.G. Crawford, and A.A. Alchian (1978), 'Vertical Integration, Appropriable Rents, and the Competitive Contracting Process', *Journal of Law and Economics*, vol. 21, pp. 297–326.

Lorenz, E.H. (1988), 'Neither Friends Nor Strangers: Informal Networks of Subcontracting in French Industry', in: Gambetta, D. (ed.), *Trust: Making and Breaking Cooperative Relations*, pp. 194–210, Basil Blackwell, Oxford.

Luhmann, N. (1979), *Trust and Power*, (translated from German), John Wiley, Chichester.

Monteverde, K. and D.J. Teece (1982), 'Appropriable Rents and Quasi-Vertical Integration', *Journal of Law and Economics*, vol. 25, pp. 321–28.

Noorderhaven, N.G. (1995), 'Trust and Transactions: Toward Transaction Cost Analysis With a Differential Behavioral Assumption', forthcoming in *Tijdschrift voor Economie en Management*.

Nooteboom, B. (1993), 'Firm Size Effects on Transaction Costs', *Small Business Economics*, Vol. 5, pp. 283 – 95.

Palay, Th.M. (1984), 'Comparative Institutional Economics: The Governance of Rail Freight Contracting', *Journal of Legal Studies*, vol. 13, pp. 265–87.

Semlinger, K. (1991), *Innovation, Cooperation and Strategic Contracting*, International Colloquium on Management of Technology, Paris.

Williamson, O.E. (1975), *Markets and Hierarchies: Analysis and Antitrust Implications*, Free Press, New York.

Williamson, O.E. (1979), 'Transaction-Cost Economies: The Governance of Contractual Relations', *Journal of Law and Economics*, vol. 22, pp. 233–61.

Williamson, O.E. (1985), The Economic Institutions of Capitalism; Firms, Markets, Relational Contracting, Free Press, New York.

Williamson, O.E. (1991), 'Comparative Economic Organization: The Analysis of Discrete Structural Alternatives', *Administrative Science Quarterly*, vol. 36, pp. 269–296.

Woodside, A.G. and K. Möller (1992), 'Middle Range Theories of Industrial Purchasing Strategies', *Advances in Marketing and Purchasing*, vol. 5, pp. 21–59.

Zucker, L.G. (1987), 'Institutional Theories of Organization', *Annual Review of Sociology*, vol. 13, pp. 443–64.

12. A Changing Japanese Market for Corporate Control

John Groenewegen

As elsewhere, institutions in the Japanese economic system change. Interesting developments take place in the market for corporate control which could have an impact on the possibility for foreign firms to take over Japanese ones. Clearly, short-run recession problems in Japan play a role in this, but also structural issues related to the keiretsu system are at stake.

For describing the changes in the Japanese market for corporate control and assessing the consequences for the internal and external organization of Japanese firms, use will be made of concepts and theoretical insights of the theory of institutional change as presented by Bush (1987).

After having discussed concepts of that theory of institutional change. I will present the history and interdependences of the Japanese business system. Short-run problems related to the recesssion and their consequences for the business system follow. Then the long run structural changes in the business system are presented. After having shown the characteristics of the system, the short-run as well as long-run causes of change, I will try to assess their implications for the market for corporate control at the end of this chapter.

THEORY OF INSTITUTIONAL CHANGE

On institutions and organizations

I prefer to start with a broad definition of institution as a set of behavioural rules that govern actions and relations. For research concerning specific organizations it can be useful to make a distinction between categories of institutions. A useful criterion is the purposefulness and, related to that, the nature of their dynamics. Institutions, like legal rules, are purposefully designed and the result of collective action. This makes them differ from values, norms and routines, which often guide behaviour (more or less) unconsciously.

Interesting is the distinction made between institution and organization (Sjöstrand, 1992). Organizations like firms are considered to be 'arenas' in which different types of institution can co-exist (see also Stinchcombe, 1990). So-called rational institutions (endogenous in neoclassical and new institutional economics) such as the market and the corporation are supplemented with the non-rational ones like the association, social movements, clan and circle. These institutions can be identified in concrete organizations.

Figure 12.1 The difference between institutions and organizations (cf. Sjöstrand, 1992).

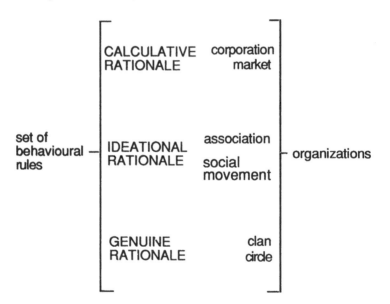

The interaction rationales behind these institutional constructs are calculative, 'ideational' and genuine. In the calculative rationale the actor tries to reduce uncertainties by calculation, aiming at the coordination of transactions in the most efficient way. The ideational rationale reduces uncertainty through the sharing of ideas and beliefs, resulting in relations of trust. Actors can also have 'genuine' close relations based on kinship, or friendship. It is important to realize that the six types of institution fulfil the same function: to reduce uncertainty and coordinate behaviour. Organizations are the arenas where the interaction rationales emerge, are designed and develop in different combinations. So an organization like a firm in Japan can coordinate behaviour through calculative rationales, but also via ideational and geniune rationales (cf. figure 12.1 above).

When we use the concept 'organization' we refer to a real life entity like a firm, a labour union or a government agency, which has sovereignty and coordinates behaviour through a combination of the institutions mentioned above. To follow Sjöstrand (1992): economic concepts like efficiency are incorporated through the calculative rationale; when calculation is difficult, impossible or not relevant, then the rationale of shared beliefs, norms and values coordinates behaviour, whereas these are supplemented by 'close relationships', in which trust and altruism are important. The set of behavioural rules is of different types (calculative, ideational and genuine), which all produce information and reduce uncertainty and coordinate behaviour. This takes place in organizations, which are arenas where different combinations emerge and are constructed by the actors involved. Which institution dominates and characterizes (more or less) the organization differs in time and space; firms in Japan have another combination of institutions than in the US, whereas the institutional combination in Japanese firms in 1993 is different from the one in 1965.

Theory of institutional and organizational change

According to neoclassical and new institutional theories, changes in institutions result from calculative behaviour. A specific type of organization will be selected, because it minimizes production and transaction costs. However, because institutions are public goods (Sjöstrand, 1993), the problem of free riding will cause underinvestment in institutional and so organizational change (Newman, 1976). Government then should provide institutional change as a public good, yet this might fail because of interest groups, ideology and limited knowledge (cf. Lin, 1989, and Bush, 1987).

For understanding the theory of institutional change, the distinction of Veblen between ceremonial and instrumental values is important (Rutherford, 1984; Bush, 1987). When institutions are defined as 'a set of socially prescribed correlated behaviour' and the values are the correlators, then ceremonial values correlate behaviour by prescribing status and privileges.

On Economic Institutions

Ceremonial values defend invidious distinctions, appeal to tradition, are formulated in rituals and above all are not subject to critical scrutiny. The logic behind ceremonial values is 'sufficient reason', contrary to 'instrumental values', which are based on 'efficient cause'.

> Instrumental values are validated in the continuity of the problem-solving processes. The criterion by which the community judges instrumentally warranted patterns of behaviour is that of 'instrumental efficiency'. (Bush, 1987, 1080)

Crucial in this is the process of goal formulation and the explicity of the objectives (which problems to be solved?) for the community. Institutionalists (Tool, 1979) have made clear that the process should be a democratic one and that systems of indicative planning are very useful in making objectives, problems and the efficiency of instruments explicit. In reality, behaviour often contains both ceremonial and instrumental characteristics.

> [...] instrumental behaviour is 'encapsulated' within a ceremonially warranted behavioural pattern, thereby incorporating instrumental behaviour in a ceremonially prescribed outcome. (Bush 1987, p. 1084)

Ceremonial behaviour often inhibits changes necessary to implement technological or organizational innovations. Innovation mostly demands changes in the combination of the institutions which govern the organization. In the dynamics of institutional change, the index of 'ceremonial dominance' plays an important role, because the 'fund of knowledge' of society (encapsulated in ceremonial patterns or embodied in instrumental patterns) is not fully available for problem-solving. Only the part that is 'ceremonially feasable', the so-called 'institutional space', allows instumental patterns of behaviour. In time the fund of knowledge grows (as the instrumental problem-solving capacity of the community grows), but ceremonialism can prevent the use of instrumental knowledge and inhibit the free inquiry necessary for instrumental valuing.

Ceremonialism is often related to vested interests that want to keep things as they are, now and in the future (for instance, the power of big business, the military-industrial complex, the bureaucratic elite, and so on). Institutional change implies a change in the value structure; an increase in the dominance of ceremonial values is a regressive change, and a decrease of ceremonial values a progressive one (the problem solving capacity increases). The first step in a progressive change is the encapsulation of an innovation:

New ceremonially warranted patterns are required to encapsulate the increase in instrumentally warranted behavioural patterns. (Bush, 1987, p. 1093)

Innovations are permitted only when it is anticipated that they will not disrupt the existing value structure of the community. After that, the community becomes habituated to the new standards of judgement in the correlated behaviour; learning and diffusion lead to the erosion of inhibiting ceremonial values (Bush, 1987). The critical factor is the awareness of the commmunity that new standards are necessary for solving the problems the commmunity is facing. Drastic changes (revolution), catastrophes and contact with other cultures can play a stimulating role in this.

Important in all this is the so-called 'institutional space' and 'principle of minimal dislocation'; the existing institutions are a more or less coherent set of rules resulting in more or less efficient outcomes. ('More or less', because full coherence in a dynamic setting is not likely.) Because of growth in knowledge, or change in conditions (for instance liberalisation of markets, or a recession), the problems to be solved or the availability of instruments change. What is considered to be the problem and what is considered an efficient instrument is mainly determined by the existing pattern of values.

Change is possible, but change demands awareness, discussion, critical scrutiny of existing institutions. The room to manoeuvre is often very limited, the more so because a change in one element of the institutional setting demands changes in the other elements. One of the related elements that is on the agenda to be changed can fulfil such a crucial function that the community does not want to give up the specific institution knowing that another type of instrumentally warranted behaviour will not be performed then.

The so-called 'principle of minimal dislocation' points to the fact that :

All institutional modifications must be capable of being incorporated into the remainder of the institutional structure. It is convenient to call this the principle of minimal dislocation. It discloses the limits of adjustment in terms of rate and in terms of degree and area. (J. Fagg Foster, 1981, pp. 933–4)

THE JAPANESE BUSINESS SYSTEM: A MARKET FOR COPORATE CONTROL?

The market for corporate control is the stock market where outsiders can buy shares (ownership) of firms which can be made more profitable by restructuring, reorganization and replacement of management. This pressure on management is said to assure efficiency. It is widely known that the market for corporate control in Japan hardly exists, because 'stable stockholders' control about 70% of the shares. The Japanese business systems have other disciplining mechanisms, of which the history and 'embeddedness' are explained in this section. Attention is paid to relations inside the firm, to subcontracting and to the role of the bank.

The Japanese firm, some interdependences

A Japanese firm has central management like all other firms, but the difference between the Japanese (J-mode) and American (H-mode) firms (Aoki, 1990) is the processing of information inside the firm and, related to that, the incentive system and the labour market. Information is produced at all levels in the organization and each level has direct contact with the customers. Lower operational levels have specific information and handle problems autonomously, whereas decision-making is a process of interaction between levels inside the hierarchy. Employees are supposed to invest in specific skills, to delegate responsibility to lower levels, to learn the next generation of skills specific to the job. Insights of transaction cost economics would point to problems of opportunism. In the J-mode these problems are attenuated because of life-time employment contracts and slow internal promotion based on a range of criteria like skills, experience, cooperativeness and the like.

Intergenerational teaching, delegation of responsibility and specific investments are rewarded with a higher ranking, whereas the slow, well-managed promotion system hinders young colleagues from bypassing older employees with knowledge they have taught them. In the J-mode, an imperfect external labour market (difficult to find a comparable rank by another firm) is necessary to prevent well-skilled employees from being bought out by competing firms. The firm itself does not recruit personnel at middle and higher level in order not to distort career perspectives of junior employees. So information processing, decision-making, an imperfect labour maket and ranking are all interrelated.

Subcontracting

The Japanese firm is capability-driven resulting in a workforce with similar skills, which is favourable for information processing, learning and decision-making. Japan has many so-called production *keiretsu* ('*sangyo keiretsu*'), where a parent firm has economic (supplier-buyer), financial (stockholding), organizational (management assistance), technological (transfer of technology) and personal relations with subcontractors, co-designers and co-makers. The relations are long term and subcontractors depend heavily on the parent company (for recent changes into a more web-type of structure, see van Kooij, 1991). Subcontractors are the cushion for conjunctural recessions. Because the parent firm has a direct and indirect interest in the subcontractors on the one hand and subcontractors depend largely on the parent on the other hand, opportunism is not likely.

The subcontracting system is interrelated with the internal organization of the J-mode; because of the tiers of subcontracting, the parent can concentrate on the activities which demand specific capabilities and can implement a ranking and life time employment sytem.

Main bank

In the *kinyu keiretsu* (horizontally structured group), firms, the General Trading Company (GTC) and the group bank (main bank) are connected through economic, organizational and financial relations. Important for assessing the market for corporate control is the position of the main bank. The firms inside the group have bank accounts with the group bank, the group bank is their major stockholder (cross-stockholding), the group bank is the most important lender to the group members, and the group bank is the one that monitors the group members and if necessary organizes a recontruction or liquidation.

The group bank is important, but that is not to imply a complete dependency of the industrial firms; group members are free to develop relations with other banks, to have stockholdings with other banks and when the financial position of the industrial firm is strong the bank does not interfere in the firm's strategies. There is an intense exchange of information (Presidents' club) and when a firm is in trouble, the group bank is responsible for restructuring, rationalization and replacement of management.

Firms are ranked by the group bank based on the financial position and duration of the relationship. Highly ranked firms are very independent and, with their stable shareholders like the group bank, these firms do not have to fear hostile takeovers. The lower ranked firms do not have much bargaining power. The group bank has a good entry to the network of parent firms and their subcontractors, whereas the subcontractor can more easily start a relation with a group bank through a parent group member. The group bank is responsible for the group members and has a reputation as efficient monitor and lender of last resort to defend. The high ex post cost of reconstruction is an incentive for close intensive ex ante monitoring.

This self-enforcing mechanism is reinforced by the administrative guidance of the Ministry of Finance (MOF); a group bank will be heavily sanctioned (no new branches) if the bank evades its responsibility. Lacking a market for corporate control the group bank fulfils an important monitoring and disciplining role, supplemented by the internal labour market (information, ranking, decision-making), the internal supply market (customer-subcontractor), the internal capital market (cross-stockholding, monitoring, efficient reallocation, reconstruction) and external monitoring by branch and government agencies such as the Ministry of International Trade and Industry (MITI) and MOF.

Internal and external developments demand changes in one part of the system, which have effects on other related parts. For instance a change in the internal labour market will affect information processing, learning, investments in specific skills and the like. There are signs of changes in the role of the main bank (bankruptcies in industrial groups?) and of an emerging Japanese market for corporate control. Where do these changes come from and what will the consequences be for the system as a whole?

From the insights of the theory of institutional change as presented by Bush (1987), we learn that understanding the change of institutions and organizations like the Japanese market for corporate control is an extremely complicated issue. Internal and external pressures are involved as well as rigidities due to existing interests and structures. External pressures on the Japanese government and business systems to change the market for corporate control can be resisted by important actors in the economic and political system.

However, other actors can mobilize internal pressures and explore the institutional space available. Important for understanding the changes in concrete organizations, like the Japanese market for corporate control in the 1990s, is first of all a good understanding of the existing organizations, the institutions (calculative, ideational and genuine) which coordinate behaviour inside the organizational arenas, the existing internal and external pressures and structures (short-term as well as long-term), and the interests of the actors (firms, banks, government).

From all that a picture should emerge of the growth in the fund of knowledge of the community (we need a market for corporate control to solve our problems), the instrumental value of a change in the market for corporate control, the ceremonial values involved and finally of the institutional space and the possibility for actors to use the room to manoeuvre effectively to change the existing market for corporate control. A complete or at least extensive institutional analysis like that requires a book; in the following parts of this chapter only a few elements are briefly explored.

SHORT TERM AND LONG TERM DEVELOPMENTS IN THE JAPANESE ECONOMY

Long term developments

Long term developments in the *keiretsu* and the relation between government and business can be briefly summarised as follows (for a more extensive discussion see Groenewegen, 1993):

1. The firms have seen their financial means grow in the last decades which made them less dependent of the main bank (Kester, 1991).

2. The bank felt pressure from the liberalization and deregulation; ranking and competition made them more critical towards group members (Kester, 1991b).

3. The General Trading Companies are confronted with a structural decline of their share in Japan's import and export (Shin, 1989).

4. Subcontracting relations are changing more and more into network relations (Van Kooij, 1991).

5. The role of government is becoming more and more indirect (Groenewegen, 1993).

These long term developments are reinforced by the short-term recession pressures.

Before the recession

The peak of the so-called 'bubble economy' was 1988–1989; firms had a lot of cash (increasing share prices and real estate prices) leading to diversification (Kester, 1991a) and the so-called *zaiteku* (speculation in high risk stocks). The General Trading Companies were particularly active in *zaiteku* mainly because the GTCs were desperately in need of new sources of revenue. Mitsubishi, Sumitomo, Marubeni and Itochu were very active; for instance, Mitsubishi *zaiketu* funds rose in 1989 to 2.6 trillion yen, which was around one third of the assets and responsible for the strong growth of profits. (For Mitsubishi the *zaiteku* was at one point in time responsible for 33% of the profits.)

Recession; collapse of the stockmarket (1990-1992)

The Nikkei index, indicator of the Stock value in Japan, fell below 16.000 in June of 1992; the commercial land prices fell by 30%, which implied a drop of $2.5 to 3.5 trillion in financial assets. Together with rising interest rates, a falling overseas demand, a falling growth of GNP (1.4% for 1993) and a rising yen (which is there to stay because of the structural trade surplus), all this caused serious problems for many Japanese firms. A few figures:

1. The assets of Mitsubishi shrank in September 1992 from 10.3 trillion yen to 6.9 trillion.

2. The GTC started to liquidate when the Nikkei index had fallen to 18.000 (September, 1992); by March, 1993 the portfolio of the top nine GTCs was reduced to half. The GTC had to raise cash by selling land and shares of long-standing business partners *Far Eastern Economic Review* (FEER 17-6-1993).

3. Pre-tax profits for 1,461 listed companies fell on average 24.9% in 1992.

4. Bankruptcies rose 22.7% in 1992 to 14.441 cases.

5. After-tax profit of Nissan in 1990 was 85 billion yen, in 1991 78 billion, in 1992 58 billion, in 1993 20 billion in the red.

The firms have high fixed obligations among which the depreciation costs are a heavy burden. The large investments in the late 1980s caused high depreciation rates, which are expected to fall in 1995 (*Asia Money*, February 1992). What are the answers of the different actors to these short term developments and what are the more long-term consequences for the changes in the market corporate control?

We are not able to deal entirely with this research agenda. In the following we will try to shed some light on the main actors in the Japanese business system, their interests and values so we get some insights in the 'institutional space' in general and in the probable changes in the market for corporate control in particular.

Government

The government took measures to stimulate the economy: tax reductions and an increase in expenditures for infrastructure. MITI and the Ministry of Finance also took measures to stimulate foreign investments to strengthen the position of shareholders and to facilitate the selling of firms:

1. In 1989, the tax law was changed: proceeds from sales of firms were taxed by 29% of the sale price. (Before 1989 the proceeds had to be added to income.)

2. MITI promoted foreign investment by allowing foreigners (owning more than one third of the stock) to carry forward losses the first three years to set off against taxable income for seven years (two years more than Japanese firms). Since 1 August 1992, foreigners are no longer banned from buying shares of partially privatized utilities to a maximum of 20%.

3. Government reduced the official discount rate from 6.25% to 2.5%.

4. Ministry of Finance supported the stock market by pouring $15 billion of government controlled savings into stocks (Nikkei + 27% from August 1992).

5. MITI launched a consulting company to advice foreign firms on takeovers.

6. The Ministry of Justice took measures to improve the position of the shareholder.

7. The costs of a lawsuit by corporations against its management decreased to 8,200 yen per case (had been a percentage of the claim).

8. Large companies were obliged to appoint an independent auditor; the tenure of company auditors was extended from 2 to 3 years.

9. Restriction on the size of bond issues by large companies was lifted.

The bureaucracy

In Japan, bureaucrats play a crucial role; according to Van Wolferen (1989) the enigma of Japanese power is largely to be found in the role of the bureaucrats with their relations to politics and big business. Because of the economic recession and problems of structural adaptation (bankruptcies of important firms), the prestige of the bureaucrats as the controllers of the economy is diminishing. In newspapers, much attention is paid to unorthodox behaviour of bureaucrats who make public statements about failing government policies. Although this behaviour is incidental it seems that the role of bureaucrats is also changing in more general terms: both politics and bureaucracy have lost prestige and control, whereas banks and large firms are becoming more independent in their behaviour. What the consequences for the relation between government and keiretsu will be is not easy to predict: are these developments only signs of a superficial change or are we dealing with long-term structural changes in the relationship between government and industry?

> Companies are aping the West to downsize payrolls, merge, and streamline production. But even as it cribs from Western economies, Japan won't change its basic tenets. It will continue close industry-government cooperation, and its cozy, corporate *keiretsu* groups will remain intact. (*Business Week*, March 29, 1993, p. 39)

The banks

The banks have to deal with difficult economic situations forcing them to restructure their own activities and to reconsider their relation with the group members. In that respect the situation at this moment is not very clear. On the one hand, banks seem to dump shares of clients, but on the other hand, banks seem to apply a stricter ranking and dump only shares of the lower-ranked firms and strengthen the ties with the higher-ranked ones. If the latter is the case then the keiretsu ties become stronger instead of weaker. The same question can be raised with respect to the support firms in the keiretsu give to each other. Again, the answer is not easily had as illustrated by the following statements:

> Japan's bear market is damaging what has long been viewed as one of the great strengths of modern Japanese industrial society: the system of cross-shareholdings that links Japanese corporations, their suppliers, customers, banks and insurance companies tightly together in keiretsu. Since the fall of 1991, these 'stable' shareholders have started to dump each other's shares. (*Global Finance,* April 1992, pp. 79-81)

> Some observers had predicted that hard times might break up the '*keiretsu*'. Instead, they are drawing together. (*Business Week,* October 26, 1992, p. 48)

The position of banks in Japan is also changing because of deregulation policies of the Ministry of Finance; the situation of specialized banks operating in closed markets is ending, which introduces more competition among banks. The increased pressure on Japanese banks to become more competitive has also led to mergers resulting in megabanks, for instance, Sakura Bank (merger in 1991 of Mitsui Bank and Taiyo Kobe bank).

The banks have also taken measures to increase efficiency and profits. They have restricted the loans, which mainly has implications for smaller firms, which then become almost completely dependent on the government Fiscal and Investment Loan Program (FILP).

The firms

Also the firms in Japan are under more competition pressures, which results in the selling of stocks and real estate and a reduction in investments. Firms behave more independently and shop around for cheap money, cut linkages with lower subcontractors, fire personnel (try to find a position for them within related firms) and are more willing than ever to look for alliances with foreign firms or take-over candidates.

In conclusion to the changing role of government, bureaucrats, banks and firms and relations between them, it is not clear at this moment whether fundamental organizational changes take place with strong implications for the relations inside the *keiretsu* and the market for corporate control, or if the changes are more superficial and the underlying linkages remain or are even strengthened. If we just look at the number of takeovers an increase can be reported, but closer examination shows that hostile takeovers are extremely exceptional and that takeovers are restricted to small, family-owned firms with no group ties. Foreign firms have more opportunities to take over these individual firms, because they are often the only ones to turn to; if a firm is in trouble and the stock market is not reacting and the bank refuses a loan, then a takeover by a foreign firm is the only solution.

CONCLUSIONS

Changes inside the Japanese economy (recession and long-run developments in the business system) together with changes outside Japan resulting in more pressure to open capital and product markets and the objectives of the 'rulers' (economic growth, competitiveness, friendly relations with US and Europe), all together demand for changes in the organizations in Japan. The different interest groups (firms, bureaucrats, politics) seem to be aware of that.

Deregulation and liberalisation resulting in the introduction of a market for corporate control is positively received by all main actors in the community. More calculative behaviour cutting linkages with inefficient firms, ranking of firms and customers is more and more accepted practice. Such calculative behaviour is considered necessary for implementing the objectives of growth, competitiveness and acceptable relations with the outside world.

However, the different interest groups are also aware of the efficiencies of the existing business system. Most of the interdependencies described above have elements of ceremonial as well as instrumental behaviour. Ceremonialism results in excluding firms from market pressures and the rescue of inefficient firms, whereas the same institutions contribute to efficient alternative disciplining mechanisms. Taking the reaction of the banks and firms on the recession into account, the most recent developments seem to result in a strengthening of the keiretsu ties instead of a weakening. Several cases (see appendix) show that the banks fulfill their role as monitor, lender of last resort and organiser of a reconstruction. Also the other group members fulfill their role in the *keiretsu*. The actors seem to be fully aware of the efficiencies of the system and they want to conserve its basic characteristics.

In respect to the market for corporate control, Kester (1991a) explains its absence as a consequence of the existence of other disciplining mechanisms in the Japanese business system. Kester points to two objectives of Mergers and Acquisitions (M & A). One has to do with 'trading hazards' (uncertainty, opportunism in the supply of intermediary products) and the other with shirking of the management (so-called 'downward opportunism'). Vertical integration through M & A often aims at avoiding 'trading hazards', which in the J-mode are efficiently reduced in the subcontracting relation. The agency problems of the large corporation can be solved by an efficient market for corporate control, but in Japan this function is fulfilled by the disciplining mechanisms in the business group. So according to Kester there was no need for a market for corporate control and that is the most important explanation for its absence. Of course, the cross stockholdings, the until recently existing government regulations, the taboos of selling a firm and the loyalty of individual firms to their group all play a role, but the absence of the economic need is crucial. The other disciplining mechanism discussed above is still prominent in Japan, which makes the development of a 'real' market for corporate control highly questionable.

The impression exists that the inefficiencies of the system of stable share holding are being carved out: the government takes measures that limit the possibilities of protecting group members from market pressures (see the case of the supermarket affair of Shuwa Corp and Inageya Co. in Appendix) and firms and banks end relationships with lower-ranked firms. The impression exists that the calculative, ideational and genuine institutions in organizations like the Japanese business group result in a reaction in favour of 'stable shareholding', which is considered economically efficient and which fits in the 'institutional space'. The opening of the capital market is relevant for the smaller and non-keiretsu firms, which offers those Japanese firms an opportunity to be taken over by a foreign company (see the case of Nomura Toy in Appendix) and which offers foreigners an entry to Japanese markets without disturbing the system.

In respect to the balance of power between bureaucrats, managers and politicians, long-term developments point into the direction of a change of power in favour of the large companies. The bureaucrats of MITI and the other ministeries had already lost much of their direct influence in the seventies and eighties and this seems to be reinforced by the way they have dealt with the 'bubble economy' and the recession. Undoubtedly politicians will promise the US and Europe to continue the process of deregulation and liberalisation, but the large companies seem to be in the driver seat more and more. It is the general impression that the opening up of markets and the introduction of a market for corporate control will be closely monitored and controlled by the large *keiretsu*.

APPENDIX: CASES

Case of Shuwa Corp

Tokio Business Today (TBT) (September 1989) reported two important events: one was the acquisition by T. Boone Pickens of a considerable ownership in Koito Manufacturing Co. and his demand to participate in the firm's management and the other was the case of Shuwa Corporation.

In January of 1988, Shuwa, owner of real estate in Japan and the US, started to buy shares of supermarket chains: 33.34% of Chujitsuya Co. and 25.01% of Inageya Co. A merger of the two companies with another supermarket chain, 'Life Stores', was proposed, but both Chujitsuya and Inageya disagreed. Because Japanese firms are not allowed to buy their own stocks, a protection against outsiders has to be organized by 'stable shareholders'. The two firms increased their capital by buying each other's shares. Without increasing the financial burden of the firm, the stake of Shuwa would diminish that way. Shuwa applied for an injunction of the Tokyo District Court. The court ruled that the two corporations violated the law, because the shares were priced far below the market price, which constituted a 'favourable issue' for specified shareholders. Moreover, the move was illegal, because only the board of directors of the two firms had taken the decision instead of a general shareholders meeting. Finally, the court cited the illegal intent of the capital increase:

> In cases of disputes surrounding management control rights, new stock issues, which have as their main objective guarding the authority of the existing management, are illegal. (*TBT*, September 1989, p. 35)

In their defense Chujitsuya an Inageya pointed out that the capital increase was meant to strenghten the tie-up between the two companies and that the prices of the shares had been driven up by Shuwa and that the stock market did not reflect real values. Court did not accept these arguments. It is expected that Japanese firms will bolster the 'stable shareholder' relations before a raider can strike.

Volkswagen

Volkswagen Audi Nippon was in the market late in 1992 for a Japanese distributor. JAX Ltd., a car importer with 21 Tokyo outlets, was in need for cash. Because of the crash of the stock market, stocks of JAX had fallen by 69% since 1989. In December of 1992 Volkswagen bought by issuing new shares a 49.99% stake in JAX for $21 million.

Nomura Toy

Nomura Toy is a small toy company bought out to one hundred percent by Hasbro, a US giant. Nomura toy had no heir and was in strong need of capital.

Itoman

Itoman is a 110 year old food-textile trader, member of the Sumitomo keiretsu. Real estate projects and risky loans caused financial trouble in 1992. Itoman invested in almost everything from Modigliani paintings to apartment blocks to stocks. It is said the firm had close relations with gangsters, also. In 1990, Itoman made a profit of 6.3 billion and in 1991 a loss of 60 billion yen. The name of Sumitomo was tarnished and its stock price knocked because of the relationship with Itoman. Sumitomo was expected to do something. Managers were sent to Itoman, but it soon was clear that more drastic measures were necessary.

Sumitomo Metal Industries Ltd. let one of their subsidiaries (Sumitomo Bussan Kaisha) merge with Itoman (April, 1992), in which transaction the personal relationship of bank president Sotoo Tatsumi with friend Tasko Shingu, chairman of Sumitomo Metal Industries, seemed to have played an important role. All the more than one thousand (1,342) jobs were saved and out of the merger the 12th largest trading company arose. The losses of Itoman were not transferred to Sumitomo Metals but absorbed by the Sumitomo Bank.

Nissan helps Fuji

Subaru made losses in 1991 and its main bank (Industrial Bank of Japan) asked Nissan (a 4.2% stockholder in Fuji) to step in. Isanu Kawai, President of Nissan Diesel Motor Co, became manager of Fuji. Synopsis (a US software firm) bought 82% of SC Hightech Center for $3 million, mostly from Sumitomo trading firm.

REFERENCES

Aoki, M. (1990), 'Towards an Economic Model of the Firm', *Journal of Economic Literature*, vol. 28, pp. 1–27.
Bush, P.D. (1987), 'The Theory of Institutional Change', *Journal of Economic Issues*, vol. 3, pp. 1075–1116.
Fagg Foster, J. (1981), 'The Theory of Institutional Adjustment', *Journal of Economic Issues*, vol. 4, pp. 930–2.
Groenewegen, J. (1993), 'The Japanese Business Group', in Groenewegen J. (ed.), *Dynamics of the Firm*, Edward Elgar, Aldershot.
Kester, W.C. (1991a), *Japanese Takeovers*, Harvard Business School Press, Ma.
Kester, W.C. (1991b), 'Global Players, Western Tactics, Japanese Outcomes: The New

Japanese Market for Corporate Control', *California Management Review*, Winter, pp. 58–70.

Kooij, E. van (1991), 'Japanese Subcontracting at a Crossroads', *Small Business Economics*, vol. 13, pp. 145–54.

Lin, J.Y. (1989), 'An Economic Theory of Institutional Change; Induced and Imposed Change', *Carto Journal*, vol. 9, no. 1, pp. 1–33.

Newman, G. (1976), 'An Institutional Perspective on Information', *International Social Science Journal*, vol. 28, no. 3, pp. 466–92.

Rutherford, M. (1984), 'Thorstein Veblen and the Process of Institutional Change', *History of Political Economy*, vol. 16, pp. 334–48.

Sjöstrand, S-E. (1992), 'On the Rationale Behind Irrational Institutions', *Journal of Economic Issues*, December 4, pp. 1007–40.

Sjöstrand, S-E. (1993), 'The Socioeconomic Institutions of Organizing: Origin, Emergence, and Reproduction', *Journal of Socioeconomics*, vol. 22, no. 4, pp. 323–52.

Shin, K.S. (1989), 'Information, Transaction Costs and the Organization of Distribution: the Case of Japan's General Trading Companies', *Journal of the Japanese and International Economics*, vol. 3, pp. 292–307.

Stinchcombe, A.L. (1990), *Information and Organizations*, University of California Press, Berkeley.

Tool, M.R. (1979), *The Discretionary Economy*, Goodyear Publishing Comp, Santa Monica.

Wolferen, van K.G. (1989), *The Enigma of Japanese Power*, MacMillan, London.

Newspapers and weeklies:

Tokio Business Today – A Court Ruling unleashes Japan's corporate raiders, Sept. 1989, pp. 34–36.

Global Finance – Cross-Holding Share Dumping Has Just Begun, April, 1992, pp. 79–81.

Business Week – Cover Story Fixing Japan, March 29, 1993, pp. 38–44.
    For bankrupt companies, happiness is a warm keiretsu, October 26, 1992, 48–49.
    Buying a piece of Japan Inc., January 25, 1993.

Far Eastern Economic Review – Lose and Learn, Japan's firms pay price of financial speculation, 17 June 1993. The Urge to merge, 28 January 1993. Fact in the door, 11 March 1993. Systematic Solution, Itoman's problems will be spirited away, 1 October 1992.

The Economist – Biter bitten, April 25, 1992.

Asia Money & Finance – Japan's corporates hit the pain threshold, February, 1992, pp. 9–13. Corporate Japan, July/August 1992, 49–54.

Name Index

231